The Complete Computer Trainer

D1113133

The Complete Computer Trainer

Paul Clothier

McGraw-Hill

New York   San Francisco   Washington, D.C.   Auckland   Bogotá
Caracas   Lisbon   London   Madrid   Mexico City   Milan
Montreal   New Delhi   San Juan   Singapore
Sydney   Tokyo   Toronto

McGraw-Hill

A Division of The McGraw·Hill Companies

©1996 by **The McGraw-Hill Companies, Inc.**

Printed in the United States of America. All rights reserved. The publisher takes no responsibility for the use of any materials or methods described in this book, nor for the products thereof.

pbk   4 5 6 7 8 9 DOC/DOC 9 0 0 9 8

Product or brand names used in this book may be trade names or trademarks. Where we believe that there may be proprietary claims to such trade names or trademarks, the name has been used with an initial capital or it has been capitalized in the style used by the name claimant. Regardless of the capitalization used, all such names have been used in an editorial manner without any intent to convey endorsement of or other affiliation with the name claimant. Neither the author nor the publisher intends to express any judgment as to the validity or legal status of any such proprietary claims.

Library of Congress Cataloging-in-Publication Data
Clothier, Paul
    The complete computer trainer / by Paul Clothier
        p.   cm.
    Includes index.
    ISBN 0-07-011639-3 (pbk.)
    1. Computer—Study and teaching.   I. Title
QA76.27.C58   1996
004'.071—dc20   96-5917
                                                                    CIP

Acquisitions editor: Brad J. Schepp
Editorial team: Marianne Krcma, Book Editor
               Susan Kagey, Managing Editor
               Lori Flaherty, Executive Editor
Production team: Katherine G. Brown, Director
               Brenda S. Wilhide, Computer Artist
               Brenda M. Plasterer, Desktop Operator
               Linda M. Cramer, Proofreading
               Jodi L. Tyler, Indexer
Design team: Jaclyn J. Boone, Designer   0116393
               Katherine Lukaszewicz, Associate Designer   GEN1*

This book is dedicated to those
who embrace not what we are but what we can become.
Those who see possibilities . . . not limitations.

Contents

◆◆◆

Preface

This book was written to be used as a resource for computer trainers who wish to improve their training skills and get the most from their training. It is a "field guide" to more effective and more creative training and is designed as an easy-to-read reference rather than an academic treatment. There have been numerous books, papers, and articles written on the training techniques and how people learn, but very few address application training specifically. This book does just that—it is written with the needs, goals, and challenges of the classroom computer trainer in mind. It is written in a simple, readable format and covers specific, practical ways of improving the effectiveness of computer training. It is designed to help you become an exceptional computer trainer.

Computer trainers rarely have the luxury of time to sit down and read much of what has been written about methods of teaching people how to use computers. The average trainer is generally busy teaching, planning, learning new software, or trying to unwind after a day in the trenches. This book has been written with the busy trainer in mind. It does not have to be read from beginning to end, although you might well choose to do this. You can pick up the book, read a section or two, and immediately have some new ideas and tips for your next computer training session. You can come home after a challenging day of training and find suggestions on how to deal with some of those challenges. You can take it with you when you train or read it on the way to work (not recommended if you're driving) and continually find some new and creative ideas to energize and improve your training.

Introduction

The first computer class I ever taught, over a decade ago, was a disaster. My overriding concern was to make sure the material was covered and that I sounded like I knew what I was talking about. My goal was to cover all the material and explain things "correctly." Covering the outline was my number-one priority; somewhere down that priority list were the students.

I sat opposite the director of education as she flicked through some of the worst evaluations she had seen in a long time. "We need to take a look at this," she said as she laid them in front of me. She was being tactful. I'm sure what she really meant was, "Keep this up and you're terminated." It prompted a certain amount of introspection. The meeting I had that day was my first step on a journey of learning how to train. I wanted to improve. This book is a result of what I learned in the 12 years that followed.

I've made all the mistakes imaginable in my computer training career (and some unimaginable), but I learned from them. One of the important lessons I learned, and a theme that appears throughout this book, is that computer training is more about communicating and relating than it is explaining facts. It is as much about empathy, patience, and respect as it is technical know-how. This book has the word *complete* in the title because it looks at the character and qualities of the trainer as well as the tools and techniques that the trainer uses. The tools and techniques, although very important, are the icing on the cake—the real substance of computer training, the cake itself, is the character and personality of the trainer. Teaching someone how to be an effective computer trainer purely by having him or her learn an assortment of presentation tips and techniques would be incomplete.

This book is written for the novice and experienced classroom trainer alike. It covers the very basics of planning and delivering a training session as well as offering some thought-provoking ideas for trainers who have been around a while. Most importantly, it is written for those who are committed to becoming more effective computer trainers and are willing to learn, adapt, and grow.

Training managers, support staff, helpdesk personnel, and courseware developers will also find this book valuable. Computer training is not an isolated function; its effective delivery and support is made possible by a team of people. To carry out any supporting or complementary function of computer training like creating courseware or providing helpdesk support, it is critical to be aware of what the end-product should look like. The end-product is the learning of computer software skills, and this book details what is required to produce a high quality and productive product.

The chapters cover the areas critical to the delivery of effective computer training. Each one is divided into easily digestible sections that address specific techniques, tips, or considerations:

- *Communication.* A look at what communication goes on in a training room and how you can best interact with your learners and adapt to their needs, as well as how we can encourage our learners to become more independent.

- *Training delivery.* How you should prepare for a training session, the four steps required for successful computer learning, and how to present information so that it is clear, understandable, interesting, and memorable.

- *Character of a trainer.* The qualities needed in a computer trainer, how the personality, attitude, and sensibilities of the trainer contribute to or prevent learning taking place, and how your personal development affects learning.

- *Evaluating computer training.* Measuring the effectiveness of computer training, whether existing "smile" sheets give any

real information, alternatives to smile sheets, the value of pre-
and post-testing software skills.

- *Trainer development.* The importance of learning and
ongoing development for computer trainers, how to more
objectively evaluate your training skills with the help of your
peers, the value of support groups and instructor meetings
and the benefits of trainer certification.

- *Courseware and documentation.* The types of courseware
and documentation used in computer training, how to choose
courseware to fit your needs and a detailed section on
designing your own.

- *Designing training.* Designing training from scratch, the steps
and pitfalls in designing computer training, and designing for
"just-in-time" training.

- *Training media.* The media used for learning software in
classrooms or individually: the advantages, disadvantages and
value of different types of learning media, including CBT,
multimedia, and electronic performance support systems (EPSS).

- *More training suggestions.* Some extra training ideas,
suggestions, and tips for computer trainers that don't seem to
fit nicely in any other chapter in the book.

- *The future.* What computer training might look like in the
years to come: the technologies and trends that will effect the
delivery of computer training and trainers, distance learning
and learning on the Internet, and some of the opportunities
and challenges facing computer trainers in the future.

- *Managing stress in computer training.* What causes stress in
computer training, the symptoms and some suggestions for
managing it, the causes of computer training "burnout" and
how to avoid it.

- *Dealing with difficult learners.* Why we call certain learners
"difficult," what the challenges are, and some original
suggestions for dealing with them including an extensive
listing of all the familiar "difficult" learners and practical
guidelines for working with each of them.

- *Teaching Windows programs.* Some effective methods and techniques of teaching Windows programs and how to avoid some of the common training pitfalls.

- *Accelerated learning.* Why traditional approach to computer training is not as successful as it could be and some accelerated learning techniques that can significantly improve the effectiveness of training.

- *The Internet for computer trainers.* How computer trainers can use the Internet and other online services to communicate, learn, and deliver training, a beginner's guide to using the Internet for computer trainers, Internet resources and sites for computer trainers, and how training people to use the Internet might develop and evolve.

- *How we learn.* A simple yet thorough guide to the principles of memory and learning: how people learn things, what determines if they remember, why concepts are so important, and how preferred learning styles affect how quickly people learn.

Before you begin reading this book, I have one request to make. Try not to just read the ideas and suggestions given. Act on them. Implement them. When you have read a section, go ahead and try out any new ideas in your next class. Then evaluate the class. Was it successful? What worked well and what didn't work? Could you adapt it in any way to work better next time? Reading this book as an intellectual exercise from an armchair will not be very effective. It's just like learning software—you need to do the hands-on to really start to improve your skills.

If some of these training ideas and suggestions work for you, blend them into your training. If not, discard them. Be willing to make a few mistakes. Be willing to learn and grow by risking falling on your rear end. Nothing promotes learning like experience. As someone once put it, "When you're green you grow, and when you're ripe . . . you rot." Stay green.

1

Communication

"The novice teacher shows and tells incessantly; the wise teacher listens, prods, challenges, and refuses to give the right answer."
— **Based on the teachings of Lao Tzu**

Encouraging independance

The ability to learn independently is crucial in computer training. People who are naturally independent and like to figure things out for themselves are generally at an advantage when it comes to learning how to use software. It is the trainer's responsibility to ensure that independent learning is encouraged.

Developing independent learners

In computer training, the trainer often promotes dependence rather than actively encouraging independence. This is not a conscious act on the part of the trainer, but rather the result of the way most computer training classes are structured. The learners walk in, sit down, and expect to be told what to do and how to do it. Learners expect to "be taught" and the trainer expects to "teach" them. The trainer takes on the role of "knowledge provider," a role that many trainers enjoy. It is satisfying to have people call on you for help and advice. Unfortunately, this standard training model is not very effective in teaching computer skills.

Computer trainers need to help learners develop a much greater sense of independence, to the point where the learners do not rely on the trainer anymore. In fact, most computer trainers did not rely on trainers—you probably taught yourself. You sat down, struggled a bit, looked at help menus and books, and figured it out. Still, many trainers don't encourage learners to do the same, unwittingly encouraging learners to be dependent.

To achieve a greater level of independence, you must do less. By assuming the provider role, you perpetuate a model where the learner looks outside for help. Stop being a provider, and be more of a guide or coach.

So how do you help learners achieve independence in a computer class? Ask questions. Do a good job of teaching vocabulary and basic concepts (the big picture), and when you get to an assisted or unassisted exercise, ask more questions than you answer (see page 7). In fact, after teaching a particular topic or a feature, try to answer as few questions as possible. Have the trainees find the answer by prompting them to think a little more, make educated guesses, use the help resources, and read the manual.

The "then what" approach

For example, suppose you have just introduced some new database terminology and explained the concept of a database query. It is time to show the trainees how to create and run a query. Rather than telling them all the procedural steps, you might say something like, "Which menu do you think Query might be in?" Then wait. This does several things. First of all, by posing a question, you have changed the mode of the class from one of passive listening to one of active participation. It is now up to the learners to talk. You have encouraged them to participate, to ponder the question and suggest a solution. In other words, they must think.

If you had immediately said, "Okay, click on Tools . . .," they would have done so blindly. They would be following your instructions without stopping to consider why. As a result, little learning would take place. By stopping and inquiring, trainees become engaged in thinking about the logic of the program—the key to learning any software.

After they have decided that Tools is the menu they need (and they might sometimes need prompting, or leading in the right direction), you ask, ". . . and then what?" Once again, you are asking them to think and consider. Continue this process of asking them the next step, and then the next, until the procedure is complete (see page 10).

Training people to learn procedures with the ". . . then what?" approach has been one of the most valuable elements of my computer classes. I have used it for many years, and highly recommend it. However, there will, of course, be times when you have to provide an answer or an explanation. I'm not suggesting you walk around refusing to answer questions, but rather that you do all you possibly can to have the learners find the answers. If you remember to guide rather than provide, your training will be ten times more effective.

From my files

I was teaching a word-processing class one day when a minor emergency occurred. I told the class that I would have to leave for about half an hour and that they should try to work through the courseware on their own. Thirty minutes later I returned, apologized, and asked them how far they had gotten.

"We finished lesson three," one of the participants said proudly. I looked down at my course outline. I was shocked. They had covered more material while I was out of the room than I had planned to cover with them. Skeptically, I asked a few questions to test their understanding. They all understood it perfectly.

It made me realize how much learning in a computer class relies on the learner, rather than the instructor—a humbling experience.

Do less telling and more asking

Computer trainers enjoy standing in front of a class and providing knowledge for hungry minds. That's probably why you continue to train: you love to communicate what you know to others. However, this zest for presenting information can hinder the learner. Trainers can get so engrossed in delivering training they forget to allow learning to take place, telling and showing rather than encouraging trainees to learn in the most effective way—discovering things for themselves. No learning can be more valuable and lasting than when the learner discovers the answers. This method of learning by discovery is more appropriate today than in the past, due to the increasing ease of use and intuitive nature of computer software.

It is a disservice to learners when you tell them what to do and how to do it. It is too easy for them to follow instructions in a classroom setting without significant learning taking place. It's easy to become attached to making sure that the trainees all get it "right" in the classroom. This type of training serves the trainer more than it does the learner. Everyone is following along, getting the right results and covering all the material, but the participants are just learning how to follow instructions correctly rather than being encouraged to learn.

Learning and retention happen when the learner is actively involved in questioning the how and the why. It is not enough, in a word-processing class for example, for you to say, "Click Format and then Paragraph and then . . ." as the steps to teach indents. You should be asking them questions and encouraging them to learn for themselves. Better to say, "Which menu do you think indents might be in?" and discuss the logic of the menu choices. When they have understood why it is under Format, you might say, ". . . and then what would you choose?" Let them suggest the answers.

The process of having them think about the necessary steps will help teach the logic of the program. Learning by blind repetition will be replaced with learning by understanding. Too many computer users are encouraged to remember steps rather than understand the logic of the software. By concentrating on having learners question and consider the steps, you ensure that the work is understood and therefore more likely to be remembered.

Reduce telling how and increase asking how. Ask questions that help lead trainees to answers—answers they arrive at primarily by themselves. A feature or function of a program that is learned in this mode will not only be remembered more easily, but will help the learner to develop the knowledge and confidence to learn other programs independently.

There are instances, however, when this approach is less appropriate. When the learners are true computer novices, they do not have a sufficient grasp of basic software concepts to make this approach as powerful. Also, more abstract concepts and features cannot initially be taught this way. Consider, for example, database concepts. Some of the terminology and ideas involved are totally new to the learners, and cannot, therefore, be related to their own experiences. However, after some initial terminology and concepts have been introduced, you can ask them how to use these new abstractions in finding solutions. Once the new concepts are understood, they can be used as the basis for new questions, such as, "Now you know what a database table is. What do you think related tables might be?"

Asking questions is a more effective way of learning than giving answers. When you tell learners how, you encourage them to remember by rote. When you ask them how, you encourage them to remember by understanding. Rote and repetition have a place in training, but learning by understanding is far more preferable.

Questions are powerful

I was asked by a training company in Oakland, California to talk with Susan, one of their new trainers, to see if I could help with some of the challenges she was having in her classes. We sat down for a cup of coffee and she began to explain, "When I teach a class, I think everything is going well. They seem to be following me okay, but when we do some of the hands-on exercises or reviews, they start to really struggle. They seem like they're getting it when I explain it, but it doesn't seem to stick."

She told me that the utility company, whose people she had been training, was concerned about how much their employees had learned in the classes. They found that many of the participants, when they returned to work, were still confused on some of the fundamentals of the spreadsheet program they were using. Susan, who was fairly new to the field of computer training, was visibly upset by the whole situation. "They're considering asking for another trainer to do the training if things don't change," she said, fighting back tears.

With some reluctance, she agreed to let me observe one of her classes so that I could get a feel for what was going on, and maybe make some suggestions. After a few nervous minutes at the start of the class, she began to relax and settled down to the business of training.

It didn't take long before I saw what was happening and why they weren't retaining the skills being taught. Susan was a very bright and enthusiastic trainer, and she knew her software inside out. Nobody could fault her on her technical know-how. In her class, she explained things logically and carefully, and then told the trainees exactly what to press or click. For example, to teach headers and footers, she instructed, "Okay, so go up to File and choose Page Setup, click the Header/Footer tab . . ." She went slow enough that everyone could keep up, and they all dutifully did as she said. At the end of the exercise, everyone had the correct results; their spreadsheets looked like they were supposed to.

We met after the class and she asked for feedback. I told her that I thought she was trying to teach too much rather than let the learners learn. "You're making it too easy for them," I said. I explained that she spent a lot of time hand-holding and telling them what to do. I suggested that she tell and direct them less, and ask them more questions. Get them to do the thinking. Instead of leading them through headers and footers, for example, she could have asked them questions about what headers and footers were, when they might use them, what menu they might be in, and so on.

The students weren't retaining the information because they spent the majority of the class being told what to do. And they were good at carrying out instructions. I suggested that in her next class, she concentrate on giving the very minimum of basic instruction and ask the participants as many questions as she could. "If there is any possibility they can find it out themselves with your prompting, don't answer any question directly. Throw as many of their questions as you can back at them. Get them to do the work. Let them figure it out," I told her. Although a little concerned about her ability to do this, she agreed to try it in her classes.

When we talked on the telephone two weeks later, she sounded very upbeat and excited: "Well, the first class I tried it, it felt weird. I guess I slipped back into my old ways, but I kept at it and yesterday I had the most wonderful class!" She went on to say that she had successfully taught mail-merging in a word-processing class in about half the time she usually took.

"I sat down the night before and figured out what I absolutely had to tell them about mail-merge—the vocabulary and some of the basic ideas. And then I went through all the questions I could ask them about doing it. To my surprise, they all got it the first time—I couldn't believe it! Some of them even figured out how to do labels on their own. I almost felt they didn't need me anymore!"

Using questions in computer training

Use questioning as your major method for interacting with the class. One of the most important skills a computer trainer can develop is the effective use of questioning in teaching. This is sometimes called the Socratic method because Socrates used dialogue and questioning to further the education of his pupils and himself. Although the Socratic method is thousands of years old, it remains a powerful tool for learning.

Why is the use of questioning so powerful in training? Consider the goal in computer training: the learner should be able to understand and apply software knowledge and skills. The key word here is understand. It is not enough to memorize keystrokes and procedures. This might have been acceptable in the past, with the many nonintuitive programs that were around, but with GUI environments like Windows, you have to ensure that understanding takes place. Understanding is the key to learning and further skills acquisition.

The best learning in computer training is active learning. It occurs when the participants are actively engaged in questioning, testing, inquiring, and discovering for themselves. The trainer needs to encourage this mode of learning by asking the learner questions. When a question is asked in a training session, the trainer temporarily suspends the role of information provider and becomes more of a guide or facilitator. The learner has to then stop, consider, and engage his or her thought processes in finding answers. This process is the key to independent learning. It is critical to understanding and applying knowledge.

Questions encourage active learning. But what types of questions should you ask and how should you ask them? The types of questions you can ask fall into these general categories:

- Closed questions

- Open questions

- Reflexive questions

- Leading questions

- Unexpected questions

- Next-step questions

Closed questions

Closed questions are those that have a yes/no response or one specific answer, such as

- "What keys do you press to bold?"

- "Is this an appropriate name for the macro?"

- "What button do you click to create a table?"

They have their uses, but such simple responses give little opportunity for inquiry, discussion, consideration, or original thought. Such questions encourage learners to concentrate on memorization of material rather than on understanding.

Open questions

Open questions have no single answer, but require discussion and consideration. Here are some examples of open-ended questions:

- "What could you use a macro for?"

- "Why are we creating a data file?"

- "What do you think are the differences between forms and reports?"

These are usually much more helpful than closed questions because they demand some original thought. In order to answer them, the learner must understand the topic being taught. By answering such a question, it is apparent to the trainer (and the learner) how much has been understood.

Reflexive questions

Reflexive questions are thrown back to the questioner or to the class. The goal is to have the person asking the question discover the answer, encouraging him or her to think. Consider these two exchanges:

Learner: "How do I set margins?"
Trainer: "Well, what menu do you think they might be under?

or

Learner: "Did I do this right?"
Trainer: "What was it you were trying to accomplish?"

Reflexive questions are another attempt at getting the learner to think and inquire independently. They are a refusal to give an answer and an encouragement to the learner to think a little more. By throwing the question back to the individual or to the other participants, you promote the habit of active learning.

From my files

Even when you try your best to encourage independence in the learner, sometimes there is resistance. I remember teaching a class once where someone asked me how to set margins. I sat down next to her and pointed to the screen. "Let's take a look. What menu do you think they might be under?"

"I don't know. That's why I'm asking you. Just tell me."

I was determined to encourage her to think for herself.

"Well, do you think it might be under File?," I said, persisting.

"I don't know!," she said, staring wide-eyed at me. "You're the instructor, that's what we pay you for. You tell me!"

Sometimes encouraging independence can be a challenge.

Leading questions

Leading questions guide the learner in the right direction. They're useful when a learner is struggling with a question and needs more guidance. Here are a few examples:

- "So, in a relational database, the individual tables can be related to . . .?"

- "What menu would allow us to *insert a picture* into the document?"

Do all you can to lead learners to the appropriate answer by giving clues, directions, and hints. Leading questions are often useful, but giving too much information up front deprives the learner of independent thinking. Sometimes an answer arrived at by leading questions has less chance of being properly understood or remembered.

Unexpected questions
It's sometimes helpful to ask questions when the participants least expect it. For example, the trainer might be providing a solution or showing procedural steps, and then turn a statement into a question:

- "You choose Tools, Macro, Record, and then what?"

- "We type =SUM, and what goes inside the parentheses?"

Unexpected questions are great to use when you feel your participants are just nodding vacantly, dozing, or just following you blindly. These questions make sure that the learners are listening, following, and thinking about what they are doing.

"Next-step" questions
Next-step questions are a variation on unexpected questions. They are a very powerful way to teach Windows programs or other fairly intuitive software. After having carefully explained the vocabulary and basic concepts of a particular task to be accomplished, you prompt for the procedural steps:

- "Which menu do you think Mail Merge might be in?"

- "What do we choose next?"

- "Then what do we need to do?"

Ask the learners what the next step would be, and wait for a response. If none is forthcoming, supply a few prompts or hints. The point is to provide minimal information and encourage the learners to constantly figure out the next step of the process.

When attempting to teach particular tasks in Windows and other GUI programs, I have found this approach to be one of the most effective. I have successfully taught mail-merging for several word processors in this fashion. I give a thorough overview of the basic concepts, ideas, and vocabulary used, and then I repeat, ". . . and then what . . .?" as we complete each step. I avoid telling them anything. At the end, they have virtually taught themselves and will have a much better understanding of the concepts and procedures because they figured it out.

Try using more questions in your computer training. It encourages thinking and trains participants to become independent learners.

Concentrate on open, reflexive, unexpected and next-step questions, while using closed and leading questions sparingly.

Asking questions

There are ways to effectively present questions to a class and ways to effectively respond to questions. Let's start by considering the ways to ask questions.

It is generally a good idea to ask a question of the whole group. Nobody is singled out, and there is no pressure for any one person to answer. Those who wish to answer will respond. Don't ask a question, wait a few seconds, and then proceed to answer the question. Ten seconds is the generally accepted time to wait before giving your answer. They need time to hear the question, understand it, think about what they have learned, and then find a possible solution.

Get an answer from everyone. When you are posing a question to a group, don't stop at the first response. Go around the group asking for each person's answer: "What do you think, Jill? How about you, Ron? Bill?"

Don't tell anyone whether his or her answer is correct until you have heard from everyone. At the end, you can give the right answer and discuss some of the other answers that were given. Listening to everyone's answers gives you a much better feel for who might be confused or what you might need to make clearer.

Quiet learners

If you find that certain people are not participating, you can pose a question to the whole class but let your eyes rest on someone who hasn't answered a question yet. Quite often this will be enough for them to offer a response, especially if you make the question a relatively easy one. If they appear uncomfortable about responding, don't push it; move on to someone else.

When you do get an answer from someone else in the room, come back to the quiet student and say something like, "Does that sound reasonable to you, Sue?" or "Does that answer make sense to you, John?" They might not say much, but it brings them into the conversation or discussion. After running other participant's answers by the quieter ones, they might begin to open up and contribute more. If not, then a break time is an ideal opportunity to talk with them privately, check their understanding, and figure out why they are not participating.

Learners who dominate

On the other hand, you might have someone who responds to each and every question you ask. This person tends to dominate the question sessions, so others might not feel motivated to think of their own responses. There are several ways of dealing with this, covered in the section "Dealing with difficult learners" in Chapter 12.

Incorrect answers

When you have asked a question and someone has responded with an answer that is inappropriate or wrong, avoid bluntly stating, "No," "Wrong," or shaking your head. Of course, you would be being honest if you did this, but it would not build confidence and self-esteem in the learner.

A far better response is to prompt and guide learners to the correct answer. For example, suppose you ask what a query is used for in a database. Someone offers the incorrect answer, "To print an output of the table?" Instead of saying no, you might say, "That's what we call a report" or, "What does the word query usually mean in everyday language?" You have avoided telling anyone they are wrong and, at the same time, guided them to the right answer.

From my files

I am reminded of a math class I taught in a school for children with learning disabilities. One boy in the class was very motivated to learn and was enthusiastic, but if he found that one of his answers was wrong, he would immediately become aggressive, breaking his pencil and smashing his fist on the desk. After realizing this, I changed the language I used when I sat beside him and checked his work. When I came across a problem that was wrong, I would say, "Great, that's completely right if we just change this to . . . what?" or, "Well done, you're almost there! All we need to do now is . . ." The result was a much happier, more self-confident, and relaxed individual. The self-criticism that got in the way of learning was reduced considerably. (We also saved on pencils.)

Responding to questions

When responding to questions that learners ask, or answers they give, try to create an atmosphere that nurtures and encourages their participation. Listen to the question, then direct it to the class. This technique is similar to a reflexive question except you direct it to the whole class rather than one individual.

Someone says, "Can I link a spreadsheet to the document as well?" You turn to the other participants and repeat, "So, do you think it is possible to link a spreadsheet as well?" Then, wait for a response. Someone will usually come up with the answer, or a discussion will ensue. This approach is much more powerful than answering the question outright because it gives an opportunity for the learners to think critically and discuss. Discussion should always be encouraged—it precipitates thinking and understanding.

Restate the question if necessary. Often, someone will ask a question that will be long-winded and unclear because of their lack of familiarity with the software. When the trainer grasps the question, it should be restated in clear, succinct terms to the rest of the class. This gives everyone an opportunity to offer a solution or learn something new, instead of just one person. It is most important that the learners in a class listen to and fully understand each others' questions. It should be the responsibility of the trainer to ensure this happens.

Treat all questions equally. It is often tempting for a trainer to listen to a very insightful question from a participant and say something like, "That's a great question, Steve!" This might certainly be the case, and Steve might have hit upon a very important point, but what happens when Susan asks a somewhat simple question that most of the class already knows? By treating this question differently and not saying, "That's a really great question!" you are making a statement by omission. Susan gets the message that her question is not as valuable as Steve's.

I am not suggesting that every question should be followed by an exclamation of how great it is, but that your responses should be consistent. Susan's question might not have been a wonderful, insightful observation by Steve's standards, but for her it might have demonstrated a new level of understanding of the work. Treating one question as more valuable than another inadvertently discourages more participation.

Never do it for them

Most trainers often come across learners who are quite slow at using the keyboard or the mouse, or just slow at understanding. The trainer sits next to the learner and tries to help. "Okay, now choose Format, and then . . . no, Format. No, this one here. No, the menu, not the button . . . this one here." We have all been there.

After several attempts at giving directions, the trainer grabs the mouse or takes over the keyboard, and completes the procedure that was causing so much trouble. "There, like that!" Finally, the learner can complete the rest of the exercise. The trainer feels relieved.

Whenever a trainer does that, the trainee is robbed of a learning experience. The trainee still doesn't know how to complete the task; it was done for them. Communication did take place, however. The trainer communicated, by implication, that the learner is inept and cannot use the program unassisted. This reinforces any inadequacy that person might feel about learning to use the computer. In short, doing it for them serves only one person: the impatient trainer.

I don't care how tempting it is—don't touch a trainee's keyboard or mouse. I tell my participants that they have permission to slap my hand if I touch their keyboard or their mouse. And I explain why.

The only time it might be permissible is when they absolutely cannot get to where they need to be and are holding up the rest of the class. In such a case, ask permission to get them caught up, and explain later, perhaps at a break time, exactly what you did. Otherwise, you need to be patient and persistent and do all you can to get them to carry out the procedure.

The same rule applies when you see someone's neighbor leaning over trying to help and using the other person's keyboard or mouse. Ask the "helpful" person not to do this and explain why. Say something like, "Jim, I appreciate you helping Bill out, but try to help without actually touching the keyboard because . . ." and explain the reason.

Although I use the term trainer in this book, words like facilitator and coach better describe the qualities needed to enable learning. The word trainer suggests a traditional model of a teacher standing before the class delivering knowledge. The teacher playing the active role and the learners, the passive. Facilitator or coach suggests an individual assisting, guiding, encouraging, and being a catalyst for learning to occur. Here the teacher establishes an atmosphere of mutual inquiry and encourages learners to take an active role in learning.

Encouraging self-evaluation

In any activity involving learning a skill, content feedback is necessary. When you learn something new, you constantly need to know if you are on track; if not, you need to adjust your course. This is certainly true for computer training. When learning a new feature or function of a software application, a computer learner receives feedback in one of two basic ways: from the software itself and from the trainer. In trying to figure out if they are on the right track, learners can either consult the trainer (extrinsic feedback) or try to figure it out for themselves (intrinsic feedback). The former, feedback from the trainer, is far more prevalent—and much less effective.

Extrinsic feedback Susan is working on a task in a spreadsheet program and gets an answer. She asks the trainer, "Is this right?" The trainer looks it over and nods, "Yes, well done." Susan sits there feeling quite pleased with herself.

What has happened here? The learner has completed a task and has looked for outside confirmation and approval. When validation is given, the learner sits back comforted by the knowledge that the work is correct. By providing this validation, the trainer encourages the participant to be a dependent learner. The trainer does the evaluating and the learner passively accepts it. This works very well for the trainer who feels needed, knowledgeable, and all-knowing, but it is done at the expense of the learner. The learner is encouraged to have someone else evaluate and approve. This is definitely not the road to independent learning.

Intrinsic feedback The best method of evaluation is self-evaluation. The trainer avoids making judgments and encourages the learner to evaluate and judge independently.

Again, Susan says, "Is this right?" In response, the trainer asks questions like, "Well, what is it that you are trying to do?" or, "Does that look like a reasonable answer?" or, "How can you tell if that is correct or not?" In other words, the trainer avoids making a judgment and encourages the learner to look critically at the work and make his or her own value judgment. In this way, the trainer not only encourages independence, but helps the learner gain a fuller understanding of the work.

This is the best way to serve the needs of the learner. Encourage them to become independent, provide their own feedback, and accept greater responsibility for their learning.

Using help systems and documentation

It is important to teach learners how to use help resources, documentation, and reference materials. Make sure they know how to access and use the Help menu, coaches, tutorials, and similar online documentation. If you are using courseware or other documentation, make sure that you show trainees how it is organized and how they should use it. At the end of a training session, instill in them the importance of the help resources by saying something like, "Suppose you get back to work and can't remember anything about macros. What do you do?"

Review all the possible ways of accessing help and finding information: the Help menu, the coaches, the tutorial, their notes, the courseware, the reference manual, online documentation—whatever is available. It is important that they leave the class knowing exactly how to find information or search for help. It is even more important that they leave with a "self-help" attitude to solving problems and know not to call the help desk until they have tried to solve a problem themselves.

To encourage them to do this, I often give an exercise containing a simple feature that they haven't covered yet. When they ask for assistance, I tell them to use their resources to figure it out. After doing it a few times, they begin to see the value of figuring it out for themselves.

When a learner asks how to do something during a training session, the tendency is to immediately provide the answer. This puts the trainer in the role of provider rather than coach. A better response in some instances, and one that promotes learning, would be, "See if you can figure it out." Too often a trainer discourages learning and independence by telling the users how to do things.

Help-desk staff are overextended, and the office computer guru has to get out of the training business and get some work done. Trainers need to teach learners to use the available resources and documentation and encourage a little more independence.

Interacting with learners

One of the most important aspects of any type of training is the inter-action between the trainer and the learner. This relationship can make or break the training. Being able to recognize and respond to verbal and nonverbal signals helps build rapport and allows the trainer to adapt the delivery of the material when necessary.

Reading your learners

Trainers can often become insensitive to learners. Not insensitive in terms of being mean or unkind, but of being unaware of their re-sponses and reactions to the training. Every learner is constantly com-municating how he or she is coping with the material. Most of the time, this is quite subtle. About 90% of this communication is nonverbal, consisting of facial expressions, body movements, eye movements, etc.

It's easy to miss these important signals when training. You get caught up in the process of delivering information and miss the subtle, non-verbal language of the learners. It becomes even harder when teach-ing new materials, new classes, or in new training environments. In these cases, it is especially difficult to give your attention fully to the learners. The key to becoming more responsive to training partici-pants, however, is getting attention off yourself and onto them.

Being able to "tune in" and read your learners will make training much less stressful for you and more rewarding for them. It will be less stressful for you because you will know immediately when there is a problem or a concern for a learner, and you will be able to ad-dress it promptly. It will be more rewarding for them because they will not be sitting there for long periods of time getting increasingly frustrated. Their concerns or frustrations will be nipped in the bud.

If you can begin to read your learners, your capacity to facilitate learning will increase dramatically. So how can you develop sensitiv-ity to these signals? Here are some suggestions:

- Be aware that there are hundreds of unspoken communications in every class you teach. Being aware of their presence is the first step in being able to interpret them.

- When a learner asks or answers a question, listen not only for the words, but how they are spoken. Does there appear to be some concern behind what is being said? Is there something you could say or a way you could listen that might address this concern? For example, suppose a class member folds her arms, sighs, and says, "I don't really think I would use this feature very much at work." What she might really mean is, "I'm frustrated and I don't understand the damn thing!" If you take her words at face value, you might miss the opportunity of clearing up some confusion and alleviating some of her frustrations. Read between the lines.

- Whenever possible, look around the room and observe the expressions and body language of the class members (when they are working independently is a good time). Does it look like someone might have a concern that he or she has not expressed? What could you do or say to address such a concern? You might walk over and quietly say, "Is this making sense?" or, "Need some help?" This often prompts participants to express concerns they might have.

- Do whatever you can to get your attention off yourself and onto the learners. Know your material inside out. Practice your training session. Be prepared. Get to the training room early. Be yourself. A good way to get your attention off yourself is to ask questions. This gives you an opportunity to look around and tune into the class. It's much harder to get your attention off yourself when you are constantly talking or lecturing.

- Practice reading other people's expressions and body language. Have fun with this one. Next time you're waiting for a bus or a plane or sitting having a cup of coffee, take a look at the expressions of the people around you. See if you can read some unspoken communications there. Are they concerned, uncertain, confident, happy, bored, upset, indifferent, or excited? Tune into other people's body language. What are they communicating?

Finding out how they are doing

When you drive along the road, you constantly observe the conditions and adjust your driving accordingly. You require constant feedback in order to navigate correctly. Computer training is exactly the same. Trainers require feedback in order to be able to adjust the training to the changing needs of the learners. Simply delivering information or lecturing is a one-way process that allows for no changing conditions. It's like trying to drive with your eyes closed.

To train effectively, you need to constantly elicit feedback from the participants to find out how they are doing. Without knowing how they are doing on an ongoing basis, you cannot satisfy their training needs. There are various ways to do this. One way is to become adept at reading the subtle (and sometimes not-so-subtle) signals from the learners and to tune into their unspoken language. The other is to ask for feedback.

When I train, I stop at regular intervals, usually before a break, and ask, "Am I going a little too fast for anyone?" I pause and look around the room. ". . . too slow for anyone?" I pay attention to their expressions as well as their verbal responses. Some trainees might not like to publicly admit that I am going too fast. If someone indicates (verbally or otherwise) that I am going a little too fast or slow for them, I acknowledge the fact. If it is appropriate, I adjust my teaching based on this feedback. For instance, if a majority of the group feels I am going a little too fast, I will slow down somewhat. If only one person in the group feels the pace is too fast, I acknowledge that fact, but might choose to maintain the pace and give that individual more personal help.

Some trainees who have concerns will, for various reasons, not speak up in front of the other participants. They prefer not to have the spotlight on them. The most appropriate way of addressing this is at a break time (see page 27). During a break the atmosphere is informal, and one-on-one conversations are not broadcast to the other participants. At the right moment, I might walk over to someone who I think might have some concerns and say something like, "Is this stuff making sense?" or "How are you finding this work?" I have found that this is usually enough for someone to unload any worries or frustrations they might have. They will feel freer talking to you personally than they would with the rest of the class listening.

By frequently asking for feedback, you can discover what might be getting in the way of someone's ability to learn. In most cases, you will be able to confront the issue and help them. In some cases, all you can offer is an understanding ear. Either way, the load is lightened and it will be easier for the individual to become fully engaged in the learning.

Remember, if you wish to have the participants provide you with feedback, you need to create an atmosphere that allows this. If they feel respected, honored, and listened to, they are much more liable to provide you with some honest feedback. They have to trust you first. If you have already developed a rapport with them, they will be much more inclined to open up and express their concerns or anxieties (see page 33).

Training tip

A great way of finding out how the training is being received by the learners is to give out cards or slips of paper with three sections labeled,

1 Keep doing . . .

2 Stop doing . . .

3 Start doing . . .

Ask them to finish the sentences, writing down

1 What is working well for them in the class and what you should continue doing

2 What is not working for them in the class and you should stop doing

3 What you have not yet done that they would like you to start doing

Collect them all and read them at the next break. I have found this to work really well. You often get some surprises, such as "Let's stop spending so much time with people who don't have the prerequisites for the class," "Give us more real exercises and examples rather than the simple ones in the workbook," or even "Stop sucking air in through your lower front teeth." This way everyone can express their concerns or make suggestions without feeling put on the spot or embarrassed.

Checking for understanding

It is easy for computer trainers to assume that the class is following along and understanding everything if the participants are smiling or nodding. They might be smiling and nodding for other reasons, however. Sometimes the nod is what I like to call the "polite nod." Participants are nodding more as a courtesy to the trainer than because they are comprehending everything. It's not a "Yes, I understand" nod, it's more of a "Yes, I'm listening" nod. Some cultures, such as the Japanese, are particularly likely to have this characteristic. Trainers should be wary of misunderstanding this gesture.

In order for any semblance of learning to take place in a computer class, the trainer has to constantly check for understanding. In most training, a grasp of the basic concepts and ideas is critical to understanding the rest of the material. Therefore, at regular intervals, you must determine whether the learners are, in fact, "getting it."

How can you know that they are really understanding? The most straightforward method is to ask them. During a training session, stop at regular intervals and ask, "Is this making sense?" or "Is that clear?" or "Any questions about that?" This is usually enough for participants to ask for clarification on anything that might be confusing them. I often use names at this point. I might ask, "Did I explain that clearly enough, Steve?" if I think Steve might be confused on a point but reluctant to ask. This might prompt him to ask for clarification. (Notice that I do not phrase the question, "Do you understand that, Steve?" where the emphasis is on him rather than me. It would be easier for Steve to say, "No, could you explain it again" than "No, I don't understand." When something is not clear to a learner, always assume it is your explanation that is at fault—not the learner.)

Also, remember to wait nine or ten seconds before moving on after asking a question. Remember, trainees need time to listen to your question, scan the work they have just been doing, consider any possible areas on which they might have questions, phrase a question in their minds, and then ask it. Asking a question and then moving on after a few seconds does not serve them.

Simply asking someone, "Does that make sense?" or, "Do you understand that?" is not always sufficient. Closed questions like this often encourage someone to answer yes even when something is not completely clear. If someone says, "Yes, I understand" you have no way of really knowing whether this is in fact the case. It is much better to ask more open, searching questions that can only be answered if there truly is an understanding.

For example, "How would you create a query to find all the customers in Reno, Nevada?" would be a better question to ask than, "Do you understand how to create a query?" Similarly, "When would you want to use a template?" would be better than "Is it clear what a template is?" To really gauge someone's understanding, ask them open questions or get them to demonstrate their knowledge.

From my files

When I first started computer training, I realized the need to make sure everyone understood before I continued. In one class, I stopped every now and then with, "Does that make sense?" I scanned the room, saw people nodding and smiling and assumed everything was clear. I moved on to the next topic. After an hour or so, I gave them a practice exercise to try.

No one could do it. Some of them clearly had not understood what I had covered. They had thought they understood it at the time, and the ones who knew they didn't understand felt embarrassed to say anything. I realized that nodding, smiling faces are not always an indication of comprehension. From then on, I tried to ask open-ended, more searching questions that would elicit a real comprehension of the work.

Training by walking around

When trainers remain at the front of the room and always teach from this vantage point, they perpetuate the "provider" model of computer training. The trainer provides information, and the participants become passive receivers. The front of the room gives the trainer authority and reinforces the idea that to learn, one must be told what to do by the "all-knowing" instructor.

This is not a good model. Whenever possible, the trainer should step into the learner's "space" and move around the room. When you are not using the projection panel or the whiteboard, walk around and teach. When the learners are working on practice exercises, walk around. Walk around when you're asking them questions. Take all the opportunities you can to get in among the learners, rather than remain up front.

Walking around as you train does several things:

- It helps develop more of an intimate rapport with the group.

- The learners will be more inclined to ask questions and interact when you remove yourself from the authority position.

- You can more easily coach and facilitate when you are on their turf.

- You can address any questions or problems that might arise in a more personal, one-on-one basis.

- You can follow what they are doing on their systems more easily and offer timely guidance.

- Movement increases interest level, so you can keep their attention better.

- You can control talkative or difficult participants much better (see Chapter 12, "Dealing with difficult learners").

The most important time to walk around is when participants are working on practice exercises. This gives you the opportunity to see exactly who needs a little more help and guidance. It is also the perfect time to help someone who might be struggling, without embarrassing them in front of the class.

Try to move from station to station, watching their progress, and asking if they need assistance. Avoid phrases like, "Are you stuck?" or "You look like you're a bit confused—let me help," or "No, not quite." When you say these, you are broadcasting to the rest of the group that this person doesn't understand. Never emphasize the negative. Use phrases like, "Let me show you something," "Try this," or "Is this clear?" This way, you are not emphasizing to the group the fact that someone might be confused.

By walking around and assisting one-on-one, you can clarify any confusions and help struggling users get back on track. Some of the most valuable learning in a computer class will take place when you are walking around giving individual guidance. It might feel more comfortable at the front, but the real learning gets done on the other side of the room. Consider spending some more time there.

From my files

I discovered the power of training by walking around when I taught a spreadsheet class to a group of attorneys. I would regularly stop and ask if anyone had questions. There was always silence. However, when I wandered around the room as they were working on an exercise, the questions would flow. "How do you copy again?" "Where's that SUM button?" "What did you say a template was?"

I began to realize how much easier it is for someone to ask a question one-on-one than in front of the class. In front of others, there is always that possibility of looking "dumb," or being embarrassed. When the trainer is standing next to you, and your conversation is almost a private one, you become a lot more open and communicative. It seems far less threatening—even for attorneys.

Generating participation

Learning how to use computer software is not a passive activity. You cannot sit in a room listening to someone lecture and expect to learn any real software skills. There needs to be a large element of participation. Not only participation in terms of "hands-on" use of the computer, but participation in discussion and interaction with the trainer and the other participants. Discussion and asking questions helps promote a fuller understanding of the software, and should be encouraged.

Often, a learner will prefer to sit in front of the computer and be a somewhat passive learner. It expends less energy and is less threatening. Learners are often more comfortable being told what to do than taking responsibility for their own learning. It is a model they have accepted for many years. You have to gently break them of this habit and encourage them to take a fuller part in the learning process. They need to be encouraged to ask questions, answer questions, join in discussions, and generally take a more active role in learning.

They won't all want to do this. It is your job as a computer trainer to encourage this involvement. So what will help generate their participation in the learning process? First of all, they need to understand that their participation is an important part of learning the software. At the start of many classes, and after I have developed some sort of initial rapport, I ask, "How many of you want to get as much out of this class as you can?" Inevitably every hand goes up. I continue, "If you want to get the most from this class, I need your input and participation—ask questions, answer questions, share your thoughts, ideas, complaints. Feel free to interrupt me at anytime."

I let them know up front how important their participation is. Having them understand this and having them actually participate are two different things, however. How do you get their participation? How do you get them actively involved in the training? Well, let's look at some reasons why they might not participate. Usually, it's one or all of these:

- Fear of speaking in front of a group

- Fear of making a mistake

- Laziness or just feeling more comfortable sitting and observing

Because of these inhibitions, you have to be sure to generate a safe, open, non-judgmental atmosphere room where the participants feel respected and that their opinions are valued. This is by far the most important key to generating participation in a class. The best possible atmosphere in which to generate participation is one in which the learners feel that they are listened to, their ideas are valued, and they will not be made to feel inadequate should they offer a wrong answer. It should be the trainer's goal to create such an environment. Keep in mind, also, that the atmosphere generated in the room is 90% a reflection of the trainer's attitude and frame of mind.

Other effective ways of encouraging participation are to ask questions and to try some group-learning activities. As discussed earlier in this chapter, asking questions is a perfect way to get your participants to become engaged in the learning. It forces them to actively take part and think rather than passively listen. Group activities where participants interact with their neighbors as well as the trainer are also a very valuable way of stimulating participation (see page 31, "Learner-learner interactions")

Don't let anyone escape interaction

Participation and involvement in training increases learning. Those learners who involve themselves in questioning, offering solutions, and participating class discussion generally gain more from the training than those who don't.

What often happens, however, is that the question-and-answer sessions tend to be dominated by a few individuals. The trainer feels there is involvement and class discussion, when in fact, many of the participants are simply sitting and listening to the more vocal members of the group. Make sure you have interactions with everyone in the room. Everyone should be included in the class, including the shy and quiet ones who prefer to sit and listen.

When you make sure that everyone participates or interacts with you at some point, you will find the atmosphere changes. After reluctant learners are encouraged to participate, you'll find the level of involvement will accelerate. People who sat there very quietly will start to open up and begin to be more actively involved in the training. Don't give up on anyone. Don't allow them to sit through a whole class just listening. Be persistent without making them feel uncomfortable. If necessary, ask them a very simple question just to get them participating and involved.

From my files

One of the most gratifying training experiences for me was a spreadsheet class I taught several years ago. A very self-conscious and worried-looking woman sat down in the back row.

In talking informally with the group before the class, I remember her saying something like, "I'm not too good at learning things. Don't worry about me."

During the class my goal was to include her in discussions, get her involved, but avoid embarrassing her. I started off by asking her some very simple, one-word-answer questions, and acknowledging and encouraging her. Later on, when she seemed a little less nervous, I began to ask her more open-ended questions. I tried to get her to think about the logic of the menus, rather than just follow procedures. At one point, after spending several minutes helping her think through a process, I realized that I might be making her feel a little uncomfortable. I felt that perhaps I had overstepped the mark.

At the end of the class, she came over to me, grabbed my arm, and said quietly, "Thanks for not giving up on me. Thanks for making me think. It made a difference."

It was one of those moments that makes it all worthwhile.

Using break times to your advantage

The value of break times in computer training is often underestimated by trainers. A break can be much more than just an opportunity to give the learners a chance to stretch and the trainer time to check voice-mail or return phone calls. Properly used, a break can be a much more valuable asset to the trainer.

Developing rapport

A break is a perfect opportunity to continue to develop a rapport with your learners. Informal conversation over a cup of coffee can be a very effective way of strengthening such a relationship. This allows them to feel more comfortable with you and much more a part of the class community. The more comfortable they feel with the trainer, the more attentive and involved they will be during the class.

If you leave the room at a break time and only reappear when the training is to resume, you have missed an opportunity to develop this rapport. Disappearing at break times also gives the learners a subtle message that the trainer's primary commitment is not with them.

Addressing problems

Break times are ideal for addressing problems that arise in the class. Software problems, hardware problems, and learners' concerns are all best tackled outside the class rather than during the class time. Most learners are not going to be happy seeing the trainer trying to fix hardware or software problems during their valuable class time. As well as being unfair to them, it gives the impression that the training setup is mediocre. Take a break—try to solve the problem then.

Break time is also a great time for dealing with learners who have problems or concerns. Rather than risk embarrassing them in front of the whole group, you can talk with them one-on-one and help them.

Perhaps a participant is out of his or her depth and really should re-take or reschedule a class. The break is a far more appropriate time to talk about this than trying to do it during the class. The trainer can sit down quietly with the learner and discuss the problem.

Checking for understanding

A break time is a good opportunity to see if your learners really are following the work and understanding it. Some people do not like to let the whole class know they are confused and so will not speak up during the class when they have questions. During the break, the atmosphere is much less formal and the trainer can talk with the participants one-on-one. It is then much easier for the learner to express any concerns or areas of confusion.

Dealing with fast and slow learners

Computer trainers are constantly challenged by trying to satisfy the needs of slow and fast learners, often in the same class. Break time can be an excellent time to deal with these learners. By the time you take your first break, it should be evident who is struggling a little with the basics and who is moving ahead quickly, then waiting for the next bit of information.

With the fast learner, you can use the break time to acknowledge that they are ahead of the game (just acknowledging that fact with them often helps prevent impatience or boredom) and offer to show them a few extra functions, features, or tips. You can also use this time to set some more advanced exercises or give them a few challenges that they can work on while they are waiting for the others.

With the slower learners, use the break to see how you might be able to assist them and get them up to speed. The work you do with them at the break might mean the difference between them understanding or being frustrated and giving up. The help and encouragement you offer during the break can be critical to ensuring that they have a successful class.

From my files

I taught a spreadsheet class several years ago, and about an hour into the class, I began to notice that a woman in the front row seemed confused and upset. She didn't seem to be understanding the work. I could see that she was ready to quit. Before things got too overwhelming for her, I decided we should take a break. I asked to talk with her privately and tried to find out how I could help. She told me she had not understood the work we did on formulas and felt she was now completely lost. She said she felt she was the only one struggling in the class and thought it would be best for her to leave.

I told her she could certainly leave if she felt she needed to—her tuition would be refunded or she could retake the class. She seemed relieved that her employer wouldn't be out-of-pocket. Then, I spent a couple of minutes clarifying the work on formulas that was confusing her. I offered her the option of sitting through the class for a while longer. She could decide if she wanted to leave at lunchtime.

She decided to stay in the class a while longer to see how it went. After the break, we continued, and by lunchtime this woman was participating in discussions, correctly completing all the exercises, and generally being brilliant. She told me with a smile at lunchtime that she was going to stay for the whole class.

What had happened? One simple concept had confused her from the outset, but she felt too self-conscious to ask for clarification. She had assumed that everyone else was more experienced than her and that she was the "slow" student. She was concerned that her company would be charged the course fee if she quit. At the morning break she got reassurance that she was certainly capable of understanding the work and that whatever she wanted to do was okay with the trainer. In other words, all the pressure and concerns she had were lifted. Feeling "freed-up," she was able to concentrate on the work, and her true abilities surfaced.

Without talking with her at the break time, I would have lost a participant and, more importantly, she would have left with little self-esteem and self-confidence. As it turned out, she was one of the stars of the class and became a regular visitor to our training center.

Don't overlook break times. They are valuable.

Using the participants' names

People's names are important to them. When you address someone by name, it changes the whole feeling of the interaction. Whenever I go into my bank, they use my name. Whenever they call me on the telephone, they use my name. It's only a simple thing, but it makes me feel I'm an important and valued customer.

It's the same in a computer training class. You use peoples names and the atmosphere changes. Instead of, "So, does that make sense?" you say, "So, Shelley, does that make sense?" You have only added one word, but what a powerful word! Shelley begins to feel part of the class community rather than just another body in the room. Using participants' names (and having them use yours) can bring a little more warmth into the training room. They will feel more comfortable and related to you. As a result, their capacity for learning will increase.

In order to use their names, you have to know them. There are several ways that you can remember the names of the members in a computer class.

Name tents are a good idea if you have a reasonably large number of participants. These are cards that sit on the desk or monitor, on which the participants have written their first names. (And specify first names, otherwise you'll get some people putting their last name, or last and first initial.) I also ask them to put their names on both sides of the card because I like to move around and behind the class when I teach. I have found this works well most of the time. After an hour or so of actively using their names, you'll probably be able to remember most of them without looking at the cards.

Remembering everyone's name without having it written for you is perhaps the best method. It is not always easy, especially in large groups, but it can be very effective and appreciated by the participants. How can you do this? I have found two ways that work quite well. One is using the room map. As people settle into different seats around the room at the start of the class, I make a crude map of the room and write names in the corresponding locations. I try to memorize the names at the beginning of the class, but if I forget I can quickly look down at my map and see who is sitting where.

The other way is to ask each person his or her name before you start the class or as you are checking them off your attendance list and take a second to look at them and associate their name with some feature. For example, Sue is wearing a navy-blue suit, so you might remember blue rhyming with Sue. Jim is a big, muscular guy who obviously works out, so you might think gym for Jim. Fred is wearing a gray sweater. You might imagine the word FRED in large neon letters embroidered on the sweater. If you've done a good job of associating, you'll be able to look at someone and very quickly remember his or her name. It sounds strange, but works extremely well.

A few words of warning about trying to remember names. First, try to get the pronunciation correct. Second, if you really can't remember a name, ask them, don't guess. I once had a class in which I would ask Terri an occasional question. At the end of the six hours when they were leaving, I turned to her and said, "So, Terri, did you find the class useful?" She looked at me, slightly embarrassed, and said, "My name's not Terri. It's Sherri."

Learner-learner interactions

Interactions between learners in a computer training class are often as important as those between the trainer and learner. You have probably noticed how teaching a group of learners who know one another can be very different from teaching a group of people who don't know each other. When the only interaction is from trainer to learner and learner to trainer, something valuable is missing.

When you have a group of individuals who have never met before, the class usually starts off on quite a reserved note. People become a little reluctant to speak or participate—they want to see what the water's like before jumping in. The trainer is, in effect, talking to individuals rather than talking to a group. I consider it a group when the people in the room start to build a rapport with each other and the trainer, and a certain unity of purpose and rapport is apparent in the room. Without this sense of connection with each other, the training is harder to deliver and not as powerful.

What do participants gain from interacting with each other that they don't gain from interacting with the trainer? When a learner interacts with the trainer, it is in front of the class. It is before his or her peers, and the pressure is turned up. Any confusion, wrong answers, or embarrassment is displayed to the rest of the participants. It is risky. As a result, conversation and participation is thwarted. In a small group, or in a pair, the interaction is with a peer, and concern for making a mistake or giving a wrong answer is reduced. It's the same difference we experience when talking to one or two people and speaking to a group.

Another reason for encouraging learner-learner interaction is that it increases the effectiveness of learning. When someone explains, discusses, asks, or answers questions with a peer, it clarifies and reinforces the learning. Verbalizing a question, the very fact action of forming a question in the mind, aids in being able to answer it. How often have you heard someone phrase a question, and while doing so, say, "It's okay. I figured it out"? (After all, isn't that how psychoanalysts make a living?)

The power of the group

A large company in San Francisco invested huge sums in creating new computer training rooms. They were spacious and well designed, had video projectors, sound systems, state-of-the-art multimedia computers, ergonomically designed seats—the lot. After a month or so of using them, the trainers started to mention how something seemed different about their classes. In the old training rooms, there seemed to be more energy and more interaction, and it was easier to develop a rapport with the group. For some reason, the new training rooms didn't promote this energy and warmth. Evaluations from the participants reflected this sterile atmosphere.

The training manager decided to sit in on one of the classes and figure out what was going on. After spending the morning sitting in the back of the room, she began to see the problem. The new rooms were very spacious, and the computer stations were a couple of feet further apart than they used to be. The participants were not as close together as they used to be. In the older rooms, people were close enough together to converse easily and help their neighbors if they got stuck. That couple of extra feet had made it a little less intimate; there was less interaction with neighbors. Participants would arrive, work on their own, rarely talk with their neighbors, and see only their screen. As a result, the room was a collection of individuals rather than an interactive group.

The computer stations couldn't be moved closer together, so the manager had to come up with another solution. She got all the trainers together, told them what she thought the problem was, and suggested that somewhere early on in the classes they introduce some paired learning exercises or group activities, something that had the trainees interact with their neighbors or the others around them. Most of the trainers were quite skeptical about this reasoning and the solution, but agreed to go along with it.

The difference was apparent after the first few days. The learners got to talk and work with their neighbors in the first few hours of the class, and this became a catalyst for more interaction with the trainers. The trainers were amazed at the difference it made to the participation level and the atmosphere in the room. Learner satisfaction increased, and the post-tests started to show much more positive results.

The instructor editions of the courseware for this company now include paired-learning exercises and group review activities. It is a simple change, but one that produced dramatic results.

Adapting to learners

Most computer training rooms are set up with rows of computer stations facing front, with the trainer's station at the head of the class. Most have rows of bright fluorescent lights. The walls are often plain and empty. Into this somewhat sterile setting walks the trainer, who stands at the front of the room. Anyone who wishes to ask a question raises his or her hand. If a learner gives an incorrect answer or makes a mistake, it will be in front of their peers.

Creating a comfortable learning environment

When someone walks into an environment like this, it is not surprising that most people are reminded of high school. For many people, it conjures up images of embarrassment, insecurity, and stress—not the most conducive learning environment. No wonder learners aren't always eager to participate—it's too risky.

To facilitate learning and encourage involvement, you need an environment that is more comfortable, less threatening, and less "schoollike." And by environment I don't just mean the physical arrangement of the room, but also the atmosphere created by the trainer. People need to learn in an environment that is nonthreatening, comfortable, and stress-free, not bright, sharp, sterile, and intimidating.

How can the trainer help create a comfortable learning environment? To begin with, you need to be able to develop a rapport as early as possible. Before the class actually starts is best. This way, participants get a feel for you and your style. In turn, you can help reassure them of any concerns they might have.

Before each class, when the group is filtering in, I like to get into conversation with them—especially someone who looks a little anxious about the class. I might say, "So have you used this software at all yet?" or "What will you be using this program for at work?" Sometimes I might just talk about the weather or the weekend—anything that gets us into a conversation and enables them to feel comfortable with me.

This conversation helps you develop a rapport before the class formally starts. The trainees start to get to know you and figure out if you are the type of person they can trust and relate to. If you seem like a person they can trust and someone they feel comfortable with, they will be much more inclined to participate once the class starts. By asking the right questions, you can also get a feel for the level and expectations of the learners. I have found the ten minutes before the class to be very valuable in this respect. When you do start the class formally, the participants already feel more comfortable and relaxed because of the rapport you have already built with them.

Compare this with the trainer walking into the room at the start of a class with the participants already sitting there. They don't know, you and you have no rapport with them. The introductions are formal as they all try to figure out what this person is like who is going to train them. It takes them much longer to warm up to you and it is much harder to develop that rapport in the group setting than it is one-on-one. The first ten minutes of the class often sets the scene for the whole day. A ten-minute investment of your time beforehand is well worth it.

The trainer can continue to build a comfortable, nurturing atmosphere throughout the class by applying the skills and developing the attitudes outlined in chapter 3, on the character of a trainer. If the learner feels comfortable, safe, and respected by the trainer, participation and learning will result.

From my files

When I first started training, I had what I thought would be one of my classes from hell. I had been teaching the class for two hours. I began to understand what "dying on stage" meant. There was no rapport. No one asked questions. No one wanted to answer questions. No one was smiling. I tried all my standard techniques, only to be met with steely stares. I could not figure out what was missing.

After our first break, someone spoke up and asked, "So where are you from?" It had nothing to do with what I was teaching, and I was thrown off guard a little. "London," I replied. "How long have you been here?" said another. "Um . . . about twelve years," I replied. All of a sudden, different people were asking me about where I had lived, how long I had been training, how I had learned what I know. We digressed from the training for a few minutes as I answered the questions they had about me.

When I got back to the topic I was teaching, a different atmosphere existed in the room. They started answering and asking questions, and they seemed much more comfortable doing so. They all started to participate. It was night and day compared to what had been happening before the break.

I began to realize that people want to "know the trainer." They want to learn a little about who you are, what you are like, and see if they can find a "real" person in there somewhere. It's very important that they can somehow relate to the trainer. When this is absent, and you appear only as a teaching machine, devoid of personality, the atmosphere is flat, academic; nobody is encouraged to participate. When you give a little of yourself to your learners, when you expose a little bit of the real you, you find that they want to relate to you and participate.

Other ways of helping to develop a comfortable environment involve the physical space in the training room.

Lighting
Consider a lower level of ambient lighting. It is much more conducive to having people participate and relax. The light should not be dim, but somewhat less than the full glare of regular fluorescent lights and bright enough to read the whiteboard or courseware easily. If the lights are on dimmers, consider bringing the level to less than their full intensity.

One way of lowering the intensity level is to cover the strip lighting with thin, white or pastel material so that the level is reduced and the light is diffused. This has been proven to create a noticeable increase in the level of relaxation and attention of the students.

Arrangement of computers

The standard setup in a classroom is to have all the stations in a line facing front. Try some other arrangements. (Several are discussed in chapter 2 and shown in Fig. 2-3.) Concentrate on ones that don't reflect the typical teacher-learner hierarchy, ones that allow the trainer to be more integrated with the learner and allow more learner-learner and trainer-learner interactions.

Walls and surfaces

Friendly-looking walls with posters or pictures give a nicer feel to the training room than stark white walls. A few flowers in a vase will also do wonders for the atmosphere in the room. Just because it's a computer training room doesn't mean it shouldn't look interesting and attractive. I know one trainer who hangs mobiles with keyboard shortcuts on them from the ceiling and sticks colorful memory aids on the walls. It creates a very stimulating and interesting setting, and people tend to learn more. All these things can bring a little more life into the room and create a more enjoyable and relaxed atmosphere for training.

Temperature

Studies have shown that a temperature slightly cooler than normal is best for learning. When a training room is warm, people concentrate less and are more prone to feel tired. A cooler temperature tends to promote attention and interest. Having said that, don't freeze the participants hoping to stimulate even more learning—just have the temperature a little cooler than normal, but comfortable.

Remember also that the temperature should be adjusted for the learners, not the trainer. Trainers usually prefer it much cooler than everyone else because they are speaking and moving around, not just sitting still. Don't wait to read the evaluations to see if the temperature was okay. Ask now and again during the class if you feel it might be too hot or too cold. Don't ask, however, if you can't do anything about it.

Using examples from the learner's world

Learning is enhanced when learners can associate new information with things they already know about. If information is relevant to your own life and experiences, you remember it; if it isn't, you generally don't.

It should be the constant goal of a computer trainer to relate the material being taught to the world and experience of the learner. When this happens, the material comes to life. It seems more real, more concrete, and therefore more easily remembered.

I was teaching a spreadsheet class some years ago. We were talking about the concept of file linking, linking information from one cell on one sheet to another cell on another sheet. I stopped and asked some questions to see if they had understood the concept. One woman said, "Yes, I understand it, but so what! How is that going to help me back at work?" It was a wonderful question. I had explained a concept and a procedure quite clearly and understandably, but had forgotten to relate it to something useful—not just something I thought useful, but something that related directly to her experience.

When I asked her about what she was doing at work and began to give examples of how she could use linking, she began to see the value. It is not until the trainer brings the ideas and concepts to the world and experience of the learner that the value is seen. Once the value is seen, the concept, procedure, or whatever is more easily understood and remembered. When you teach software, make sure that you demonstrate the value of the information and how it directly relates to the learners' experience.

In most computer training classes, trainers work from a particular piece of courseware and use the example exercises in that. Some trainers develop their own printed exercise sheets to work from. These work reasonably well in most cases, but I suggest that whenever possible that the trainer use examples and exercises that reflect the experience of the learner. This will take a little more effort on the part of the trainer, but it will bring the material to life and be more than worth the investment. Here are a few examples of real-life exercises you can use with various types of software:

- *Charts and graphs.* Instead of using a standard example or an example in the courseware, ask the learners for examples that they might actually want to use back at work. Ask them what type of chart would be appropriate for their example. Would they need to label it? If so, how? Would they need to add any explanatory text or annotations?

- *Presentation graphics.* Have the participants create a real presentation that relates to their work. Get them to plan out each slide or overhead for their own, particular presentation. By the end of the class. they can have a partially completed presentation that they can save on a floppy and take back to work.

- *Macros.* Ask them, "What macros would be useful to you at work? What shortcuts would you like to have?" "What do you find tedious in your work that a macro might be able to simplify?" Help them create macros that they would actually use at work, rather than your examples or the examples in the courseware.

- *Project management.* What project are they working on? What tasks and resources are required? Forget the examples on the data disk; get them to create a mini-project of their own. What information do they want to track? What types of reports do they want to print?

I am not suggesting that you ignore all the practice exercises in your handouts or courseware, but that you try generating a few real-life examples suggested by the participants. You'll find it will generate more interest, assist understanding, and improve retention. This is another reason why it is so useful to find out a little about the background and needs of your participants beforehand, as mentioned earlier. When you have an idea of what type of work they are involved in, you can arrange for your examples to relate to this.

The needs of the learner

A casino wanted to train a large number of their office and administrative staff on the presentation software program they had just invested in. There were two computer training centers in the area. In order to decide which one to use for their training, they decided to initially send a few employees to each and get some feedback from the participants. They scheduled each group for the introductory class at each center.

A week or so after the classes, the training coordinator at the casino talked with the groups to get some feedback. She found quite drastic differences between what each group had learned. The group that attended training center A felt the class was okay, a little bit slow, not too exciting, but they felt they had learned a few things they might use. None of them had used the program since they took the class. The other group, from training center B, had already started creating presentations for meetings and were very excited about what they were going to use it for. They had found the class fun, informative, and extremely valuable. It turned out that they had covered a lot more material than the group at training center A.

The choice was clear, and the training coordinator paid a visit to the successful center to learn more about how the classes were taught. She was intrigued by how different the responses from the two groups were. The training center manager sat down and explained how they did things.

"No one gets standard, off-the-shelf, training here. Each of our classes is customized before and during the training. Every instructor spends at least 15 minutes finding out what the participants' job functions are, what their skill levels are, what they hope to use the software for, and what they would like to have accomplished by the end of the day. When it's possible, we do it on the telephone before they ever enter the classroom. When we have a feel for what they want to know, we adapt the class objectives. We avoid using any 'standard' practice exercises and try to create exercises that fit what's needed at that moment in that particular class. In a nutshell, we find out what our learners' needs and wants are and adapt the training on the spot. The trainer or the courseware doesn't determine the class—the participants' needs do."

Adapting to your audience

As any professional speaker or presenter will tell you, you must know who your audience is. By knowing who they are, you can adapt your presentation appropriately. The same applies in computer training.

Without knowing a little bit about the background, preferences, and attitudes of your participants, it is difficult to train effectively.

You don't need to run them through personality and IQ tests before the class, but before and during the class, try to get a feel for their style of learning, their expectations, and their concerns, and adapt your training accordingly. At the beginning of a class I often start off by saying, "Have you ever attended a class or training session that was terrible?" This usually gets their attention. They think for a moment and then some of them nod or raise their hand. I then ask, "Tell me about it, what was it that made it so bad?"

I have a few of them relate their stories. This usually involves some trainer either confusing them, going too fast, going too slow, boring them, being condescending, or being impatient. I explain to them that the reason I am asking is to get a feel for what works for them in a class and what doesn't work. I continue, "What do you hope I don't do for the next six hours?" I look around the room, and gradually people begin to say things like, "Go too fast!," "Read the book to us!," "Lecture," "Confuse me." Then I do the same with, "What do you hope I do for the rest of the day?"

This can be a very valuable exercise for you. It accomplishes several things. The first is that it immediately lets the learners know that you are committed to teaching them effectively. It also gives them an opportunity to express those things about trainers and training that frustrate them. They find it very refreshing and, often, a relief. You have, in effect, told them up front that you will do your best to address their needs and wishes. By listening to their responses, you get a pretty good idea of the types of learners you have and their preferences.

When someone says that they hope you don't go too fast, tell them that they are responsible for letting you know if you move ahead too quickly. If someone says that they hope you don't confuse them, tell them that they are responsible for interrupting you at anytime and asking you to clarify. Because you give them "permission" up front to keep you on track, they will be much more likely to interact and ask questions during the class. It is a wonderful way to build rapport and minimize any learning anxiety they might have. It also helps you to adapt to and appreciate the needs of your learners.

Another way to adapt to the audience is to listen carefully during the class to the subtle hints the learners give you about how they like to learn. You might hear something like, "Where is that in the handout?" When you hear that, you know that this person is interested in having the information written down somewhere that he or she can refer to later. This person usually also likes to have step-by-step procedural instructions. Make a mental note to make sure you provide precise information about where to find topics in the handout, and write up step-by-step procedures on the whiteboard, when appropriate.

Another phrase you might hear when you go over to help someone is, "No, don't tell me. Let me figure it out!" This type of person prides him- or herself on being independent and being able to work things out. Such learners get a great sense of satisfaction when they come up with the answer. When you come across someone like this, make sure to give them the occasional challenge and give them lots of positive strokes when they succeed. Make an effort not to spoon-feed them in any way.

Often, you'll come across learners who make comments about reading manuals or Help menus. They might say, "They don't make any sense to me," or "It's just a bunch of computerese." These people like simple, clear explanations with the minimum use of jargon or technical terms. They value pictures, diagrams, analogies—anything visual they can relate to rather than the written word. Make sure these people get just that. If they ask for an explanation or have a question, try to illustrate the answer in a diagram or in some visual form that seems tangible to them (see page 76, "Teach more visually").

Many other comments and cues like these will undoubtedly occur throughout the class that can give you an insight into the personality and learning style of the participants. If you pick up these subtle messages, you will be able to adapt the delivery of training so as to best complement the needs of the individual learners. With experience, you can learn to answer someone's question in the form that will be best understood by that particular learner. For one participant, it might be enough to answer the question verbally. The same question asked by another participant might require a diagram sketched out on the whiteboard. For someone else, you might need to write up a few step-by-step procedures. However you do it, you should continuously adapt and tailor the delivery to the individual learners.

Personality styles

The way people learn is influenced by their personality. Introverted people tend to ask fewer questions, sit at the back, and participate less. Bold, assertive people ask questions, challenge the instructor, and make certain their needs are served. "Warm-fuzzy" people want to be accepted and encouraged, and want everyone around them to feel okay. I could go on describing different types of personalities and their typical behavior. Many researchers have spent years trying to categorize and generalize personalities. The important thing for the trainer to understand is that:

- People have different personality styles.

- These personality styles affect the learning process.

- You need to make allowances for these differences.

The trainer can try to recognize the personality traits and use this information to fine-tune communication. For example, you might have Jim in the back row of the classroom who is quiet, shy, and seems quite worried about doing the right thing. Up front, Sue is a very verbal, confident individual who asks lots of questions.

To serve the learning needs of the latter the trainer can, to some extent, reflect the style of the learner. It would be acceptable to say something like, "So Sue, what's the point of using a template?" The question is directed at Sue by name, and is open-ended. It needs explanation. This is perfect for Sue; she is comfortable being singled out and has no problem thinking on her feet. Her mode of learning and interacting are served best by such a question.

Jim, on the other hand, would probably find the question intimidating. It would put him on the spot and would make him feel uncomfortable. A better way to relate to Jim's personality style might be to ask a closed question (discussed earlier in this chapter) such as, "What do you call it when you create a blank skeleton of a document that you fill in?" Also, rather than asking him directly, ask the class while looking in his direction.

This way, Jim has not been singled out. He has the option of answering or not. If he chooses to answer, it is a one-word answer to a simple question. With pressure off, he will most likely answer the question. Now he has answered correctly, participated, and become a little more confident. With a few such questions, Jim's participation and comfort level will grow and his ability to learn will be enhanced.

Very often, the communication style of the trainer clashes with the personality style of the learner. In such cases, it's not a question of changing who you are, but simply matching your mode of communication to the learner's personality style. This way, you can make it easier for your participants to interact with you and thus promote their learning.

Juggling ability levels

Screening learners and making sure they have prerequisites is of paramount importance in computer training. However diligent you are in doing this, however, you inevitably have some imbalance of ability levels within the class. It is one of the unwritten laws of computer training: there will be those learners who will be there with you every step of the way waiting for more information, and there will be those who struggle through the class. You might have learners who are very familiar with the logic of using software applications and others who are perplexed by it.

How do you deal with this imbalance in a training session? How can you serve all the learners, regardless of the level they are at? Do you have to sacrifice the fast learners to help the slower ones, or vice versa?

It is possible to serve all the levels of learners in a class and have them get what they came for, but it does take a little effort on the part of the trainer. You have to be prepared, flexible, and willing to adapt quickly. You have to be a juggler.

Should they be in the class?
First of all, if you have a participant who does not have any of the recommended prerequisites or cannot use the keyboard or mouse properly, try to have them reschedule. This is most important. It is not kind, understanding, or fair to have someone in a class who is totally out of their depth without the requisite basic skills. Any trainer who allows such a person to remain in the class is asking for trouble and definitely not serving the participant.

If it is apparent that someone does not have any of the prerequisites, talk to them privately and encourage them to reschedule or somehow get them up to speed on the basics. Be honest with them about your concerns as a trainer, but at the same time, don't be too brutal. Don't say something like, "I'm going to have to ask you to leave, Jim, because you don't know any of the basics." This immediately invalidates Jim and will most likely embarrass him. Rather, say something like, "Jim, I'm concerned that I might confuse you with some of this. It looks like there are some of the basics that you're not that familiar with. Rather than have that happen I am going to suggest that . . ." This way, you avoid embarrassing Jim and protect fragile egos.

Dealing with the extremes

Let's assume that you have tried to implement prerequisites for the training and have dealt with anyone who really should not be in the class. You still have different levels of ability for which you must adapt. Dealing with these different levels should not be seen as a problem in training—it's what training is about! Training always entails dealing with different ability levels. Successfully being able to address the needs of those different levels can make your training challenging but very rewarding.

During the training, it is most important that your pace is geared toward the mid-range of the class, not to the fastest or the slowest. Some trainers feel comfortable directing their training to the higher end because these people pick up the information quickly, ask perceptive questions, and often interact more than the others. The trainer then runs quickly through the work. Other trainers, being overly concerned that the slower learners understand and are happy, direct their training at this group and go at a snail's pace.

Neither one of these is appropriate and should be avoided. The trainer ends up focusing on a particular group and excludes the rest of the learners. Ask any group of learners about some bad training experiences and you will no doubt get stories of how the trainer went way too fast by concentrating on the more advanced learners or way too slow by focusing on the beginners. Stick to the middle ground.

But if you go at the average speed of the class and gear your training to the middle, aren't you going to bore the fast learners and confuse the slow learners? Not necessarily. What you need to do is gear the training to the middle ability range but make allowances for the extremes. Throughout the class, you can address the needs of the slower learners and the faster learners but never focus on them exclusively.

In order to address the needs of the slower and the faster learners you need to adapt on the fly. You need to be able to fashion the example or exercise you are giving them to their level. It also helps if you have a range of exercises available for the different levels of ability. Some commercially available courseware includes "challenge" exercises that can be used for the more advanced user in addition to the regular exercises.

Suppose you are teaching a group how to create macros. You set an exercise to practice creating some useful macros. Eric is struggling with the steps and needs constant help. Anne is ahead of everyone else and finishes the exercise in a few minutes. Most of the class are following at a reasonable pace.

Eric is going to need more of you time. Anne will need less of it, but is going to want to learn more than just the basics. It always takes less time to address the needs of the faster learner than it does the slower learner, so you can deal with Anne first and then devote some more time to Eric. You give Anne another, more challenging exercise to work on or, if you do not have one, create a challenge or show her something new.

You might say, "Now see if you can figure out how to edit the macros." Don't give her any information because most fast learners enjoy the challenge of figuring it out themselves. It only took a few seconds, but now Anne is engaged in trying to solve a problem, and in the process will probably learn a new feature or function and gain the satisfaction of having taught herself. Later, you might walk over to Anne, ask her if she figured it out and give her a clue if she hasn't. You might quickly show Anne a few more advanced features or functions, saying, "Take a look at this, Anne."

Now you can spend most of your time with the rest of the learners and particularly with Eric. (Spending more one-on-one time with a slow learner during a practice session is very different than spending more class time with that slower learner.) If Eric is struggling with the practice exercise, go over and assist him. If you can see that he will not be able to complete the whole exercise in a reasonable time, suggest (quietly, so as not to embarrass him) that he just complete a few of the most important sections. It's better to have him complete a few parts of the exercise and succeed rather than try to complete the whole thing and get left behind or confused. Try to spend more time with Eric while everyone is working on the exercise, but make sure you wander around and check to see how everyone else is doing, too. Make sure you don't give too much time to Eric to the detriment of the others in the class.

Developing flexibility

Flexibility is a very valuable quality for a trainer. Developing flexibility in training can reduce stress and help you adapt to whatever is needed in the moment. What do I mean by flexibility? Flexibility could be being able to change your class outline or your teaching plan when the need arises. You might have spent many hours the night before studying the software and planning the training session. You might have created an outline and plan of action, only to find the next day that your learners did not have the knowledge or skills that you expected. You were hoping to get into some wonderful advanced features and functions, only to find that the majority of the class is still struggling with the basics.

Here you have a choice. You can go ahead with the class as planned and cover all those wonderful features you wanted to, even if you confuse them. You could proudly say at the end of the class that you covered everything on the outline; you did what you set out to do. Alternatively, you could forget your original plan, adapt to the situation, and alter the structure of your outline to reflect the needs of the learners. This is obviously the more appropriate course of action, to look at the level of competency in the room and adapt your training as needed.

For many trainers, this is hard. After working all night and planning such a wonderful class, a trainer is apt to feel upset and a little disgruntled about teaching a group that isn't familiar with the basics. In such a situation, you need to be flexible. Forget your own intended agenda and look to see what would benefit the learners most. If you need to spend an hour reviewing the basics, then do it. If you end up covering only 70% of the material you hoped to, then so be it. Far better for the learners to leave and know 70% of the work well than to cover all of the work and leave confused, frustrated, or over-whelmed.

Sometimes you need to be flexible in the other extreme. You might be confronted with a class where everyone happens to be very adept at using software, very sharp, and able to move through the work at a rapid pace. If you stick to your original teaching plan, the speed would be far too slow and they would probably be bored. Once again, you need to adapt to the learners' needs.

Another situation where flexibility is important is when you have a course outline that does not reflect the needs of the learners. This might happen when the learners are all from the same business or department. For example, you are ready to teach macros, tables, print merge, styles, and templates. You cover the objectives at the beginning of the class, and the group explains to you that in fact they are not that interested in macros or templates but definitely need to master everything else—especially print merge. What do you do? You don't say something like, "Well, I'm afraid that's what the outline is, and I really do need to stick to those topics." No. You adapt.

Make a note of what is important to them and offer a suggestion, "How about if I give you just the basics of macros and templates and spend a lot more time on print merge? It won't be in the handout you have, but I can go over merging with envelopes and labels too, if you wish." You have just made their day. They have been struggling at work for some time trying to merge envelopes. They will get to learn the easy way to do it in your class. Already, they are excited and enthusiastic about taking the class.

Continue this flexible attitude throughout the class. You might be halfway through explaining simple tables when someone asks how to paste the table into another program. If it is pertinent to everyone in the class and you could do it without spending too much time or causing any confusion, then go ahead and show them. Once again, a simple digression from the course outline can make the whole class a lot more useful and valuable to them.

It is also important to know when not to cover features and functions that are requested. Suppose you are in the middle of teaching simple macros in a word-processing program and someone asks you how to write some macro commands. If you went ahead and did this, you might bring in new concepts and procedures that would not be appropriate. You would risk losing the group. You don't want to digress from a topic that is being taught if there is any chance of causing confusion. It would be much more appropriate in this case to offer to go through the procedure at break time or lunch with that individual.

Being flexible doesn't mean doing and covering everything the learners want you to. It means being willing to forget your own agenda and adapt to what best serves the learners at any particular time.

From my files

A class that sticks in my mind was one that I agreed to teach on short notice. I received the call on Friday for a Windows-based project-management class on Monday, and spent the whole weekend planning and organizing materials. The class was to be held at the client's site, and I had been told there would ten computers in a training room with an overhead projector.

When I arrived, I discovered things were quite different. There was, in fact, no training room. No ten computers. There was one computer sitting on the end of a long boardroom table in a very small room. There was no overhead, no whiteboard, and only six chairs. Later, the participants arrived. Some had been using the software for a few months, and the rest had never used Windows.

The training manager walked in and said, "I know it's a three-day course, but we need to get it done in two. We have a board meeting Wednesday."

Ten years ago, I would have packed up my things, told everyone what to do with their project, and tried to strangle the training manager. Instead, what I actually did was adapt to the situation. I decided that since I was there, I may as well make the most of it. I tried to do what has never come easily to me: be as flexible as I could—and keep calm. I found more chairs, stole a flipchart, taught a quick introduction to Windows, and eleven of us sat around staring at one monitor.

Incredibly, the class went extremely well. The "intimate" atmosphere helped us develop a great rapport and encouraged participation. The trainees all took turns on the computer, and all got a little hands-on experience. We actually finished the course in two days, with everyone excited about what they had learned. It was one of the most satisfying classes I have ever taught. My willingness to be a little more flexible and adapt paid dividends.

Addressing fears and concerns

Many learners have fears and concerns when they are in a classroom environment. It might be a fear of looking "dumb" in front of their peers, getting lost, not understanding, having the trainer lose patience with them, or being called upon to do something. This should be addressed as soon as possible. The sooner the trainer can reassure the participants that they are in a safe and threat-free environment, the sooner effective learning will occur.

What can you do to reduce these concerns and anxieties before and during the training? By far the most important is to develop a good rapport with the group, as discussed earlier in this chapter. It is much easier to reduce anxiety when there is a good level of rapport between the trainer and the participants. The first 15 minutes of the class are critical in this respect. How you come across in those first minutes of the class effects how the learners relate to their fears and concerns. If you appear to be hurried, impatient, concerned with own agenda, and "covering the material," then their fears and concerns are likely to remain. If you can demonstrate in the first 15 minutes that you are a good listener, patient, sympathetic, and care that they truly understand the work, some of their fears and anxieties about learning will be reduced.

A typical concern of computer novices—those that have little or no experience using a computer—is the fear of damaging the system. You've seen them sit there, hands clasped to their chests, staring wide-eyed at the keyboard, terrified that the wrong keypress will cause sparks to fly from the monitor and cause major power outages. When you get beginners like this, consider having them "play" with the keyboard and type in anything they want. I often say something like, "Okay, press any keys on the keyboard you feel like. See what happens, type something in, click a button. See if you can cause a problem." (Make sure they are real novices!) I let them know that in the very worst-case scenario, all you would have to do would be to reload some software. After they do this, they begin to realize that the machine is not as fragile as they thought. It starts to give them a little more confidence and boldness using the computer.

Another approach for minimizing learning anxieties is to relate some of your own experiences of being a novice or "screwing up." After talking with the class about making mistakes and how useful they can be, I often relate some incident or mistake I made when I was learning a particular program. I tell them about some "dumb" thing I did once that turned out to be a valuable learning experience. Let them know you're human and that you can relate to some of their concerns. Making a mistake when you are training is a perfect opportunity for this.

Often, when a trainer makes a mistake, the tendency is to cover up or quickly get back on track without too many people noticing. A better idea is to stop and say, "Just a moment—I've screwed up." Apologize and let them know what the correct steps are. You might even want to let them know why you made the mistake—what it was that confused you (without making excuses). Trainees will always respect this. It makes them think, "Wow, if this guru makes mistakes, then maybe there's hope for me!" It makes the learners see that the trainer is not that different from them—making mistakes and correcting them. The distance between the trainer and the learner is reduced. They get to see that making mistakes is not uncommon or something to be avoided, but a natural part of learning software.

A common concern among learners is worrying about whether they are going to remember everything. What if they get back to work and can't remember everything they did in the class? I broach this subject when I start giving procedural steps or shortcuts, saying, "You probably won't remember all this stuff after the class—no one ever does. How do you really get to become proficient at a program?" Someone comes up with the answer, "You use it and practice." Tell them not to worry about trying to remember every procedure or shortcut they use—they can always use their "cheat-sheet" at work. Remind them that the most important thing to do is to understand the work as they go through it. The remembering procedures will come if they concentrate on understanding the work as they do it. The trainees thought that the key to learning the software was remembering, and you just told them not to worry about it. One of their loads has been lightened, and with a freer mind their capacity to learn has increased.

The keys to reducing someone's concerns about learning is to bring their fears out into the open, talk about them, let the person know that these concerns are shared by others, and through your actions and words, demonstrate understanding and empathy for wherever they might be.

Computer jargon

Many people end up becoming computer trainers because they are very quick at learning and understanding computer software. They might have been the office gurus or the computer-support people. They are very often people who enjoy computers and feel comfortable with the logic and predictability of software. They are often technically oriented.

Such a computer trainer is careful to use the correct terminology when teaching concepts or procedures. In an effort to ensure that the learners understand the software thoroughly, the trainer is apt to use terminology or jargon that interrupts the learning process rather than assisting it. The trainer might have been very precise and accurate in an explanation, but because of the use of jargon or technical terminology, the learner becomes confused or intimidated. The trainer has been thorough and accurate at the cost of being simple and understandable.

Consider two trainers. One I'll call the "hi-tech" trainer, the type I have just outlined. The other I'll call the "hi-touch" trainer, the trainer whose goal is to relate and communicate effectively at the level of the learners in the room. Someone in a word-processing class asks, "What exactly is a macro?" The hi-tech trainer replies, "A macro is a sequential set of software instructions that can be initiated by a combination of keystrokes." The hi-touch trainer might reply, "Oh, macros are great little shortcuts to help you do things. You press a key and it does a whole bunch of stuff for you, just like the speed dial on your telephone!"

The hi-tech trainer's answer was the more accurate and correct. If you looked up macro in a dictionary of computing, it wouldn't be far wrong. The other trainer's answer was perhaps not as accurate or exact, but it conveyed more to the learners in the room. They might have heard the term macro often and needed a simple, understandable explanation that they could relate to. The simpler explanation was grounded in their experience. It wasn't perfectly accurate, but it made sense.

A technical explanation might sometimes alienate the audience. The words used are from the world of the trainer, not from the world of the learners. Learners hear such an explanation and it confirms their suspicions: a macro is something high-tech and complicated that you need to have a degree in computer science to understand. Computers become more esoteric and distant. Learning anxiety is increased. Learning is inhibited.

Try introducing technical terms afterwards

Before teaching a class, look at the vocabulary that needs to be understood by the learners. This should be vocabulary that absolutely must be used. Look next at the level of expertise, background, and ability of the participants. It might not be easy to gauge accurately, but you need some basic idea of their experience.

Avoid using any technical terms or jargon that are not absolutely vital to teaching the class. The ones that are vital should be clearly defined and explained. If possible, explain the concept, idea, or feature, followed by the correct terminology. This way, the learners get the conceptual understanding and then attach a name to something known. If the jargon or technical term is introduced before the explanation, the learner is caught off-guard, and the term becomes a source of distraction until finally understood.

For example, when teaching about relative and absolute cell addresses in a spreadsheet program, I avoid using these words until the concept is understood. I set up a simple worksheet that causes an error to occur when a formula is copied. (The error occurs because an absolute cell address has not been used.) I ask the participants what went wrong and why they got an incorrect answer. They discover that a cell address that they wish to stay fixed is changing. I tell them to put a dollar symbol ($) in front of the part they do not want to change, explaining that it "freezes" part of the cell address. (I purposely use a word they can all relate to.) They adjust the formulas, recopy them, and everything works out. They understand the concept of placing dollar signs before parts of a cell address.

Then, and only then, do I introduce the correct terminology. "By the way," I say, "the term for this is an absolute cell address because it absolutely does not change." I have introduced the correct terminology after the concept is understood. This way, the new term is added to a known concept.

Try using the learner's vocabulary

Get a feel for the language that your participants are comfortable with, and adapt accordingly. When someone uses the incorrect term for something, don't immediately correct them but take advantage of the vocabulary they use. For instance, in a Windows class, you ask how to close a program and someone says, "You double-click the gray thing top left." The best response would be, "Exactly, you double click the gray thing!" and then at the appropriate moment you can say, "By the way, the name they call the gray thing is the Control menu because it controls the window." Use vocabulary that the learners are comfortable with and that makes sense to them, but make sure the correct term is introduced shortly afterwards.

When you teach a class and use vocabulary that is familiar to your audience, it is somewhat like finding someone that speaks your language in a foreign country. There is a certain sense of relief and familiarity. Your audience feels more at home and more comfortable, and their capacity to learn increases as a result.

What learners want from trainers

In a survey of what trainer qualities, methods, and skills worked best for learners, the following came at the top of the list:

- *Knowledge.* People want a trainer to be knowledgeable about the software. You must have not just a teaching knowledge with enough to get by, but a good, well-rounded knowledge, including quick ways of doing things, tips and tricks, and a knowledge of the different versions of the software.

- *Organization.* It is very important for learners to feel that a computer training class has structure and that the trainer has good organizational abilities. They like to have a clear idea of what is to be covered and how the training will be structured. They like to have the trainer deliver the training in a consistent and organized fashion. They like to see the training well-planned and well-executed.

- *Ability to capture and hold attention.* Learners want lively and interesting trainers. They like a trainer who, in some way, can stimulate their interest, capture their attention, and constantly offer something fresh, interesting, and engaging. They appreciate a little of the "dramatic" in a presentation—they like to be entertained as well as learn.

- *Relevant examples.* Sometimes in computer training classes, trainers use generic or textbook examples to illustrate software procedures or processes. Most learners prefer the trainer to relate the training to "real" examples relevant to their work and interests.

- *Genuine enthusiasm.* Notice the word genuine. Sometimes trainers feel a need to be "up" and excited, and try to appear enthusiastic when they really are not. People see through this type of enthusiasm very quickly. They like to see trainers who are truly enthusiastic about what they are teaching. Enthusiasm is contagious, and learners like to be infected.

- *Involvement.* Most learners like to feel an active involvement in the training. They want to be an integral part of what is going on and feel that their opinion counts for something. They dislike demonstrations or lecturing where they take a passive role in learning.

- *Answering questions with respect.* Many learners are afraid of asking a "dumb" question in front of others. Many people can remember experiences they had back at school when a question they asked was ridiculed, or they were made to feel "stupid." This fear often surfaces in a training room. Learners value highly the ability of a trainer to answer all questions respectfully and without condescension.

- *Patience.* Patience is highly valued in trainers. You must be able to persist in an explanation or continue to assist someone who is struggling without becoming frustrated or making the learner feel uncomfortable. Being able to listen carefully to each question that is asked without interrupting.

Take a look at your training, and compare it to this list. How do you rate? Which areas could you improve in?

Just for the record, here's the list of the mistakes trainers make and what drives a learner insane:

- Impatience

- Lack of involvement with learners

- Lack of knowledge

- Lecturing

- Disorganization

- Being unprepared

- Trainers who can't use audio-visual aids properly

- Getting off track

- Blaming others for problems with hardware or software

- Assuming that everyone is following

- Inflexibility

- Talking "down" to learners

- Lack of enthusiasm and energy

- Lack of a sense of humor

Age differences

Reaction times, manual dexterity, and coordination often vary with age. Your training should always take into account the age of your audience. On the whole, older people find it harder to understand someone who talks fast. Trainers need to slow their speech down a little when explaining things. Hearing and vision sometime pose a problem as well; you might want to rearrange seating so that the overhead and whiteboard are clearly visible and the trainer is closer to anyone with less acute sight or hearing.

The age of someone also brings other considerations into training. Generally, younger learners will be much more familiar with information technology and computers than older learners. Younger learners will understand concepts, ideas, and vocabulary that the older learners might not. Your training should account for this.

On the other hand, some older learners have a much broader range of experience and expertise in their own field than some of the younger, more computer-literate individuals. It is important that you recognize such experience and encourage them to contribute their own comments and perspectives on the work being covered. Very often, an older participant is apt to feel that his or her accumulated knowledge and expertise is not valued as highly as the ability to be computer literate and speedy with the mouse. The trainer has an opportunity to include such a person, whenever possible, in class discussions and have the class benefit from their knowledge and expertise. Knowing one's skills are appreciated and valued gives anyone renewed confidence. This confidence furthers any individual's ability to learn.

2

Training delivery

"In teaching it is the method and not the content that is the message . . . the drawing out, not the pumping in."
— **Ashley Montague**

The four steps to effective computer training

There is no one way to teach a computer class. Different trainers use different approaches, and to suggest that there is only one correct method for presenting information or learning skills would be misleading. However, certain elements in the process of learning how to use software should be present in order for the concepts and procedures to be clearly understood and remembered.

Here are four critical steps in computer training that should be included, in this order, when teaching software skills (shown in Fig. 2-1):

1. Overview of concept or procedure

2. Assisted exercise

3. Unassisted exercise

4. Review/clarification/questions

Step 1: Overview of the concept or procedure
Before teaching someone how to carry out a procedure, you need to provide an overview of the concepts involved and explain any new

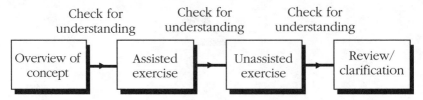

Check for understanding	Check for understanding	Check for understanding

Overview of concept		Assisted exercise		Unassisted exercise		Review/ clarification

2-1 *The four steps to effective training.*

vocabulary. The overview should be enough information for the learner to appreciate the core ideas and the intended result of the procedure.

For example, if you are teaching how to create mailing labels in a word-processing program, you might draw a diagram of a document containing names and addresses, and a document containing the label formats, and show how these are combined to create the final product: a merged address-label document. Give the appropriate vocabulary, such as data file, main file, merged file, fields, and records, and define them.

Make sure that everyone understands the core concepts—that of merging a data file and a main file to produce the address labels. Only when the concept or "big picture" is clearly understood should you move to the next step, the assisted exercise.

Check for understanding. Check that everyone in the room has a clear understanding of the vocabulary and the concept (see page 21, "Checking for understanding").

Step 2: Assisted exercise
Once everyone is clear on the basics, go through the procedures with the learners and have them follow along. And I don't mean just have them follow your every instruction, but have them work with you to suggest and discover the procedural steps.

Avoid telling anyone exactly what to press or click. Get the learners to think it through rationally. If you have done a good job of explaining the concepts and the vocabulary, they can quite often figure a lot of it out for themselves. Try not to tell them; guide them instead.

The assisted exercise is useful because you are helping them make their first steps and supporting them if they begin to stumble. You guide and prompt them until the procedure is complete and the result obtained. If a procedure is quite involved, you might consider going through another assisted exercise with a similar example.

Check for understanding. Don't continue to step 3 until you are sure that they have understood each step of the procedure.

Step 3: Unassisted exercise

Step 3, the unassisted exercise, is perhaps the most important step. They have understood the concept and the vocabulary, and have been through an assisted exercise. They are now ready to go it alone. You give them with an exercise or worksheet where they must figure it out themselves.

This is the part of the training that best indicates what participants have really learned. Often, more valuable learning occurs here than in the overview or the assisted exercise. Whatever problems, confusion, or lack of clarity they might have will become apparent here. This is the time when it is critical that you walk around and assist people one-on-one (see page 22, "Training by walking around").

Walking around will give you a good idea of who is struggling and needs extra help, and who is doing just fine. Often the most effective and lasting learning takes place when the trainer is helping someone one-on-one with an exercise. You can completely personalize an explanation for that individual. Often, when you wander around the room assisting, it is the first time that a learner can feel comfortable enough to admit that he or she is lost.

Because this is such an important step in computer training, be sure to provide ample time for the average learner to complete it. Don't rush them through an exercise so that you can cover all the material.

Check for understanding. Make sure that any concerns, questions, or confusions are cleared up before you move on to step 4.

Step 4: Review, clarification, and questions

You have given the learners an overview of the work and the necessary vocabulary. You have guided them through a class exercise. They have successfully completed exercises on their own. You have checked their understanding throughout each step.

It is now time to review the work—the concept and the procedural steps—answer any questions, and ensure that everyone's understanding is clear.

Review the concept, any vocabulary, and briefly run through the procedure again. It's also a good idea at this point to try to relate the work to what they may be doing back at the office. When you've done a brief review and everything is clear, you can move on to the next topic and start with step 1 again.

Varying the steps

In certain cases, it is more effective to have the learners go through the procedural steps before explaining the concept. This is often appropriate when the concept is complex or difficult to explain and must be seen to be understood. An example of this is pivot tables in Excel. Explaining the concept of pivot tables is sometimes challenging for a trainer and confusing for the learner. However, when a pivot table is demonstrated so that learners see the data rearranged, it becomes very clear what it is. The usual comment is, "Oh, I get it!"

In this case and similar cases where the concept might be slightly obscure, carrying out the procedure first actually clarifies the concept. Demonstrate the procedure so that the concept can be understood, and then go back to review the concept in a little more detail, as shown in Fig. 2-2.

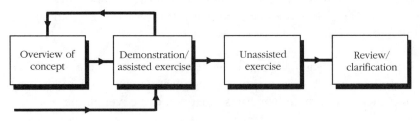

2-2 *Teaching procedures before concepts.*

The preparation

The success of a training class is usually directly proportional to the amount of preparation beforehand. Unsuccessful training is often the result of poor planning and the unexpected. Spending the time to prepare is always worth the effort. It is an investment that always pays dividends.

The environment

Preparation of the training environment is critical in computer training. When the training session begins, you should be concerned with training, not adjusting the overhead, checking the software, or counting to see if there are enough handouts or diskettes. You are not serving yourself or the participants if you wait until you're teaching to see if you have everything organized. The first 10 minutes of the class set the stage for the rest of the day, so be prepared.

Preparing the room means arriving early at the training site and making sure the equipment, materials, and resources are organized and functional. Arriving 10 minutes before a training session and hoping things are in order, like some trainers do, is not recommended.

Are all the teaching aids in working order?
Don't make any assumptions. Check overhead projectors, projection panels, presentation monitors, or whatever you're using. Get familiar with any adjustment controls on the overhead or projection panels. Do you have any spare OHP bulbs, or do you know where to get them? Is your screen focused and visible to all the participants?

Is the trainer's area organized?
Can you sit or stand in easy reach of your computer and see both the participants and the large-screen display? Can you easily move to the screen display to point out things without stepping over power cords or cables? Is there enough room at the trainer's station to place your manual or notes? Is there enough light to read them when the lights are dimmed? Is it easy to get up and walk over to the learners, or are there obstructions?

Do you have the requisite supplies?
Do you have enough copies of the courseware? Consider having them next to each computer when the session begins rather than having to hand them out during the class. How about floppy disks? Do you have name tents, sign-in sheets, evaluation forms, and certificates? Are there enough dry-erase markers? Do they work? Do you have an eraser for the whiteboard? Does the flipchart have enough paper?

Is the hardware and software functioning correctly?
Just because you might have trained in the same room before, don't assume that the hardware and software are functioning as they should.

Turn on all the systems and run the software. Are the defaults set? Do all the screens look the same? Has someone forgotten to run the refresh program? Make sure all the systems are consistent before the class starts.

Is the lighting adequate?

Where are the lighting controls? Do you have the facility to dim the lights rather than have them on or off? (If you do, try not to work all day in a dim environment; it is not good for your eyes.) Is the front of the room spotlighted appropriately so that everyone can see what you are doing or writing? Walk to the back of the room and see if everything seems clear and readable. Make sure you are familiar with the lighting controls before you start training. Don't wait until the end of the class to realize that every station had its own desk light, while you were sprinting back and forth to the light switches.

Can you adjust the temperature if necessary?

It is often a challenge in a training room to get the temperature just right. The heat from monitors and a room full of warm bodies can drastically alter the temperature. What seemed like a cool room in the morning can turn into a sauna by noon. Are you able to adjust it if necessary? A room slightly too cool is preferable to one that is very slightly too warm—it is more conducive to learning when the temperature of a room is slightly cooler than normal. If you do not have a full class, consider turning off some of the extra monitors—they act as heaters.

When you prepare your training room before you teach, you can alleviate many of the concerns and stresses of training. It will help you start your class in a more relaxed and confident manner and help you focus more fully on your training.

From my files

Try not to gauge the right temperature for the training room by how you feel. Trainers generally prefer it to be a bit cooler than the participants because the trainer is moving around, speaking, and generally being active, while the rest of the class is usually just sitting. Ask them if the room is at a comfortable level; don't just adjust it to suit yourself.

One trainer I know has a habit of turning up the air conditioner before he starts teaching. He likes a very cool room. His students rarely appreciate this. In one spreadsheet class that I sat in

on, he moved over to the thermostat and turned the temperature down. When it began to get colder, the woman nearest the
control at the back turned around and moved it up. Fifteen minutes later, he wandered back and increased it again. This went
on for an hour or so, with the trainer somewhat perplexed as to
why the temperature wasn't changing. The woman at the back
was getting tired of playing this game. The trainer started on the
next topic, "So, does anyone know how to freeze the titles on a
spreadsheet?" The woman at the back took advantage of the opportunity, "Yeah, just keep 'em in this room long enough!"

Training room layout

The location and arrangement of the computers in a training room is important. Most computer training classrooms are set up in the standard
"classroom" format, with all the students facing front toward the trainer.

This usually works quite well—the learners can look up from their
monitors and see what you're doing in the front of the room. However, one of the drawbacks of this type of setup is that it reminds people of being back at school. It projects a formal learning atmosphere,
promoting the image of the trainer as the authority figure in the room.
This is not always the most conducive atmosphere in which to learn.

There are other alternatives. If a large part of your training consists of
hands-on exercises, independent learning, and one-on-one coaching,
you might consider choosing one of the "learning center" arrangements
for your computer stations shown in Fig. 2-3.

These arrangements are designed to give a much more informal feel
to the training environment and one in which the trainer is not the
only focus. If interaction with other learners is part of the plan, then
have a fairly open system so that the learners can interact easily. However you place the computer stations, make sure that you can move
freely around the room and get to anyone who might need help.

The chair, the keyboard, and the monitor

Once you have the computer stations suitably arranged in the room,
consider the positioning of the chair, the keyboard, and the monitor.
Make sure the chair can be moved easily towards or away from the
desk. Make sure the chairs are comfortable—there is nothing worse
than having to sit in a hard, uncomfortable chair for a whole day.
Make sure the height can be adjusted simply, if need be.

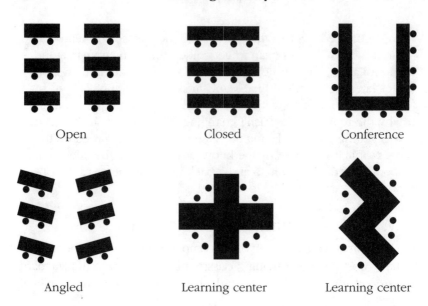

| Open | Closed | Conference |

| Angled | Learning center | Learning center |

2-3 *Classroom arrangements.*

How about the keyboard? Is it at the right height and angle for the users? Can they adjust it if necessary? Consider investing in some wrist rests. Also, look at the position of the monitor. Is it approximately at eye level? Try not to have a setup where the users have to look down at their monitors. Is the monitor image clear, focused, and easy to read? Arrange for it to be about 14 to 24 inches from the user's eyes. If possible, have a document holder adjacent to the screen and at the same level as the screen. This avoids having to make frequent head and eye movements. Document holders that attach to the side of the monitor work well.

Free space
Make sure there is enough room at each learner's space for the keyboard, the pointing device, and a notepad or courseware. Avoid having the computer stations so close together that there is too little room to make notes. A cramped environment detracts from the training. On the other hand, in a large room, don't place the computers too far apart. It can have an adverse effect on the interaction in the room when people tend to feel more isolated and less inclined to participate and interact.

Create a training guide

Computer trainers teach classes in their own unique ways. Most tend not to follow the courseware page by page, line by line. In fact training page by page is often the exact opposite of what most learners want to do in a class. Trainers usually follow the sequence of topics in the courseware, but often choose their own examples and explanations, returning to the courseware for the exercises and practice sessions.

When you do this and use the courseware as a guide, as opposed to the page-by-page approach, make sure that all the relevant topics are covered in the right order, so that when you get to the practice sessions, the learners have the requisite knowledge to complete them. It is also useful to be able to know quickly how far along you are in the course outline and what topics are still to be covered.

A way of doing this is to create what I call a "training guide" like that in Fig. 2-4. Create this the night before the class or in the morning before the class. (Give yourself enough time!) Get a sheet of paper, fold it in half, and write down the section or chapter numbers on the left side. By each section or chapter number, write down the main topics or concepts that you need to teach. If there are any example files or data files that you need to use when teaching that section, write their names down with a box or circle around them. Include the page on which that section begins, and on the right side of the paper, show the page on which the practice exercise for that section begins. Feel free to create your own version of this, something that works well for you, but make sure it contains these basic elements.

When you begin the class, you can use the guide to write up a list of objectives. As you teach, you can glance at it and easily see what section you are on, the page number in the book, what topics you must cover, the names of the example files, and the page number for the practice exercises. It helps you keep track of where you are in the timeline of the class, helps you look ahead at what is coming up, and is a very simple and efficient way of guiding you through the training.

When you create a training guide and teach from it, make absolutely sure that you have gone through every page of the courseware yourself and tried every single example and exercise. Be completely fa-

EXCEL INTRO

① Basics (p.2) ITEMS.XLS
   Cursors
   Worksheets
   Windows
              Exercise ————————— p. 15

② Worksheets (p.16) PAYROLL.XLS
   Data Entry
   Editing
   Basic Functions
   Save/Open/Close
              Exercise ————————— p.26

③ Editing Worksheets (p.28) PRODUCT.XLS
   Insert/Del/Rows/Cols
   Undo/Redo
   Col width/Row height
              Exercise ————————— p.37

④ Formatting (p.39) FORMAT.XLS
   Copy/Move
   Drag/Drop
   Format #'s
   Fonts/Styles
              Exercise ————————— p.54

2-4 *A simple training guide.*

miliar with the courseware before you teach your own version of it. The purpose of the training guide is not to avoid using the courseware, but to help you use it appropriately.

Figure out what they know before the class

How often have you stayed up until midnight preparing the next day's advanced-level class, only to find the next morning that none of the participants know the basics?

Sometimes the opposite happens. You are told by your training manager that the group you will be training are beginners. You discover that although they're beginners in learning the program you're teaching, they are all experienced C programmers.

The time to find out who you will be training is before the class. The time to discover that they have not seen a mouse before is definitely not during the class. To provide the very best learning experience you can (and to lower your blood pressure), you need to gauge the level of competency of the participants before the training takes place.

Sometimes in a public class, this is not possible. In that case, you have to make do with adapting on the fly and being flexible. However, when possible, attempt to get a feel for the expertise level of a group by using a preclass questionnaire, a pre-test, by speaking with the training contact, or by speaking with the actual participants.

Questionnaire
A questionnaire sent out to all the participants of the training session can give you a good idea of competency levels. You can create one yourself or use those provided by various courseware publishers.

The questionnaire doesn't have to be too detailed or extensive. It just needs to elicit some information about the skills the learners possess and the features of the program with which they are familiar or unfamiliar. This information can be given to the trainer (or summarized) prior to the training so that any changes of material and approach can be planned ahead of time. It can sometimes be time-consuming and requires organization, but it is well worth the effort.

Pre-test
A pre-test can be any test that is set up before the class to determine the current skill levels of the learners. This could be as simple as writ-

ten instructions asking the user to carry out certain procedures or as sophisticated as a computer-based, interactive version of the software that monitors skill levels. As well as being a tool to help you plan the class, the pre-test can be part of a pre- and post-test system that shows what skills have been mastered in the class, as discussed in chapter 4.

Interview

Another useful method of gauging competency and skill levels is to talk with the person responsible for setting up the training or with the participants themselves. This is not accurate or reliable, but it can give you a good feel for what to expect before training. This is especially useful if a particular customized class is set up for a company or a department, where the needs of the learners in the group are similar. When it is possible, a conversation with a few of the participants over the telephone will be very valuable in gauging what skill levels to expect and what topics are of particular interest.

Here are a few useful questions to ask in such an interview:

- How long have you been using the software?

- What other programs do you use?

- What features are you particularly interested in learning?

Planning a class

Do you really plan your classes, or do you just learn your material, take a look at the courseware, and improvise on the day? Many trainers choose the latter, but planning your training a little more carefully not only benefits the learners, it can make your training run much more smoothly. It takes time, but the investment is worth it.

When you sit down to prepare your class, consider the following:

- What are the objectives for the class?

- What are the core concepts your learners need to understand?

- What diagrams could help clarify these concepts?

- What new vocabulary is to be introduced?

- How much time are you planning to spend on each topic, task, or lesson?

- Do you have exercises for different levels of learners?

- Would a cheat-sheet or quick reference for procedures help?

- Who are the learners, what are their abilities, and what might their concerns be?

- What instructional media do you have to use?

- What energizers, quizzes, or learning games could you include?

Being prepared is half the battle.

Broaden your knowledge

If you are teaching a particular application, it is useful to have a certain degree of knowledge outside of the software you are teaching but that relates to it. Try to gain a knowledge and understanding of the operating system it runs on, any software it is often used in conjunction with, and other software from which your learners might have upgraded.

The program you are teaching might be your specialty, but for the learners, it is usually one of many packages they use, and so it is not used in isolation. It might be one of a suite of programs that are used in conjunction with each other, and which share data. It might be a new version running under Windows that used to run on some other operating system. When you are familiar with related software, competing products, and other systems, you can relate a little more to real-life applications and challenges the users might have. Learning a program in isolation limits your ability to relate it to the real world.

For example, you might be teaching a presentation graphics program, and someone asks you if it is possible to link spreadsheet data to it. Having a broader knowledge than just your favorite presentation graphics program will enable you to answer this and show how it's done. Showing this might be the single most valuable part of the class for this person, even though it might not be part of the class outline. Your wider knowledge of software has provided the learner with a solution to a real-life problem.

Or you might be teaching a Windows spreadsheet class with a group that used to use a DOS spreadsheet. Some knowledge of that old spreadsheet is invaluable to you when teaching. The features and functions of the new spreadsheet can be related to the older one. "You know when you used to press F3 for Help? Well, now what you do is. . . ." The training is easier for the participants because it reflects their experience and their concerns.

I like to teach "incidentals" during a training session, such as, "By the way, did you know that you can import WimWam files into this word processor? If anyone's interested, I'll show you how you can do it this afternoon." Having a wider knowledge of programs and systems gives you an edge in training. It gives you the ability to show how applications work together, lets you relate to older ones, and helps you to provide more real-life scenarios.

The beginning

The first 15 minutes of a class are crucial; they help set the stage for the rest of the day. The learners need to be oriented to you, the facility, and the material. Starting the training off on the right foot can make the difference between a successful class and mediocre class.

How to start the class

There is more than one way to start a classroom training session. Every trainer has his or her own particular method. However, there are a few important things you should include, whichever approach you choose:

- *Be there before they arrive.* Always be there to greet participants when they arrive and help them get comfortable with you and the surroundings. This is the perfect time to start to develop a rapport with them. Be there at least 20 minutes before the start of the class. Arriving five minutes before the class is due to start will not serve you or your participants.

- *Introduce yourself.* A simple introduction is all you need. You don't have to mention all your degrees or qualifications. The focus of the class is them, not you.

- *Orient participants to the facilities.* Let them know where things are in the building, such as the restrooms, break room, and telephones. If necessary, orient them to the training room.

- *Inform them of class timing and breaks.* Let them know about break times, lunch times, the duration of the training, and when the class will finish. People sometimes have days, times, and even classes confused.

- *Introduce the courseware.* Refer to the table of contents when talking about the class objectives. Let them know how they can use the courseware back at work and how you are going to use it in the class (see Chapter 6).

- *Let them know your style.* Trainers use different approaches when training. Some stick closely to the courseware while others prefer to refer to it only at certain times. Some trainers have quite a formal, conventional method of training; others have a relaxed and very informal style. Let them know your style so that they know what to expect.

- *Find out about them.* Make sure you know the participants' names, what company they are from, and what they hope to gain from the class. You don't have to have everyone introduce themselves formally to do this. It can be done in a casual, conversational way, or even by doing some type of ice-breaking activity such as those given in chapter 9.

Include each of these somewhere at the beginning of the class—not necessarily in this order. It orients the learners to you, the training, the materials, and what to expect. This way, there are no surprises later on like, "I have to leave now—I thought we were finishing at four," "Is this stuff in the book?," "When are we going to take a break?" or a question I remember well from my early, nervous training days, "So . . . what's your name?"

Introductions

At the start of a training session, you might typically introduce yourself and ask the learners to introduce themselves. This is the usual, formal way of introductions. Sometimes it doesn't work as well if you haven't talked with them casually first. Sometimes it establishes a formal atmosphere that is not conducive to learning. It is much better to greet people informally as they arrive, introduce yourself, and ask them a few questions about their work and their experience. After the informal conversations, the formal introductions are much easier for both you and the participants. To walk into a class, step up to the trainer's station, and begin with introductions does not allow the participants time to know or trust you. It will take longer to develop an easy, comfortable rapport.

Some trainers, in their introductions, make the mistake of giving a long list of impressive credentials in the hope of demonstrating to the participants that they have a knowledgeable instructor. Rather than be comforted by this knowledge, the learner is often intimidated. I had a colleague who used to start the class by saying, "Hi, my name is Sally Smith-Carpenter, and this is WordPerfect Introduction. I have been training for ten years, and I have a degree in computer technology and biochemistry. I've been using WordPerfect since it first came out, and you'll see that it's a very easy program to learn!"

Sally thought that this would help inspire their confidence in her ability and teaching talents. It might have done this for some, but it probably also made others think, "Oh great, I need to have a couple of degrees to understand this stuff!" Rather than help develop a rapport, it developed a distance between the learners and the trainer.

The learners want to know that you know your stuff, but at the same time, they want to know that you are not too different from themselves. An introduction that omits qualifications and certificates and emphasizes the qualities that you have in common with the participants is much more effective. Don't worry about letting them know how much you know. They will discover it within the first half-hour, anyhow.

One of the most effective introductions I ever saw was from an instructor with numerous certifications who started with, "My name's Tom and I'll be helping you learn this program today." "A year ago, I was sitting where you're sitting, pulling my hair out," Tom said, rubbing his bald head, "trying to create a database. Then someone showed me the easy way. I'm going to teach you the easy way today." With a couple of sentences and a few gestures, he had communicated a lot. He seemed down-to-earth and approachable, and had addressed some of their concerns. The program might seem confusing, he was saying, but I'll show you an easy way of using it. No one doubted that he could make it easy for them.

It is very useful for you (and also the other participants) to get to know a little about each of the learners. Knowing their job functions and experiences can help you direct the training and choose relevant examples. Finding this out informally as the participants arrive is quite effective and can be less threatening for the learners. When you ask for the learners to introduce themselves at the start of the class, don't go around the room one by one. Some people do not have a problem with this, but many feel uncomfortable and put on the spot. Instead of listening to all the other introductions, they are sitting there nervously, figuring out when their turns will be, and frantically trying to remember their names and where they work.

A much better way is to ask for introductions to the group as a whole, not to ask any one individual. I usually say something like, "So, give me a brief idea about what you do at work, and what you hope to get out of the class," and then I scan the room. The more confident ones speak up first, and gradually each person speaking seems to act as a catalyst to the others. If one or two participants haven't spoken up, I glance over in their directions, and they invariably speak up. The end result is the same as more formal introductions, but it avoids starting off the class by making some of the participants uncomfortable.

State the objectives

State the objectives of the training session before actually delivering the material. This lets the participants know what to expect and gives them an overview of what will be covered. It helps them see the big picture of the class, and how their individual needs might (or might not) be met. Objectives should drive the class, but never be set in stone. Often, the objectives need to change or be adapted according to the immediate needs of the group. It is important to allow a little flexibility in this regard.

When writing up objectives, make sure you go through them with the class rather than just have them on the flipchart or whiteboard. Briefly mention each topic you intend to cover, but avoid any unnecessary detail about the features. Rather than saying, "We're going to cover saving, opening and closing files, justification, and setting the margins," say something like, "We're going to learn how to create simple letters and memos." Covering objectives is not the time to get into any specifics.

If a topic is unfamiliar to the participants, explain briefly what it is. Make sure that none of the terms or topics are confusing to them. Don't leave them hanging as to what a term or topic means. Avoid saying something like, ". . . and then we'll cover parsing external data. I know you don't understand that right now, but it'll become clearer when we get to it." The whole purpose of stating objectives is so that the learners can get an overview and know what they are working towards. The participants must be clear about what is to be covered. It's also a good idea to summarize the objectives, such as, "What we're going to do today is cover all you ever wanted to know about tables, creating form letters, and how to customize the buttons." This helps put it all into perspective.

As you run through topics to be covered, stop and ask a few questions: "Have any of you created form letters before?" "How many of you are familiar with what a table is?" This helps you gauge the knowledge of the group and pitch the class at the right level. It also helps the learners relate what is to be covered to what they are doing back on the job.

When you have run though the course outline, ask, "Which of these do you feel are going to be most valuable to you?" or some such question. The response gives you an idea of what's important to them. This information can help you decide which topics to spend a little more time on and which to spend less.

When you talk about the objectives, you might hear, "Are we going to cover . . .?" or, "Will you show us how to . . .?" Participants might mention topics or features that are not in the class outline. If you can cover these without sacrificing the existing content, confusing anyone, or getting too sidetracked, try to do it.

You might also consider asking something like, "So tell me, exactly what do you hope to get out of this class?" or, "What do you want to have achieved by four o'clock this afternoon?" You will usually find that their objectives are not exactly the same as yours. They might be expecting more emphasis on one topic and less on another, or something that has nothing to do with any of the stated objectives. Once again, if you can find the time during or after class, at break, or at lunch to address topics that they wish to learn, the class will be much more valuable to them. Something that took you two minutes to explain could make the world of difference to a learner.

At intervals throughout the class, it is worth quickly recapping the objectives and stating what has been covered and what is yet to be covered. This gives the participants a feel for how the class is progressing, what they have got to look forward to, and how the last few topics fit into the scheme of things. When the class spans several days, it is especially important to recap what has been covered, what objectives have been completed, and what are still to be completed. Always start the next day of a multiple-day class with a review, recap, and restatement of objectives so that learners can orient themselves once again to where they are in the training.

The presentation

Explaining something to a group of people does not constitute training. We need images, interest, clarity, interaction, and variety. We need to bring information to life and deliver it to our audience in a simple and understandable form. The way we present our material is as important as the material itself.

Gesticulate

Communication is the process of getting what's in your brain over to another person's brain. Words are the most commonly acknowledged way of doing this, but 90% of communication is nonverbal. Part of this nonverbal communication is how you use your hands.

Hands can be an effective tool for computer training. You can use the hands for emphasis and for painting pictures in the air. Using your hands can bring energy, interest, and clarity into your training.

Most people are familiar with using the hands for emphasis, but let's consider the "painting pictures" part more carefully. As I have mentioned many times in this book, use every opportunity to help learners visualize pictures and images. The hands can help achieve this. When I talk about a linear process, such as the steps involved in recording a macro, I might place my left hand palm-down in the air at eye level. "Step one, we turn the recorder on." "Then, we carry out the keystrokes we want to record." I move my right hand down below the left hand. "And then we turn the recorder off." I put my left hand down at chest level, below my right hand. Crude, I know, but the learners immediately construct a visual image in their minds of the three steps.

When I talk about linking a cell from one spreadsheet file to another, I sometimes draw the spreadsheets in space. "Here's the spreadsheet file with the cell you want to link from . . ." I move both hands over to the right, as if holding a spreadsheet. "And here's the spreadsheet

file you want to paste the link to." I move my hands over to the left.
"We copy the cell contents from this file." I pretend to pick up a single cell from my file. "And paste a link . . ." and so on, moving my
hands around as if there really are spreadsheets suspended in the air.

Painting pictures and miming like this can produce a memorable image and assist your verbal explanations. I realized the power of this
when I was teaching a DOS class years ago. I was explaining the concept of a directory structure and used the analogy of a filing cabinet.
I walked over to the corner of the room, and I asked them to imagine a four-drawer filing cabinet. I pulled out the top drawer to illustrate a directory and then "held up" a manila folder inside the drawer,
the subdirectory. I then "pulled out" a piece of paper, the file itself. I
constantly referred back to this filing cabinet in the corner of the
room when any questions were asked about files and directories.
Later on in the class, when I reviewed some of the directory structure
ideas, the participants would point to the corner of the room "where
the filing cabinet was." I asked a challenging question. "I can explain
that," said Steve in the front row. He got up out of his seat, went over
to the "filing cabinet" and proceeded to pull drawers and file folders
out. The rest of the class sat there nodding as if the virtual cabinet had
been there all the time. Images are powerful.

Teach more visually

Software has become more and more graphical and less text-based.
Your training should reflect this. Graphical user interfaces (GUIs) are
used because people respond better to pictures, symbols, and icons
when learning, than they do words. A picture or a symbol can convey more information, more quickly than written text. When people
see an icon with lines on it that represents right-aligned text, they immediately get the idea. When they see the words "right-aligned text,"
they have to read them, understand them, and create a picture in their
minds of what the words represent.

Diagrams and visual images are powerful. Signs on the freeway, the
dashboard of a car, and the controls on a photocopier are all sym-
bolic rather than textual. Computer trainers need to incorporate more
visual explanations than they do. We deal with GUI software and our
goal is to develop a level of understanding and expertise, yet we insist on using words to teach this. Someone asks a question in a class
about linking files, and we give a verbal explanation. If they are
lucky, we might throw in a little hand movement. A simple diagram

to explain the concept of linking not only makes it easier to grasp in the moment, but it is much more memorable.

Whenever you can, use visual ways of explaining ideas or answering questions rather than purely verbal explanations. Consider using diagrams on overhead transparencies to explain some of the more elaborate concepts you teach. The next time someone asks you a question, try giving your explanation by sketching a diagram on the whiteboard or flipchart.

When you do draw simple diagrams and sketches, make sure they are clear and simple. Don't add to the learner's confusion by having them try to figure out what your artwork is supposed to represent.

The power of pictures

A utilities company decided to create a multimedia application that would teach its employees about new company policies and procedures. They wanted to create the application in-house, so they sent four of their people to a local training center to learn a popular multimedia authoring package. The first few days of the week-long course went well, but there were complaints about the courseware being difficult to follow when help was needed. The trainer, Joan, who had spent many hours putting the custom courseware together, was perplexed. Joan had spent a lot of time making sure the courseware was clearly laid-out and well designed, and had a good index and table of contents.

During a break, she asked one of the members of the group what he found difficult or confusing about the courseware. He thought for a second and said, "I think it's because there are no pictures. It's a real graphical program—really easy and fun—but you get to the handout and it's a bunch of words. I guess we like diagrams and pictures rather than reading." Joan took another look at the courseware and realized he was right—it was a whole bunch of words.

After a week or so of editing, a new piece of courseware emerged. She added screen shots, diagrams, pictures of icons, and tables, and cut down on some of the less-critical text. She sent her utility group the updated manual and a few days later got telephone calls from each of them thanking her and raving about the "cool manual." They even purchased extra copies of it for other people in the department.

Joan ended up becoming a full-time courseware developer because of the popularity and quality of the documentation she produces. I asked her once how her courseware has changed and matured since she first began writing. She didn't hesitate, "My courseware now has twice the number of illustrations and half the amount of text that it used to have. I've managed to halve the weight and double the effectiveness. I used to concentrate on explaining concepts accurately with words. Now, I concentrate on pictures and screen shots."

Organize your whiteboard

You would never think of handing out courseware with illegible or hard-to-read printing. You wouldn't hand out courseware with poorly drawn illustrations, or with a totally inconsistent format. However, quite often, when trainers get in front of a whiteboard or flipchart, they lose all sense of clarity and organization. Words are scribbled all over the place, diagrams are hurriedly sketched, there is no consistency and no format. Yes, it's only temporary, but it's nevertheless important.

A well-organized and consistent use of the whiteboard can make a difference in how easily a concept or procedure is understood. It can give a sense of organization and structure, and it can help people take notes. When using the whiteboard, make it

- Legible

- Simple

- Organized

- Consistent

Make sure your writing is clearly legible—no excuses about poor handwriting. Write in all caps if you have to, but make it easily readable to everyone in the room. Try not to write at angles; keep it all straight and horizontal.

When you draw a diagram, make sure that each part is labeled clearly and that the diagram is drawn accurately. If participants wish to make notes or diagrams, they need to copy something clear and readable.

When you write something on the board or flipchart, choose just one or two words to describe a step or part of a procedure. Don't get wordy. If you are describing a step that involves highlighting cells, write down "Highlight," not "Highlight the range of cells you wish to change." If you do a good enough job explaining concepts, one word should be adequate.

When you are drawing a diagram or a sketch, only include the most important features. Don't provide too much detail. Draw simple shapes—squares, circles, triangles, rectangles—don't get carried away by trying to get too artistic. Think of the symbols on highway signs or the dashboard of your car. They are very simple, yet convey the required information.

Good courseware has organization. There is some logical structure to it. It has headings, subheadings, diagrams, and captions that are consistent. They are always in the same format. A well-organized whiteboard should show some consistency. When you write up the name of the topic you are going to teach, try to always put it in the same place on the board. When you write up step-by-step procedures, have a place and format for those. When any new vocabulary words are introduced, have a place for those. If a learner asks you to cover something later in the class, have a place for "things to cover later."

The idea of organizing the whiteboard is to offer the learners a clear and consistent presentation of information. They will follow along more easily, will be able to interpret your notes and diagrams better, and will have some sense of continuity. They will know how to read your whiteboard: where the procedural steps are, which are the shortcut keys, and where the vocabulary words are. It truly is a service to your participants. Keep in mind that some of the learners' fears of being in a classroom situation relate to memories of teachers and lecturers scribbling incomprehensible scrawl all over the place. Give them legibility, simplicity, organization, and consistency, as shown in Fig. 2-5.

Draw effective diagrams

When you draw a sketch or diagram to assist understanding, it needs to be simple and clear. Sometimes a trainer draws a quick diagram to help with an explanation, but ends up complicating the issue because of a poorly drawn or poorly chosen image.

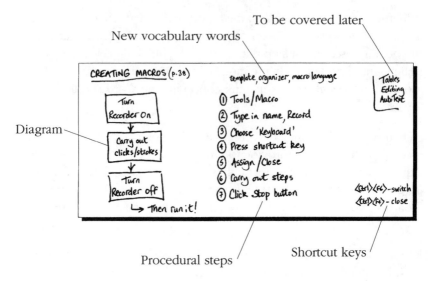

New vocabulary words

To be covered later

Diagram

Procedural steps

Shortcut keys

2-5 *Organizing the whiteboard.*

A diagram should be as simple as possible and yet contain the essential information (Fig. 2-6). The words that you use to label it should be kept to a minimum. Trainers often feel inclined to include as much information on the diagram as possible—they think that the more information they give, the better it will be understood. This is not the case. Remember, people can take in a whole picture in one blink of the eye, while a group of words have to be read and are not as immediately accessible.

When you draw a shape to represent a file, document, table, picture, step, or whatever, try to choose a shape that best represents the idea or object. If it's a document, a rectangle might be appropriate. If it is a disk, a circle would work. Don't choose a symbol that has very little relationship to the actual idea (a circle for a document or file, for example). Also, make sure that the positioning of the shapes is logical. If your diagram describes a process, make sure the logical sequence of each step is evident.

Ensure that symbols are large and clearly drawn, and that any text is readable. Don't sketch a tiny little diagram at the edge of the whiteboard.

If you start by drawing a rectangle with horizontal lines on it to represent a document, stick to this convention. Don't draw a circle next

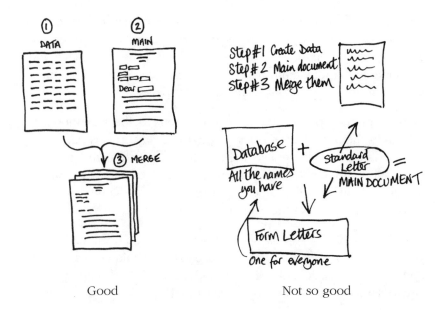

Good   Not so good

2-6 *Keeping it simple, clear, and consistent.*

time. If the courseware or software shows a graphical representation of a feature or concept in a particular way, stick to that format when you draw a diagram. Make sure that the pictures and diagrams you draw reflect any the learners might see in the courseware or on their screens. When you review a concept or procedure, make sure you draw the diagram the same way you originally drew it.

As with everything else in computer training, put yourself in the learner's seat. If you stepped back and took a look at your diagrams, would they be understandable? Do they contain the essentials? How clear, direct, and to-the-point are they? Are they well-drawn? Diagrams can make the difference between understanding or not understanding. They are worth doing well.

Vary your presentation

After you have been training for a few years, it's easy to get into a training rut. You have developed a style of teaching and a way of presenting information that you feel comfortable with. Unfortunately, this is not necessarily a style that works best for the learners; it's just one that seems to work for you.

For example, some trainers love to use the overhead projection system and do lots of demonstrations and assisted exercises. Other trainers concentrate more on exercises and worksheets to give their participants the maximum hands-on experience. Still others concentrate on following the courseware page by page.

Trainers often adopt a training style that reflects the way they learn and gives them the least-challenging training day. This is particularly so when you have been teaching the same class so many times, you can teach it in your sleep. You know the exact comments you are going to say, you draw the same diagrams, you do the same practice exercises, and you make the same jokes in the same places.

I used to do this with spreadsheet classes that I had been teaching for years. I was convinced that my approach and technique was perfectly fine. Participants seemed to understand the work, could apply it, and always laughed at my three spreadsheet jokes.

I then had an opportunity to sit in another trainer's class and watch her teach the same class. The same topics were covered, but what a difference! She used the overhead much more creatively than I ever did. She used a flipchart to review the work—I never used the flipchart. She would have review games at the end of each section—I never even thought of learning software by playing games. I would always explain carefully how to tackle the practice exercises. She gave the learners hardly any direction until she was helping them one-on-one.

In short, she taught the same class, but in a very different way. She used different media, provided different examples, and used different training approaches. Not necessarily better—that is not the point—but different. In the next spreadsheet class I taught, I tried some other approaches and found that in many cases, I could present the material more effectively.

Vary your presentation from time to time. Try some new approaches, new materials, and new ways of explaining things. It will help your learners, develop your own creativity, increase your enthusiasm, and give you an extra training edge.

Helping learners "link" ideas

When adults learn, they learn differently than children. When provided with new information, children can assimilate it quite quickly.

They do not have the wealth of experience and accumulated knowledge that an adult has, and therefore the information is often unrelated to previous experiences, as discussed in chapter 16.

A child's motivation for learning is also different from an adult's. Because adults have a wealth of experience to call upon, they need to be able to relate new information to information already clearly established in their memories. Once this link has been made, the new information is more readily absorbed and can therefore be recalled more easily. If the new information seems unrelated to ideas already established in the memory of the learner, understanding and recall are not as effective.

It is crucial for you to be able to associate or "link" new information with information that the learner is already familiar with. The more you know about the learners, the better you can link information. This is another reason why it is good to get to know a little of the background and experience of learners before a class.

For example, suppose you are teaching a group of salespeople how to carry out a mail-merge in a word-processing program. You draw a very simple diagram on the whiteboard of a data file and a letter being merged into multiple copies of the letter. You tell them the data file is much the same as a Rolodex file (an analogy relating to their experience). You give them the example of having to send all their customers a promotional letter about a new product (relating to their experience). You start to talk about querying the data file by giving an example of sending promotional material only to those customers in California (again relating to their experience). You use the word _filter_ to explain the concept of querying (linking to a known idea).

To give you another example of how valuable linking is, consider something that happened to me in a spreadsheet class. I was teaching a group from the accounting department in a casino. We were covering relative and absolute cell addresses. I had explained the concept a few times, and everyone but Jim in the front row had grasped the idea. I tried several more times with Jim, but was unsuccessful. Finally, a woman in the class asked if she could try to explain it to Jim. I told her to go right ahead, thinking that she would have no more success than myself.

"Jim, you know the AB341 form for revenues? Well, the tax rate cell in that is constant, and. . . ." In about 20 seconds, Jim knew exactly what absolute and relative addressing meant. He couldn't grasp the concept while I used my examples, but as soon as it was related to his experience, it became clear.

Have learners verbalize the concepts

A very effective way of reviewing concepts and procedures is to have participants say them aloud to the group or to each other. Have you ever noticed that when you start verbalizing ideas or confusions to someone else, things start to fall into place and become clearer? In order to communicate information in words and sentences, you have to first form clear concepts in your mind. When you encourage learners to verbalize the concepts you are teaching, it will help them gain a better understanding of the work and will also assist them with remembering. This concept is discussed in detail in chapter 14.

Ask the learners to explain a concept or procedure they have just learned. (Let them volunteer—don't put anyone on the spot.) As they do so, they will be clarifying and consolidating the information in their own minds as well as helping everyone else review the work. When this is done, they might find that there is something they didn't quite understand fully. Speaking it aloud will bring this to light. If it wasn't verbalized, the misunderstanding might never have been cleared up.

When someone has just finished explaining a concept, turn to the group and say something like, "Does that sound right to you?" This usually prompts a few people to add to or concur with the explanation. This is a great way of reviewing the work, discovering any gaps in the learners' understanding, and generating participation.

Another method is to pair people up and have each person explain the concept or procedure to the other. This has an advantage over the previous method in that it involves all the participants and no one escapes being involved. Many people will find it far less intimidating talking with their neighbor than they would in front of the whole group. When this is done, each person tends to assist, guide, and add to the other person's explanation. They have, in effect, a learning partner with whom they can discuss the work. In addition, it creates a rapport between the learners and brings a certain liveliness and vitality to the training.

Pictures, patterns, and structure

When you teach people how to use software, be sure to provide them with a recognizable, structured pattern of information (see chapter 16). Simply providing a sequential list of procedural steps and encouraging the learners to remember this is not the best way of learning. They must be encouraged to see some overall pattern or structure in the information, as shown in Fig. 2-7.

Many learners are left scratching their heads after being taught a new software feature or function because the trainer has omitted to illustrate the overall structure, the "big picture," and has instead simply provided a set of keystrokes or mouse-clicks to follow. In emphasizing the steps, this trainer has forgotten to put them into the larger context (the *pattern*) of how they all fit together. Interestingly enough, most trainers gained their own knowledge of computers in a very nonlinear, nonsequential fashion, but pass this knowledge on to a learner in a totally different mode. Most courseware also reflects this linear, discrete-step type of learning.

Of course, a certain amount of procedural steps are necessary, but these are much more valuable and understandable after the learner has first been shown a pattern of how everything fits together. By going straight to the procedural steps without first providing a pattern, you encourage memorization of the material rather than understanding.

Suppose, for example, that you are teaching the concept of copy-and-paste. Before any information about procedural steps is given, a clear idea of the concept of copying and pasting must exist in the learners' minds, along with the necessary vocabulary. They need a mental image or an actual diagram showing the idea of copying and pasting. It is important that they have an image or structure in their minds that is clear and understandable. This is the critical part of the learning process, not the procedural steps.

The procedural steps will make sense and be easily remembered once the conceptual pattern is clear. In fact, learners can often figure out the procedural steps with only the minimum of guidance if the trainer has done a good job of presenting the initial pattern.

The pattern or structure presented to the learner does not have to be a picture or diagram; it can be an image in their minds' eye. You might be teaching how to create a macro in a program and relate it

A

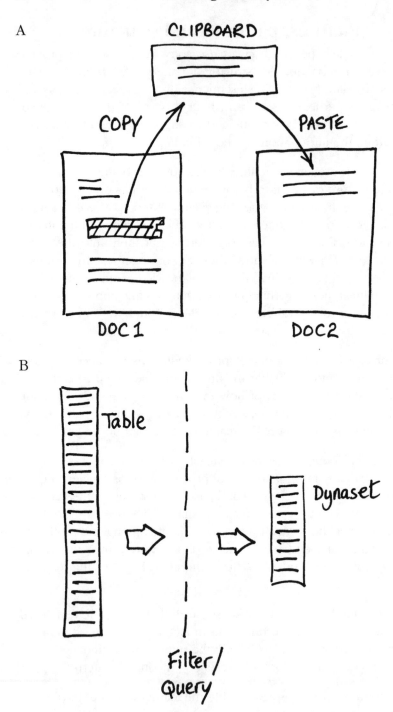

2-7 *Creating a pattern.*

to a handheld recorder. You hold your hand up as if you were holding the recorder. "I start the recorder," you say, pressing an imaginary record button. "I speak into it and it records what I say." You bring the recorder to your mouth. "And then I stop the recorder." You pretend to press a stop button. You then explain how you can replay macros just like rewinding and playing the handheld recorder.

As you act this out, your audience is building an image in their minds of the recorder and you speaking into it and replaying it. It is a familiar and understandable image that makes sense to them. You have created a meaningful pattern so macro recording and playback steps are not just separate, unrelated events, but form a structured whole.

To have procedures learned, the starting point, as shown in Fig. 2-8, is to have the concept understood. To understand the concept, you need to create an image, a structured, meaningful pattern that learners can relate to. Without some form of pattern and structure, the procedural steps are unconnected and relate to nothing.

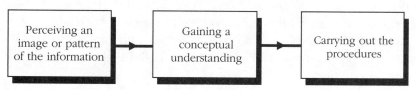

2-8 *Three steps to learning.*

"Incremental" training

When most trainers train, they tend to do it in a somewhat linear and sequential fashion. You cover all the basic topics, and when you feel these are understood, you move onto the next topic and so on until we cover everything. In a spreadsheet program, for instance, you might talk about the screen layout and the menus. You might then cover the different types of mouse cursors there are, and what each of them is used for. Then you might cover basic cell entry and editing. Finally, after having a good understanding of the basics, you would put them all together and create a simple payroll worksheet.

This is teaching from the logic of the program rather than teaching from the logic of the learner. When people write books or handouts for a software application, they generally start with a good discussion of all the basics, then move on to the next topic and discuss that, then move on to the next, and so on. This very sequential presentation is not the way people learn, however. When you learned to drive a car, you didn't study the gas pedal for a day, get thoroughly acquainted with that, and then move onto the brake pedal the next day. No; you learned a little about everything, practiced, and then got out on the road, gradually expanding and fine-tuning your learning.

People don't learn in any remotely linear fashion. They learn a little about everything, and then expand their learning incrementally in all directions. In a spreadsheet class, this would be a much more appropriate way to learn. Instead of teaching all there is to know about cursor movements and then spending an hour talking about text entry and editing, give participants a real example or exercise that calculates something in the first 20 minutes of the class. Already they are working on something valuable and real, and can see results. They might not know all there is to know about cursors and editing yet, but that can come later when they start expanding their knowledge incrementally from this basic working example. After this simple example, you might then go on to talk about using the cursor for moving the cells or copying the cells. You might continue by talking about changing and editing cells. You have started with a real, understandable, working model, and gradually increased their knowledge by building on this original model.

Think about learning in terms of ever-increasing concentric circles as opposed to learning along a straight line. People learn very little in life in straight lines, they naturally learn in this ever-expanding, incremental fashion. This is how your computer training should be, following the form of the way people learn.

Nonlinear learning

Eric is one of those people who masters anything that has a logical structure in a matter of days. He started to play with the Hypertext Markup Language (HTML) the day he got his account with an Internet service provider, and a week later he was creating Web pages. Training was not his field, he was the network guru for a small college, but because of his knowledge of the Internet and his Web skills, he was asked to teach an introductory class in HTML. He created an outline of everything he wanted to teach and created some very comprehensive documentation.

The training manager stopped by after Eric's first half-day of train-ing and asked how the class was going. Eric gave the thumbs down. He said he thought he was losing them and that they didn't seem like a very enthusiastic group. The training manager knew some of the participants of the class and knew they had been very excited about learning this Web language. She de-cided to sit down with Eric at lunch to see how they could re-vive the class.

At lunch, Eric pulled out a copy of his class outline and ex-plained what he had covered so far. Eric had given a brief, 30-minute introduction to the history of HTML and had spent the remaining three-and-a-half hours listing and explaining each of the basic tags. Eric's class outline was very comprehensive and started with all the basics, moved onto the more advanced tags, and ended up with them putting it all together the second day. The problem was that they hadn't done anything yet. So far, they had spent half a day learning the syntax of tags.

The training manager suggested that Eric try teaching just a little bit of everything the participants needed to see a basic Web page appear, "Forget about covering everything in order, just get them creating a very simple page so they can see the effects of the tags. Then do some fine-tuning, using the other tags and techniques. Let them see an end-result before providing any more detail. Teach them the way you learned it, Eric, by gradu-ally expanding your circle of knowledge. Don't teach it like you're writing a book on it." Eric agreed to give it a try, although he was a little upset about changing his nicely structured teach-ing plan.

That afternoon, he helped the class create a simple Web page with a few links and a graphic. When the participants saw what their collection of little tags did on the screen, they got excited. The atmosphere in the room changed. Throughout the after-noon, questions flew. "How do I get it to . . .?," "What happens if I want to . . .?," "What's that tag that changes the . . .?" The learners were all hooked. Eric abandoned his outline and ended up just going around the room answering questions.

The next day, he built upon what they learned from the first day. By 4:30 that afternoon, he had covered more material than he had planned. It was covered in a very nonlinear, sometimes

unstructured fashion, but they all "got it" and wanted more information. He had a wildly enthusiastic group of HTML users.

When Eric teaches his Web publishing classes now, he has participants build a simple page within the first hour of the class.
He gives them just enough information to create something real.
When they can see a result, he gives them the next layer of information and then the next, and so on. It works perfectly.

Use analogies

As mentioned earlier in this chapter, when adults learn, they need to
link new ideas to those already established in their minds. Once some
sort of link has been formed, they can grasp the new material more
readily.

Analogies help the linking process. An idea or concept is explained or
made clearer by relating it to something we know about. You have
most likely used the filing cabinet analogy for directories. It works
because a new idea has been related to something very familiar.
Analogies are perfect for computer training. There are hundreds of
opportunities in teaching software concepts where analogies can be
used. Whenever possible, try to use them in your explanations, especially when people seem a little confused.

So where can you get some good analogies? You can create them yourself, or you can steal them. Some of the analogies you already use in
your training you probably heard from someone else. Others you
probably made up on-the-fly in a training session one day—these are
often the best!

The next class you teach, go in armed with some new analogies. Sit
down sometime before the class with a piece of paper, and on the left
side, write down a list of all the most important concepts that need to
be understood in the class. On the right side of the page, invent an
analogy (or two) for each concept. Use the following guidelines:

- Make the analogies as visual as possible. When people see a
  picture or can visualize an image, they will remember more
  easily.

- Make sure they relate to most people's experience. Don't use
  analogies that some of your audience might not relate to,
  such as sports analogies.

- Make sure your analogies are simple and clear. A complicated analogy that takes a while to explain will not simplify a concept, but instead obscure it.

- Make them a little bizarre and unusual. The more visual and ridiculous, the better. People remember strange and unusual images—they have more impact.

Make a special effort to create analogies for concepts you teach that often cause confusion. Try doing this with a group of other trainers— it works even better with everyone's input and creativity. Once you have created them, how do you know if they are any good? The only valid way to tell is to try them out in your training. If the learners understand and learn from an analogy, it's probably a keeper. If they still have blank expressions on their faces after one of your "new" analogies, throw it out. The only real judge is your learners. Don't keep using an analogy because you like it.

Another way of adding to your repertoire of analogies is to ask the learners, "What can you think of that this is similar to?" or, "How could you simply explain this concept to one of your coworkers?" I have got some wonderful analogies this way. If it comes from the participants, it is more valuable because it lives in their world of experience, not a computer trainer's.

Don't be shy about asking other trainers what analogies they use. Better still, sit in one of their classes and observe them in action. Share your analogies with other trainers during an instructor meeting (see page 139). Get together with all the other trainers in your department or company and just talk about training methods, tips, tricks and analogies.

Analogies and humor

A computer training company in London, England decided to schedule instructor meetings once a month. The purpose of the meetings was for instructors to get together somewhat informally to discuss and swap training methods, approaches, and ideas. When the trainers heard about the proposed idea, they were not in the least bit enthused. Most of them had been teaching for many years and did not feel they would benefit from such a group. All the same, they were obliged to attend.

In the first meeting, Deborah, the training director, tried to get the ball rolling by talking about teaching Windows programs. She asked what topics, concepts, or procedures the students had most problems with. Slowly the trainers began to make a list: selecting text, when to click or double-click, multitasking, remembering to select something before formatting it, and so on.

Deborah picked the first problem mentioned, selecting text, and asked how everybody approached that. (The problem was that many new users try to highlight text from the middle instead of starting at the ends.) One trainer said something like, "If you go over it enough times, they'll eventually get it." Another mentioned that she spent some time with the overhead display showing them the correct way.

Then it was time for Pete, one of the new instructors, to contribute. Somewhat diffidently, he told how he liked to give analogies and get the students to visualize pictures of things. For selecting text, he told his class to imagine painting a hallway. You would have to start at one of the ends; it would be silly to start in the middle. The others laughed and asked if he had any others. He liked to explain multitasking, he said, by telling them to imagine being at a cocktail party, talking with a guest, and then some very attractive member of the opposite sex walks in. He moved his head from left to right. "Your processing is shared—multitasking—you see!" The room broke out into hysterics and they pressed him for more of his wonderful analogies. Pete spent the next 20 minutes going through his list of strange and wonderful analogies with an attentive and smiling audience. He told them how he tried to make the analogies as bizarre as possible because the learners seemed to remember them better. The others asked him if he wouldn't mind them stealing a few for their next class. Pete was delighted and said he would write them all out and give everyone a copy.

The first instructor meeting at this company turned out to be a great success, and Pete's list got circulated. I talked with some of the instructors at the next meeting about the success they had with the analogies. Those who had used them said they had worked extremely well, in addition to bringing some humor into the class. Some of the trainers had created new ones for the programs they taught.

With the help of Pete and the rest of the instructors, Deborah now has a file with analogies for every class that the training center teaches—and every new trainer gets a copy.

Engage all the senses

Learning is most effective when as many senses as possible are involved in the process. When you learned to drive a car, many different senses were engaged:

- Sight, in viewing the traffic conditions and the dashboard
- Hearing, in the sound of the engine, the traffic around you (and maybe the instructor shouting at you)
- Touch, in the steering wheel, the gear stick, the foot pedals
- Emotion, in anxiety trying to avoid pedestrians

These all combined to make your first driving lesson memorable.

Now imagine it is your first driving lesson, but your instructor sits you down at a desk in a room and starts explaining the theory of good driving. For the first half-hour you grasp the basic ideas of the clutch, accelerator, brakes, and steering. The instructor explains how you should use the indicators correctly and asks you to read a section in the driving manual about making left turns. After two hours of this type of instruction, would you be an adept driver? Of course not. It doesn't work like that. You need to be in the car, feeling the steering wheel in your hand, touching your feet on the pedals, listening to the engine, and watching the road. The more senses that are involved, the better. Learning a skill has to be experienced as fully as possible.

Computer training is much the same. The more senses involved the better. Unfortunately, the default mode for the learner is often listening. Because many trainers like to talk, this verbal mode of training tends to get overused and the learners' other senses get overlooked. Engaging other senses, particularly the visual, is a much more powerful way of training.

Use more visual images in your training—data displays, overheads, diagrams and pictures on the whiteboard and in the courseware (see page 85), wall posters, and gesticulations. Use more kinesthetic work for the learner—moving the mouse, typing on the keyboard, writing down shortcuts, and drawing diagrams. Encourage more verbalization from the learners—have them take a more active role in asking and answering questions and explaining concepts. Use more emotion in your training—anticipation, excitement, humor, involvement, and drama! Relying on words alone is too limiting and ineffectual.

Even with higher-end "technical training" when the subject matter might be a little drier, you can still inject a more sensory stimulus into your training. The following are some suggestions.

Develop some vocal variety

As you inevitably talk a considerable amount in training, you might as well bring a little variety into your speech. Have you ever recorded your voice on tape? It is sometimes disconcerting how lacking in energy and color one's voice is. It sounds fine when you are up there in front of the room—you think you sound interesting, engaging, and enthusiastic. But dare to tape one of your next classes, and you might be surprised. Play it back when you get home. Do you accentuate important points or words by changing tone and volume? Do you sound enthusiastic and energetic? Would you feel comfortable using this tape to promote your training services?

If the answers are all yes, then I congratulate you. If you are like most of us, though, you could do a little fine-tuning of your verbal presentation. I don't mean overdo it like a television commercial for used cars; just turn up the contrast and brightness a few notches. The emphasis and emotion you put into words is often as important as the words themselves. Words with energy, enthusiasm, and vigor behind them multiply their effectiveness.

Be passionate

Bring some excitement, anticipation, inspiration, and drama into your training! I know a trainer who, when he teaches a class how to delete a file, picks up a sheet of paper, screws it up into a ball, tosses it into the garbage, and shouts, "Delete!"

Another trainer, before teaching a particular spreadsheet function, points to the overhead screen and says, "Watch this—you are going to be amazed." She has everyone's attention and they are all wondering what they are going to see. She looks around the room with an excited grin on her face. She demonstrates the feature and then turns to the class, "How do you like that? Impressive, eh!?" She then goes on to explain what she did and how to do it. She has a way of bringing a sense of anticipation and excitement to her training. At break times, I hear her learners say things like, "What's this surprise she says she has in store for us this afternoon?" or, "What's this feature that will change our lives forever?"

She brings humor and a little drama into all her classes and is frequently requested by clients. Not only are her participants excited and entertained by the class, their ability to learn and remember is increased.

Use more visual explanations

Cut down the amount of words you use in your training and increase the number of images you use. Have you noticed how the more popular computer books are full of pictures? People can assimilate, understand, and remember a diagram or picture far more easily than a bunch of words. Draw more diagrams on the whiteboard or flipchart when you are explaining a concept or idea. Put some more posters and visual aids on the training-room walls. Paint pictures in the air with your hands and gesticulate more.

When someone asks you a question in a training session, try giving the answer with the aid of a diagram or by drawing images in the air. You will find that they will more easily grasp a concept if they can see it or see something that represents it. When you are explaining a concept or idea, use a diagram rather than a purely verbal explanation.

Get their bodies involved

Don't just let the trainers watch you do it—have them grab the mouse or the keyboard and do it themselves. Don't have them sit there and listen—get them to write something down. Get them to draw a diagram. Get them to work with their neighbors. Get them moving or doing something! Passive listening is far less effective than active involvement. Learning and retention increase when learners are physically involved in the learning process.

Writing is an example of this. The act of writing something down, rather than just hearing it or thinking it, causes it to be more permanently imprinted in the mind. It is proven that when you write your goals down you are 10 times more likely to achieve them. This gives you some indication of the power of transferring thought into writing.

Get your learners more physically involved in the work—it will improve their retention and keep them awake.

"Mind" breaks

The length of study time in a class versus the ability to recall what is learned is shown in Fig. 2-9. After about 30 minutes, a learner's attention and ability to focus starts decreasing. As a result, the effectiveness of learning and ability to remember are reduced.

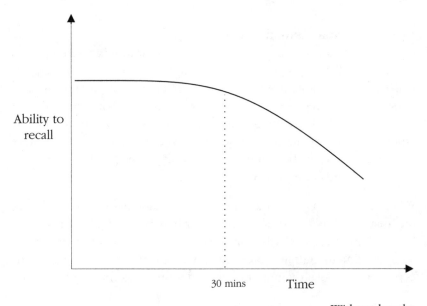

2-9 *Recall versus time without breaks.*

However, if a short break or change of focus is introduced approximately every 30 minutes, the learner's ability to focus and attend is reset back to its original level, as shown in Fig. 2-10. This does not have to be a complete break, such as a coffee break, but can simply be a change in focus. It would be unreasonable to provide coffee breaks for participants every 30 minutes, but you can provide "mind breaks."

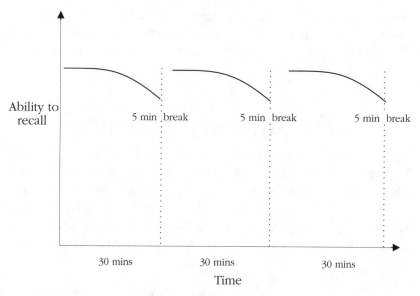

2-10 *Recall versus time with breaks.*

A mind break is simply a change of focus—a different activity, a shift of attention, or maybe a stretch. You can create short mind breaks in your training every so often by doing things like these:

- Tell learners you are going to give them a five-minute mind break. Do nothing for five minutes. Tell them to sit back and relax.

- Have them do a paired learning exercise as discussed on page 31, "Learner-learner interactions".

- Tell them to stand up, stretch, yawn, shake their hands—whatever they want to do to relax.

- Have them try an exercise or worksheet.

- Tell them a humorous story.

- Ask them how what you're teaching relates to what they do at work.

You get the general idea. You don't have to have them leave the room. You arrange a change of pace, direction, or focus. You have them think about something else. Done effectively, this can be as good as a break.

Ending and follow-up

How you end a class and follow up afterwards can make a big difference. People who leave your class excited, energized, and satisfied will remember you, the material, and your organization. How people feel walking out of a class is as important as how they feel walking in. Following up and supporting learners after a class can help your training organization more from being a good one to being a great one.

Ending the class

Don't let your class fizzle out at the end. The beginning of a class and the end of a class are memorable for people. Don't have an anticlimax; let them leave on a high point with enthusiasm, confidence, and a clarity about what they just learned. I've seen trainers teach great classes and then at the end say something like, "Well, I guess we're done . . . er . . . don't forget to switch the computers off. Bye."

Make sure when you finish the class, that you have reviewed what was covered and have cleared up any confusion or answered any questions. Don't let anyone leave with an unanswered question or concern. Offer to stay around for five or 10 minutes after the class to answer any other questions they might have. Encourage them to use and practice the skills back at work—let them know that taking the class is only one element in learning the program. The most important part is using and applying the skills back at work, where they will continue to expand and refine their knowledge.

Let participants know about the next class they might want to take to enhance their skills or any learning resources available to them. Tell them about any support services they can use or help desks. What can they do when they are back at work and have a problem or question? Will you be available to help support them?

Finally, acknowledge and thank them. Most of us are in training because we enjoy teaching, seeing different faces each day, and the interactions with other people. Let them know how much you enjoyed teaching them (if you did!) and compliment them as a group on their abilities, persistence, questions, friendliness, or whatever made a difference in the class. When they leave, use their names and say goodbye to them at the door rather than from the front of the room. This ends the class on a much more personal level and also gives them the opportunity to thank you and shake your hand if they wish (and many will want to do just that).

Follow-up after training

Everyone involved in the training function in an organization wants to develop a good relationship with their clients. This is vitally important before and during the training, but what is often overlooked is the relationship with the client after the training has taken place.

Training should never be seen just as an event that comes and goes, but as part of a larger learning process. One of the most important parts of this process happens after the class, when your participants get back to the office and try to implement some of the skills they learned. To help provide a complete learning experience, it is necessary to follow up after the class.

The training provider can contact the person responsible for setting up the computer training and have a brief conversation about how the training went. This is more appropriate for private classes than it is for ones offered to the public. You can ask things like, "How did the class go—did they learn anything?" "Have they had an opportunity to put any of their new skills into practice yet?" "Did they feel the class was valuable?"

This does a couple of things. First of all, the call itself demonstrates that your company, department, or organization is concerned about the quality and value of its training. Second, it provides an opportunity for the client to provide valuable feedback on what the participants felt they gained from the class, whether they found it useful, and if they are actually using any of their new skills. Class evaluations are one thing—using the skills back on the job is something else.

A call like this also provides an opportunity for clients to express any concerns they might have had about the training that otherwise would have gone unspoken. Many a training relationship has been saved by doing exactly this and addressing an issue that was worrisome to the client.

Many training managers complain that they haven't the time to follow up on all their clients. They are swamped, too busy, or have more important things to do. This might be the case, but the return in terms of rapport, repeat business, and evaluating your training product, a follow-up call can't be beat. A five-minute telephone call can be the best investment that you make all day.

Support after training

After taking a class at a training center, many learners become concerned about whether they will remember all the skills they learned. They worry that they will get back to work, get stuck, and not be able to complete their work. You've shown them how to use the courseware, the manual and the Help menu, but what they really want is a person to help them if they need it.

Offering some type of support after the training reassures your participants that they're not alone. They will be a lot more relaxed when they leave the class if they know that you, your department, or your company can offer help and support. This does not have to be anything fancy like a 24-hour support line. You can simply let them know that they can call if they encounter a problem, and whoever taught the class will get back to them within 24 hours. This is usually workable with most trainers.

Another great way to offer support after a class is to use e-mail. When learners have questions, they can send an e-mail message to the trainer—a sort of "e-mail helpdesk." The trainer can also easily distribute additional information to the learners through the e-mail channel.

Just like follow-up, this service can help you develop a closer and a more supportive relationship with your clients. Once again, a small time investment yields a large return.

3

The character of a trainer

"The mediocre teacher tells. The good teacher explains. The superior teacher demonstrates. The great teacher inspires."
— **William Arthur Ward**

Developing you

Becoming a better computer trainer is not just a question of learning new presentation skills and studying adult-learning theory. The greatest difference that you will notice in your training comes as a result of a change in you, in your attitude towards other people and your relationship with them.

Your ability to train more effectively and become a master at what you do cannot develop just by reading about some creative training tips and techniques. That is just frosting on the cake. The real substance of effective training is who you are. Your ability to train develops to the extent that you develop yourself. Call it personal growth, self-development, or whatever, but when you start to make positive changes in you and your relationship to other people, your training improves.

When thinking of how you can improve your training, get better at what you do, and deal with all the challenges you face, it's natural to look outside yourself for solutions. It's easier to think of what you can do instead of who you can be. As long as you concentrate on the doing, however, you'll find that your solutions are only short-term. Take developing effective listening skills, for example. You could study all the tips and techniques in this chapter for fine-tuning your ability to listen and try to implement them, but if at your core you don't believe that others have much to offer, then all this research will have no lasting effect. If, on the other hand, you come to really appreciate the contribution that others make to your life, listening won't be a thing to do, it will be a natural expression of who you are.

Developing communication skills as a trainer requires a certain amount of self-examination. Striving to become a more effective computer trainer involves being willing to look more closely at who you are and scratch beneath the surface. Take every opportunity to develop you. Attend workshops, read, listen to tapes, discuss, and reflect. Be committed to your own personal growth. When you change, your whole world changes.

Developing your listening skills

There is a difference between hearing what people say and listening to what they say. Hearing happens unconsciously. Listening involves conscious attention. In a computer training class, the default model is that the trainer talks and the learners listen. Trainers are good at talking; it is easy for them, and they are used to having learners listen to them. Trainers are often not used to listening, however. You hear what your learners say, but you might not always listen as powerfully as you could. When a question is asked, a trainer has usually made up his or her mind within the first five seconds what the learner is asking, what they are confused about, and what the trainer's answer is going to be. Often, trainers answer before the question has been fully expressed. We make assumptions, we judge, we interrupt, and we don't listen. Most people do this in their lives everyday, when they talk to others. What we call conversation is really waiting for a break in the other person's speaking so we can give our opinions.

To be effective in computer training, you need to listen more powerfully. Magical things happen in your training when you really listen to people. Here's some suggestions for listening powerfully:

- When someone asks a question, wait for him or her to completely finish before replying. Never interrupt a trainee.

- Never assume you know what someone is asking or talking about until you have let him or her finish speaking.

- Try to turn off your biases and opinions when listening. They get in the way. Try not to judge what someone is saying—just try to understand it.

- Maintain eye contact with the person you are listening to, and don't do anything else but stand there and listen.

- When a question is being asked, try to listen to it from the trainee's point of view rather than yours. Try to stand in their shoes.

- Listen to the slower, less experienced learners the same way you listen to the faster, more experienced ones. Don't judge anyone's questions as more or less valuable than anyone else's.

- Listen to those challenging, "difficult" learners with the same level of openness and patience you would grant anyone else.

Developing your listening skills will further your goal as an effective communicator more than anything else in your training. You'll find that your ability to listen powerfully to what others say is proportional to the level of commitment you have in your relationship with them. The more committed you are to really contribute to the learner, the easier it will be to listen. The more you are tied up with your own concerns and agenda, the harder it will be.

Being generous

To become an exceptional trainer, you must develop a generous nature—and I don't mean give away ten-dollar bills before you have participants fill out their evaluations. I mean that you should give freely of yourself to others, and be understanding when other people don't match your ideals. When someone expresses something, states an opinion, or asks or answers a question, it's too easy to make judgments about them rather than consider what they are saying. These judgments and evaluations of people color your ability to listen to what they are saying.

Be generous when a learner consistently fails to understand what you are explaining. Try not to make it mean anything about that individual other than that they don't get it. As soon as you begin to make it mean something like they are apathetic, inattentive, stupid, or whatever, your ability to help their learning diminishes.

Be generous when a learner challenges you or tries to argue with you. Try to see their point of view. Consider the possibility that you can make mistakes. Allow someone the benefit of the doubt for a change. Don't be attached to being right all the time. Listen carefully to what they have to say.

Be generous with your time. Offer to help some of the slower participants at a break, during lunch, or after class. Demonstrate the commitment you have to making sure they learn. Try to be available to them when they need assistance.

Being committed to your training

The extent to which you are committed to something is usually reflected in your success at it. When you have a small commitment to something, you get small results. When you have a powerful commitment to something, you get powerful results.

Take a look at your computer training. What are you committed to? Some people are committed to surviving the day intact, some are committed to getting the best evaluations they can, some are committed to having the class run smoothly, and some are committed to covering all the material. Whatever your commitment is, your results will most likely be consistent with it.

What would your training look like if you were totally committed to empowering everyone to learn? What if your only goal was to have each person get the absolute maximum from their time with you? How would you do things differently? What would you do that you don't currently do? What would you take responsibility for that you currently do not? How differently would you relate to your learners?

I like to pose a question to computer trainers who say they wish to improve: "If I said I would give you $10,000 if you taught your next class so that everyone learned and understood all the material and had the most fulfilling and empowering learning experience they've ever had in training, would your next class be any different than the last?"

"Well, of course it would!" they say. They start to tell me how they would plan, prepare, design learning aids, develop a better rapport, be really patient, offer extra help, etc. I ask them why they don't teach every computer class that way. "Because they don't pay me $10,000 per class!" is the reply. Ask yourself this same question, and you'll see that part of improving your performance as a trainer is a decision away. It is a question of motivation as well as learning new skills and techniques. When you are truly committed to your training, you'll get the same results as you would with the $10,000 carrot.

Take an honest look at the commitments you have in your training. What is important to you? Do these priorities match what is desirable for your learners? Are you more concerned about being liked than being effective? Would you be willing to embarrass yourself rather than risk embarrassing a learner? Are you relieved when 4 p.m. rolls around?

One of the most important steps in becoming an exceptional computer trainer is the commitment to serve and empower every learner you teach. As W. H. Murray puts it:

> *Until one is committed there is hesitancy, the chance to draw back, always ineffectiveness. Concerning all acts of initiative, there is one elementary truth, the ignorance of which kills countless ideas and splendid plans: that the moment one definitely commits oneself, then Providence moves too. All sorts of things occur to help one that would never otherwise have occurred. A whole stream of events issues from the decision, raising in one's favor all manner of unforeseen incidents and meetings and material assistance which no man could have dreamt would have come his way.*

Once a genuine commitment is there in your training, magic will start to happen.

Being yourself

To be effective in training, or anything for that matter, you need to be yourself. One of the reasons why some of the more experienced trainers and speakers are so effective is that they have learned to relax and be themselves. Tools, techniques, and training methods are all valuable, but when you're not being the real you, whatever you do comes across as unauthentic and forced.

I used to become a different person when I was training. I knew the way trainers should be, how they should respond, and how they should react in certain circumstances. When I taught, I would take on the demeanor of what I thought a trainer should be like. My training had no "me" in it at all. As soon as I walked into a training room, I put on my trainer persona. I thought I was being effective, but all I was doing was putting more distance between my learners and myself.

To train effectively, try to put a little more "you" into your work. Be honest and straightforward. If you make a mistake, admit it. If you want something from them, request it. If something strikes you as funny, share it with them. You'll find that your rapport with your learners will improve. They will feel more comfortable around you.

I learned the power of this by accident. Whenever I used to teach a class after getting very little sleep, I discovered that my effectiveness and my rapport with people improved. I could never figure this out—why should my being tired actually improve my training? I later realized that when I was tired, I didn't have the energy to play "trainer" and was just my plain old self. It worked so much better.

When you feel exhausted or drained after a training session, it is often because you have been playing a "part" all day. Acting takes energy and effort. You'll find that the more of yourself you express in the class, the less exhausting your training will be. To put it another way, "Your training won't be draining if the 'you' they view is true."

Being assertive

A degree of assertiveness in training now and then is necessary. When you are teaching a group, you will inevitably encounter situations that need to be addressed and things that need to be said to ensure that the most value is gained from the training.

Trainers who fail to be a little assertive now and then can lose control and direction of the class and end up feeling like they are fighting the tide. The class becomes difficult to teach, communication becomes harder, and the trainer finishes the class feeling exhausted.

People, understandably, are sometimes reluctant to be assertive for fear they will offend someone or be unpopular. If done in the right way, however, this never need happen. The effectiveness of being assertive is determined by the commitment behind it. Some people try to be assertive, but end up being pushy, opinionated, or slightly aggressive because the motivation behind the assertiveness is the need to make themselves right, and others wrong. Assertiveness that rests on this is not productive; it pushes people away. Being assertive to be right never works. When the assertiveness is driven by a genuine commitment to empowering someone else—in this case, the learners—it becomes much more effective.

Let's say it's morning break time, and half the class wanders back five or 10 minutes late. You are upset because the class is now 10 minutes behind schedule. You decide to say something. "The next time we take a break, can you make sure you return on time? Thanks." In the learners' hearing, it sounds like a reprimand, a slap on the wrist. You have passed judgment on them and made them wrong.

Consider the same situation, but as a trainer whose prime concern is having the participants learn as much as they can. The fact that they are 10 minutes late is still an issue that needs to be addressed. You are concerned that they might not have time to cover as much material or might miss some important concepts. The concern is for the success of their learning, not for your convenience. You might say, "I know that you want to get as much out of this class as you can, so when we take breaks throughout the day, I'd like you to get back here promptly so we can get started. Everyone okay with that?" You do not consider it a personal inconvenience, but simply something that gets in the way of the learning. Nobody is judged wrong; nobody feels reprimanded. Your concern for the learners is understood and respected.

Developing real patience

Patience is a necessary prerequisite for training. Patience is a passive way of honoring and respecting another. Learners value a trainer's patience very highly. When they encounter something in training that they do not understand or that needs clarification, they will be much more inclined to ask questions and participate if they feel the trainer is a patient and sympathetic listener.

Most trainers have a sense of this, but often end up developing what I call "fake patience." Someone will ask a question, and you'll repeat an explanation or try to clarify an issue. The learner still does not get it. You make another attempt to explain or elucidate. The learner still doesn't get it. As this continues, you make an effort to maintain the appearance of being patient (like you know you should), but underneath you are beginning to get a little frustrated. You might start saying to yourself, "Why can't you get this? It's pretty straightforward!" "How can you not know where the Escape key is!" Although you try not to show it, your posture and tone of voice change slightly. You try to appear patient, but what you really want to do is give this person a shake!

Real patience develops from an understanding and sense of what it is like to be on the other end, to understand what it feels like to be confused in a group. It comes from having empathy for others. It comes from not judging others by how intelligent or articulate they are. It comes from being committed to serve every learner, not just the ones who are keeping up with you.

When a trainer has empathy for the learner, then real patience develops naturally. You can stay calm no matter how many times you are asked a question or confronted with someone who doesn't get it. Real patience is not a question of practicing intense self-control when you've told someone where the Escape key is 10 times. It develops from being truly concerned about having someone understand the work and having their temporary lack of understanding be perfectly okay with you.

Real patience grows from understanding and appreciating others regardless of who they are or what they know. It is not a question of learning a specific technique, but of developing yourself and your relationship with others. As mentioned previously, the growth that you experience personally will always manifest itself in your training.

Here are a few ways to help develop patience:

- When a question is asked, listen like your life depended on it. Make sure you understand exactly what is being asked and what the confusion or concern is.

- Wait for someone to completely finish when he or she is asking a question. Don't assume you know what people are talking about before they have finished talking. (Trainers are great at answering questions before the learner has finished talking.)

- Take a class in a subject you know nothing or very little about. Find out what it feels like to be confused or a little intimidated.

- The next time you feel a little impatient with someone in your training, stop and try to focus only on what you could do or say that would serve that person.

Developing enthusiasm

Nothing is more interesting, engaging, and motivating than listening to someone who is genuinely enthusiastic about what they are doing. It is infectious. Someone's enthusiasm can bring subjects to life that at first seem dull and uninteresting.

I once spent an hour listening to someone talk about cardboard boxes. This person knew everything there was to know about cardboard boxes; the weight, texture, tensile properties, thermal conductivity, composition, and so on. He loved his work. I stood there, held by his interest and enthusiasm, and listened for an hour to the past, present, and future of cardboard boxes. I was not bored once. I never come across a cardboard box without thinking of that character. Enthusiasm is the spice in training. It can turn a seemingly bland subject into something exciting and engaging.

Here are some suggestions for developing enthusiasm:

- *Maintain a balance.* You can't be that enthusiastic when you are teaching and working too much and have an imbalance with your work and leisure time. You need a balance. You need sleep! You can't be enthusiastic when you're stressed. (See Chapter 11 for more on this subject.)

- *Keep up with the latest software.* Read and learn as much as you can about the software you teach. Learn new tips, tricks, shortcuts. What "cool" features does a program have? Learn some lesser-known shortcuts.

- *Remember why you train.* Most computer trainers stay in the profession because they gain a real sense of satisfaction from helping other people learn. Remember the excitement and sense of satisfaction you felt after teaching some of your first classes? Take a moment to appreciate the contribution you make to others when you teach.

- *Try new ways of training.* If you've taught that spreadsheet class a hundred times and can do it in your sleep, then try a different approach. Teach the class in a different way (see Chapter 9). Use different exercises, teach in a different order, introduce a game. Make each class unique. Sit in one of your peer's classes, and find out how they teach the same class.

One last note on enthusiasm—sometimes people are very excited, enthused, and interested in what they do, but they haven't notified their face about it. Don't forget to smile now and again and look like you are enthused. Your learners love to see you smile.

Respecting your learners

Respect means to show understanding, consideration, and to allow people to be who they are without personal judgment. There are two types of judgment. One is where you make an observation of what is occurring, e.g., "This learner is slow." You are stating what you observe to be so. You are "judging" this learner to be slow. The other type of judgment is the personal judgment, when you turn an observation into a criticism of the individual. "This learner is slow because . . ." he or she is a poor listener, stupid, lazy, or whatever. Personal judgments have an emotion associated with them. Frustration, impatience, and anger are often present when trainers make personal judgments about their learners.

Respecting your learners means letting them be who they are—slow, fast, attentive, inattentive, quiet, loud, accepting, argumentative—without letting it mean anything more than that. As soon as you make it mean something and attach personal significance to it, your ability to communicate and relate to that person is diminished. Letting go of such judgments is by no means easy, but certainly worthwhile.

Avoiding putting anyone on the spot

A prerequisite of learning efficiently is an environment free from perceived threat. Although a mild level of stress is often useful and motivational when learning a new skill, anything that causes undue concern or worry gets in the way of learning. The biggest fears of people in a classroom situation are having to speak in public and looking "dumb" in front of peers.

Trainers sometimes forget what it is like to be on the other end. When you train, you are in control of the environment. You have the power to bring attention to anyone in the room for whatever reason. The learner, on the other hand, has a more passive role by default. Every time the trainer asks a question, looks at a participant, or uses someone's name, there is the possibility of being singled out, and the fear of saying or doing the wrong thing. This becomes even more of a threat for some learners when they are unsure of whether they can trust the trainer. This is one of the reasons why it is critical to build rapport as early as possible—so that the learners can ask and answer questions in a "safe" environment.

Do what you can to minimize these fears. Without thinking, sometimes a trainer will ask a question of a quiet, diffident person in an effort to bring him or her into the discussion. This trainee might be confused, self-conscious, and embarrassed. However, the trainer might persist in having this person find the right answer, when the best course of action would have been to move to another person, and return to the quiet one later. When someone seems to be uncomfortable answering a question, avoid putting him or her on the spot. A learner who feels embarrassed or pressured by the trainer (whether the trainer intended it or not) will cease to participate fully in the class and will avoid further interaction.

A trainer should be particularly careful about this when:

- *Asking a question.* "Overhead" questions or questions to the group in general are less intimidating than questions asked of individuals. If you do wish to ask an individual, state the question first, and call upon them, never the other way around. When someone answering a question becomes visibly uncomfortable, help him or her get to the answer. Don't let this person sit there sweating.

- *Listening to an answer or a question.* As someone is asking or explaining something, he or she is looking at your expression and body language to see if the question or explanation is valid. A frown, smile, or shake of the head can often be seen as an invalidation.

- *Dealing with a challenging learner.* Difficult learners can sometimes be a source of concern and embarrassment to the trainer. In order to maintain control and save face, a trainer will sometimes say things designed more for his or her own benefit than the learner's. Avoid this at all costs.

  When the learners in your class realize they are in a safe, nonthreatening environment, and have the sense that they can trust you, you'll begin to develop a very powerful rapport and level of participation.

Avoiding making the learner wrong

Try to avoid the terms *good, bad, right,* and *wrong,* when responding to questions in your training. When you ask a question to the group and someone gives an incorrect answer or is way off track, don't shake your head or indicate that the answer is wrong and move on to someone else. Instead, stick with this person, leading him or her to the answer. "Well, that's correct, apart from the last part. What do we need to include?" When this person gets to the answer, finish with something like "Exactly!" or "Great!" The learner is left with a far more empowering attitude than when you simply let them know the answer was wrong. Try to have them succeed regardless of where they start.

Also, when listening to explanations, don't make someone wrong for simply using different vocabulary or expressing something poorly. An answer like "Double-clicking the gray thing up there . . ." rather than using the exact terminology should be perfectly acceptable if you are sure the learner understands the concept. You can always mention the proper vocabulary after you have affirmed the answer.

Simply considering "right" and "wrong" answers limits the creativity and independent thought of the learner. Painting everything so black and white gives the learner little encouragement to inquire further and learn. "That's not the right way of doing it . . ." can invalidate, whereas "There's a better way of doing that . . ." encourages them to learn more.

Developing a new attitude toward slow learners

Slow learners are often a challenge for computer trainers. Trainers usually prefer to train the "sharper" ones, where you can zoom through the material quickly and answer some quite insightful questions. You explain a concept, and they immediately grasp it. You tell your fellow trainers, "I had a really good class—they were all really sharp!"

When confronted with learners who don't catch on so quickly and struggle to follow, the temptation is to give an inward sigh. Slow learners appear as problems, interrupting the flow of the class. You try your best to appear as patient as possible for as long as you can. If they would only get it, you think to yourself, then things would run more smoothly, and you could get on with all the material you want to teach.

Trainers need to change their attitudes toward slow learners. Slow learners should be seen as an integral part of computer training, not an interruption of it. In fact, you should welcome slow learners in your training. They are an opportunity and an asset to you. One of the greatest contributions you can make as a trainer is to facilitate someone's understanding and learning. When you have a room full of fast learners, you often end up "showing" them the software. The opportunity you have to exercise your training skills is not as great as when your participants struggle to understand. When they do struggle, you have to put your training expertise into action and really teach. You start to use analogies, diagrams, mnemonics, stories—whatever you can to get a concept or idea across. This is when you really are training—leading someone from confusion to understanding using your experience and teaching expertise. It's on these occasions that you really can develop and perfect your training skills. Empathy, patience, listening skills, the ability to communicate, the ability to think on your feet—all those skills are brought into play. Here is your opportunity. When you are training the slower learners, you are putting your training skills into high gear.

So, welcome slow learners in your classes! Get excited when some-one doesn't follow or understand something. Never view a slower learner as a problem or interruption. See them as a perfect opportunity to perfect your training skills. You will grow and develop your skills more with your slow learners than you ever will with those "good" classes.

Using humor

People learn better when they smile and laugh. When you laugh, your body's chemistry changes. Endorphins, the body's own painkilling, learning-enhancing, "feel-good" drug, are released. People feel better, their immune systems improve, and they relax more. When people find something amusing, they put themselves into a more conducive state for learning. Humor has been proven to increase the effectiveness of learning. One university carried out an experiment by coaching professors in using humor in their lectures. When tested, the students from the "humorous" group did 15% better on all the tests. It's powerful!

Humor can

- Add interest to the training

- Engage and motivate learners

- Help build rapport

- Help people to relax

- Increase the ability to learn

Natural humor is much better than telling jokes. There is much more humor in what naturally happens in the training room and how you respond to it. An occasional joke might be okay, but I generally recommend against it (unless you are a natural). A joke has a story and a punchline. There is an expectation that people will laugh. This puts pressure on them and you . . . and who needs more pressure? I have always found the most effective humor involves telling the truth about something or pointing out something that everyone has thought but never expressed. Ask your next class if any of them "jiggle" the hour-glass in Windows programs to try and speed things up. Everyone has done it on occasion, knowing it makes no difference whatsoever.

Some trainers make an effort to be funny. They try hard to make people laugh. Generally, it doesn't work. Being yourself and telling the truth about a situation provides the best humor. Think of the last time you rolled on your sides laughing until your stomach hurt. Was it because of a joke? No, some situation arose out of the blue that just tickled you. Something someone said or someone's expression just set you off. No joke, no story, no punchline—just real life. It's the same in training. The most humorous times are when there is a relaxed atmosphere in the class, the trainer has a good rapport with the group, and an incident happens that provides the opportunity for a comment or reflection.

Recently, I was observing a trainer's class, and one woman looked at what had happened on her screen and said, "How do I get out of here?" The trainer looked up and said, "Just use the door back there, it'll take you to the main office." She smiled, "No, I mean this menu!" It was a simple little wisecrack but they all found it quite hilarious.

Another time, I was showing an enthusiastic, excited group how to develop a presentation slide, and one woman kept insisting we use more creative color schemes and fonts. "Can't we use a script font for that?" I stopped, looked over at her, sighed, and said, "Are you always this picky?" Everyone had been thinking the same thing, and the whole room fell into laughter. The woman broke into a broad smile.

One morning, I was teaching the second session of a project-management class. The day before, we had finished late, and the group (who were all from the same company) explained how they would have to go back into work that night to take care of some emergency.

The next morning, I was looking out at some unmotivated, tired individuals who probably had not gotten much sleep. "How many of you can remember how to schedule tasks?" A few hands crept up. "How many of you can remember how to assign resources?" Still fewer hands went up. I paused. "How many of you don't really give a hoot about tasks and resources this morning?" It had a wonderful effect on the group. They laughed, became a little more responsive, and it changed the whole atmosphere.

You can develop humor in your classes by putting yourself in their shoes, guessing what they might be thinking or feeling, and saying it aloud. You don't have to be a comedian. A friend of mine often stops in the middle of her training, looks at the group and says, "Do I sound like a computer nerd?" She expresses what they might be thinking and exaggerates it a little. When something is quite involved, she says, "Don't worry. We'll finish this by midnight—did you all bring sleeping bags?"

Listen for the comments and situations that happen naturally in the class and try a little exaggeration. But most of all, be yourself—that's where the best humor comes from.

A word of caution when using humor: Never embarrass anyone or put them on the spot. Avoid sexist, off-color, ethnic, or religious humor, regardless of who your audience is. If you ever have a doubt about making a particular comment, don't. One final word: Don't try to be humorous if it doesn't come naturally. The more you are like yourself, the funnier you'll be. The more, genuine, straightforward and honest you are, the more natural humor you'll develop.

A wonderful resource for humorous materials, books, seminars is

The HUMOR Project, Inc.
110 Spring St.
Saratoga Springs, NY 12866
(518) 587-8770

4

Evaluating computer training

"Life is short, the art long, opportunity fleeting, experience treacherous, judgment difficult."
— **Hippocrates**

You can only evaluate the effectiveness of computer training when you know exactly what the goal of the training was. It's hard to tell if something is successful if you don't know what you wanted in the first place. If you have analyzed the participants' needs before the training, then you already have something objective to work towards. If not, then the course objectives provide some guidelines—but only some. The course objectives aren't always a valid criterion for evaluating the effectiveness of the training. Learners could successfully achieve the training objectives without necessarily increasing productivity or providing value back at work.

As well as knowing what you need to evaluate, you need to consider who the evaluation is designed for. The goals and objectives of the training will be different to different people. To the learner, the goal might be to begin to understand the program a little better. To the trainer, it might be to have successfully taught the skills outlined in the course objectives. To the training manager or supervisor who scheduled the training, it might be to have the learner use new computer skills at the workplace. To the organization, it might be to have seen a measurable return on the training investment.

Each different objective requires a different form of measurement. The first thing to do, then, is to decide who you are evaluating the training for. Are you evaluating in order for the trainer to gauge the effectiveness of his or her training? Are you evaluating in order to see that skills learned in the class have been transferred to the workplace? Or are you attempting to evaluate what effect the training has had on the organization's bottom line?

Before going any further, let's look at the difference between *measuring* training and *evaluating* training. Measuring involves ascertaining that particular skills have been learned. Evaluating is the process of interpreting this information and determining its value to the individual or organization. Measuring is one thing. Considering what the measurements mean and what their implications are is something else.

The "smile" sheet

It is dubious how much value the typical evaluation, or "smile sheet," has. Unfortunately, far too often, it is a token, some hastily conceived set of questions that focuses on how well the instructor did, whether the instructor was liked, whether the courseware was "useful," and other such vague questions. It is often used by training centers to see if the customers were happy and by trainers to see how much they were appreciated. These evaluations don't measure much that could indicate the true value of the training. If anything more valuable than this is needed, the method of evaluation must change.

A much better idea for in-class evaluations is one that focuses not on whether the courseware was great or the trainer was liked, but on what was understood clearly. The evaluation would take the form of a list of topics, features, and functions covered in the class, with checkboxes or columns for the learner to indicate the level of understanding of that particular topic or feature. The emphasis is then on how well the participants understood the work, rather than whether they enjoyed themselves and or whether they thought the trainer was nice.

This type of evaluation can be much more useful because

- It helps the trainer focus more on making sure that the work is clear and understandable.

- It attempts to measure learning and comprehension of skills instead of feelings about the class.

If you do stick with smile sheets, keep in mind that their ability to measure the true effectiveness of training is very limited. The comments and responses end up being more a commentary on the learner than the trainer.

Redesigning your evaluation forms

If you are unhappy with the standard smile sheet and are considering creating a new evaluation form, the first step is to decide what you want to evaluate. After being absolutely clear on this, you can then structure some appropriate questions, keeping in mind that these questions address the perception of the learner, not the truth (as will all of these types of evaluations). It is sometimes the case that a learner thinks he or she understands a topic, when, in fact, this is not the case.

If the goal is to measure the learning of particular skills, then the questions can address each topic covered in the class and the level of understanding of the learner, as shown in Fig. 4-1.

In this sample evaluation form, the columns on the right-hand side specify the level of understanding the learner achieved for each topic on the left-hand side. The topics listed should be the most important "core" concepts and procedures. As with all evaluation forms, space

Course Evaluation

Your Name: _____   Date: _____

Instructor's Name: _____

Workshop Attended: Introduction to PowerPoint

How clear is your understanding of the following?

Topic	very clear	a little confusing	very confusing	not covered
Creating a new blank presentation				
Adding text to a slide				
Copying and moving text				
Using the outline feature				
Inserting and deleting slides				

4-1 *Topics evaluation sheet.*

should be provided for general comments if the learners have any particular likes and dislikes they wish to express.

This type of evaluation is very valuable to the trainer. Not only do you get an idea of which areas seem to be giving the learners problems, but the form can be used as a guide for training, reminding the trainer which specific topics and ideas must be covered in the class. These types of evaluations are also useful for reviewing important topics at the end of the class.

When creating evaluation forms, remember to keep them simple and easy to fill out. Most learners, at the end of a long training session, are not overly excited about having to fill out evaluation forms. The simpler the required response, the better. Ask a question and have them check an appropriate box or column. Use graded responses like a scale of 1 to 5, where 1 is "strongly disagree," and 5 is "strongly agree," as shown in Fig. 4-2.

Course Evaluation

Your Name: _____   Date: _____

Instructor's Name: _____

Workshop Attended: _____

	strongly agree 5 4 3 2 1	strongly disagree
The course objectives were clearly stated.	☐ ☐ ☐ ☐ ☐	
I found the course valuable.	☐ ☐ ☐ ☐ ☐	
The course was relevant to my work.	☐ ☐ ☐ ☐ ☐	
The instructor was knowledgeable in the subject.	☐ ☐ ☐ ☐ ☐	
I found the handouts useful.	☐ ☐ ☐ ☐ ☐	

4-2 *Checkbox evaluation sheet.*

Make it easy for the person to fill the evaluation sheet out, while at the same time making sure the responses provide you with valuable information. Evaluation forms with levels or numbered responses are also useful when trying to consolidate the results. Useful statistics can be generated from this type of form. In contrast, if the form is predominantly "wordy," then summarizing responses can be difficult.

Make sure all the available responses make sense. I once came across this question on a training center's evaluation: "Do you feel the trainer's communication skills were excellent, good, or satisfactory?" To answer, however, you were required to check a grid that had "strongly agree" through "strongly disagree." Keep it clear.

If your evaluation form is of the 1 through 5 type, or the agree/disagree type, make certain that at least one question is a "reversal," so that you can tell if a learner has just checked what he or she thinks is the best (or worst) category. An example of the agree/disagree type would be, "I felt the instructor went too fast for me." If you got a "strongly agree" here with all the other "strongly agree" reactions, the responses may be suspect.

Use language that is clear and concise. Say something like, "The instructor explained things clearly," rather than, "The instructor demonstrated a commitment to providing information that was clearly understandable."

Try to avoid questions that are not directly related to the rest of the evaluation form or are designed to be used for sales follow-up like, "What other classes might you be interested in taking at the ABC Training Center?"

Re-evaluating evaluations

Cher was a new instructor at Professional Computer Training in Reno, Nevada. She had been with the company for two years as the office manager and then tried her hand at teaching. She loved it—and was good, too. She had a real feel for what it was like to be a beginner in a class. She was supremely patient.

Cher mainly taught WordPerfect classes. Her favorite thing to do was to create WordPerfect tables. All of a sudden, all the company forms and memos were redesigned in tables. A common comment around the center would be, "Ask Cher to put it in a table!"

One day, after attending a computer training seminar in San Francisco, Cher announced that she wanted to redesign the class evaluation forms. When everyone heard this, they assumed that in a few days they would see the same old evaluation forms . . . but in tables. At the next staff meeting, Cher was eager to show the redesigned forms.

They were not as everyone had expected. Yes, they were all nicely laid out in tables, but the evaluation was a totally different concept. Before, the evaluation had questions like "Were the handouts useful?," "Was the instructor responsive to questions?," "Did the instructor explain things clearly?," and so on. The new evaluations had nothing like that. Cher explained that she felt the old evaluations had always been asking the students to evaluate the instructor instead of evaluating what they had learned. All they did was give an indication of whether the students liked the instructor.

The new ones she had prepared were quite different. There was a different evaluation for each class that was taught. In the first column on the left were the major topics that were covered in the class. The next four columns were headed "I understand," "A little confused," "Very confused," and "Not covered." There were lines at the bottom for comments. Cher explained that the center should be trying to evaluate what the students learned, not what they felt about the instructor. Also, instructors would be able to glance at the blank evaluations to make sure they had covered the appropriate topics and not overlooked anything.

Everyone was quite impressed with Cher's new evaluations. They had been using the old ones for many years and never thought to question them. The old ones addressed the question, "What did you think of the instructor?" The new ones asked the question, "What did you learn?" Quite an important difference. Now, all the evaluation forms at Professional Computer Training are of that same format. The trainers love to compete with each other to get all the checkmarks in that "I understand" column. More importantly, everyone knows exactly what is to be covered in each class, and the training is consistent from trainer to trainer.

Handling the evaluations

Avoid giving out evaluations before the end of the training. Some people ask for the evaluation ahead of time and fill it out partially or completely. Avoid this—no one can effectively evaluate a computer training class before it is complete.

When you do give out the evaluation form, make a point of asking the participants if they wouldn't mind filling it out. Explain how useful it is for the trainer and the training organization to be able to continually improve the quality of training. Encourage them to write any comments regarding things that did or didn't work well for them. Consider having anonymous evaluations. People will be much more open, expressive, and truthful if the evaluation doesn't identify them.

When the evaluation form has been handed out, don't continue talking. Let the participants sit quietly for a few minutes, and read and consider the questions. Don't walk around the room looking over their shoulders, either. If possible, leave the room while they fill it out. The presence of the trainer sometimes affects the results of the evaluation. A participant might feel uncomfortable writing a complaint or concern down if the trainer is hovering.

When they have finished, either ask that they pass them into the center of the room and collect them, or ask them to place them in a box or on the side as they leave. Avoid collecting them individually from each person and particularly avoid reading any until everyone has left. (Some people are concerned that the trainer might see a negative comment or suggestion about the class and confront them with it before they leave.)

Make sure you read every evaluation that you get. Make a mental note of anything that is mentioned consistently, and consider making changes if necessary. Don't concern yourself too much with an occasional "bad" evaluation. Evaluations are sometimes more a reflection of the evaluator than they are the person or thing being evaluated. Don't let a "bad" evaluation ruin your day. Read it, consider it, resolve to take a different approach next time if you feel it is valid. If the comments do not seem valid (and only you will truly know), then forget them. A "bad" evaluation once in a while does not mean you are a poor trainer. Read your evaluations, consider them, make mental notes to change if necessary, and then, move on.

Pre- and post-testing

A valuable way of measuring the impact of training is pre- and post-testing of computer skills (see Fig. 4-3). Testing a learner's skill level (or perceived skill level) after training can only provide useful information if you have an initial skill set to compare it with. The pre-test provides this. The pre-test, carried out before the training, measures

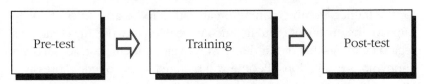

4-3 *Pre- and post-testing.*

initial skill levels. After the training, a post-test is given that measures, or tries to measure, skills that the training provided. By comparing the two, you have an indication of the impact of the training. The pre- and post-tests can be implemented using questionnaires, task-completion exercises, or testing software.

Questionnaires

Paper-based tests like questionnaires can only really address the learners' perceived skill levels. They ask the learner to check appropriate boxes ranging from poor level of understanding to excellent level of understanding on each of topics that are to be covered or were covered. The pre-test is usually done immediately before the training and the post-test immediately after the training.

What information can a paper-based pre- and post-test give? They can give you the learners' perceived level of change in their skill levels. Some companies, organizations, and training managers use these tests to provide evidence of the impact of the training. As you can probably guess, this method is faulted and only gives a subjective view of the effect of the training. A learner can feel very confident about what was covered in the class and still be unable to perform back on the job.

Of course, these types of tests can provide some valuable data, and many publishers provide them with the courseware. Many training organizations are beginning to use them, but like smile sheets, this sometimes becomes an exercise in organizational correctness rather than a genuine attempt to measure and evaluate training effectiveness.

Carrying out tasks

Another method of testing is a set of questions that asks the user to complete certain tasks and carry out certain procedures using the software. The resulting files are saved and later reviewed to see if the end result is correct. It is very difficult with this type of test to gauge how efficiently or quickly a task was completed. It is a step above the purely paper-based test, but still does not provide an effective way of gauging real on-the-job computer skills.

Testing software

A much better way of pre- and post-testing is using testing software that tests the learner's ability to actually carry out tasks. These can either be simulations of the software or tests that integrate themselves with the actual program itself. The software simulations sometimes expect the learner to carry out tasks a particular way, and they don't allow much freedom for different approaches to solving the same problem. The "integrated" tests, where the learner is using the actual software, are much better. The learner is free to do anything with the actual software and use any approach to solve a problem. The software can record each keystroke and the time taken, and calculate efficiency as well as whether the end result is correct or not.

This method is far better than the other types of testing, but still has its drawbacks. One problem is that the software confronts the user with instructions on what task is to be accomplished. If these instructions are poorly written or are misunderstood, the user "fails." The system ends up giving a poor score to someone who might be competent, but didn't understand the instructions.

Delayed post-testing

Up to now, we have been looking at measuring the skill levels of the participants immediately after the class. This is certainly valuable, but what if you want to evaluate the effect of the training on skills the participants can perform back at the office? This becomes a little more challenging. You need to allow a reasonable amount of time to elapse after the training, and then test the computer users in their work environment to see what skills have "stuck." This can be done by one of the methods outlined already in this chapter, or by interviewing them to get a feel for the value of the training.

Productivity and return on investment

Suppose you test the learner at a later date back at work and find that, yes, many of the skills taught in the class have indeed "stuck." Does this indicate that the training was successful? On one level, yes—you successfully helped the learner gain new computer skills.

But if the goal of the training was to have the computer user be more productive at work, then you have to dig a little deeper.

To determine if the user is more productive, you have to have some objective measurement of productivity at work before the training, and then a similar measurement after the training. You can see that it starts to get a little more complicated. How do you quantitatively measure output or performance on the job before and after training? If you do measure it, how do you determine which skills were a direct result of the computer training? It gets to look more and more like a Swiss cheese.

Suppose you can accurately determine that the individual who completed the computer training is now more productive. Can we now say for sure that the training was successful? Perhaps, but someone in the organization will want to look at the total investment in training and determine if this investment has seen appropriate returns. How do you determine the overall return on investment?

The more levels you take it to, the more nebulous such evaluations become, and the harder it is to accurately measure. There are also some intangible results from training that cannot be easily measured, such as gaining confidence, feeling more comfortable with technology, interacting with other employees, and feeling valued as an employee.

It's difficult to objectively and accurately evaluate the impact of computer training at all levels. The more accurately you wish to gauge the effect of the training, the more time, money, and effort the organization has to invest.

Most organizations don't get much past the pre- and post-testing mentioned earlier. Most work on a more subjective evaluation of training. If the trainee appears more confident and comfortable with the software, felt the class was valuable, and is using some new skills, then the assumption is that the training was worthwhile.

In considering a meaningful evaluation, then, you must first determine what you wish to evaluate: perceived skill levels, skill level back on the job, or increases in productivity. You then need to know the current skills levels before any training takes place. You need to determine a method for measuring these skills. Then, after the training, you need to implement similar measurements to determine what effect the training has had.

An increasing number of organizations want to look at their return on investment for computer training. It can be a considerable investment, and they obviously want to see if their investment is paying off. Right now, there are not many simple, precise, and inexpensive ways to do this, but with the increasing sophistication of network systems and the economic incentive, training professionals will begin to develop new ways to accurately measure skill and performance changes in the workplace.

Good books on measuring training's impact and evaluation include *Evaluation: 10 Significant Ways for Measuring and Improving Training Impact,* by Sandra Merwin, and *Designing and Delivering Cost-Effective Training—And Measuring the Result,* by Jack Gordon, Ron Zemke, and Philip Jones.

5

Trainer development

◆◆◆

"It is much more difficult to judge oneself than to judge others."
— **Antoine de Saint-Exupéry**

Becoming a better computer trainer involves an ongoing commitment to developing your training skills and yourself, updating your technical knowledge, and continually looking for ways to improve. Successful trainers, speakers, and presenters constantly critique themselves and strive to improve. It's this drive to learn and refine your skills that can bring satisfaction and fulfillment to what you do for a living.

If you wish to improve, you must be willing to elicit the help and guidance of others. It's difficult to improve when you don't know what your strong and weak suits are. Sometimes, this is the hardest part of striving to improve—accepting other people's evaluations of what you do. Most people have a tendency to become slightly defensive about their methods and ways of doing things. However, to develop your skills as a trainer, you need to put defensiveness aside and accept that your peers have a lot to offer you.

Evaluating computer trainers

It is critical that a trainer's skills be evaluated at intervals in any organization where training is provided. It is necessary for the organization to know that training is being delivered effectively, and it is necessary for the trainers to develop in their profession. Although "smile sheets" and other learner evaluations give an indication of a trainer's skills and competency, something more objective is needed to help the trainer truly assess his or her training skills. You must, of course, take learner evaluations into consideration, but trainers need to be evaluated by someone who understands training—trainers or someone who has experience training. Other trainers will be able to notice some of the subtleties of a trainer's presentation and communication skills that would go unnoticed by those who have never trained.

When evaluations are carried out by peers or training managers, try to keep the observations of performance on an objective level. It's all too easy to be swayed by someone's personality or your relationship with them. You need to make sure that your evaluations are clearly based on observable facts rather than general feelings.

Look for the following when evaluating a trainer:

- *Show knowledge of software.* Does the trainer demonstrate a thorough knowledge of the application being taught?

- *State objectives and overview.* Have the objectives and goals of the training been stated and discussed?

- *Use training materials/media appropriately.* Does the trainer use the overhead data show or other media effectively, and in a way that advances the learning?

- *Stay focused.* Does the trainer have the ability to answer questions incidental to the class material and then get back on track?

- *Encourage questions.* Are questions from the learners encouraged and welcomed? Does the trainer regularly ask the learners for questions or clarifications?

- *Respond to questions appropriately.* Are learners' questions answered with respect? Does the trainer listen carefully and patiently to any questions?

- *Manage time of instruction.* Does the trainer demonstrate the ability to manage the time constraints of the class?

- *Adapt delivery to learner level.* Does the trainer adapt the training delivery to reflect the learners' ability levels and needs? Does the trainer adjust the speed of the delivery of the material to complement the audience? Are the needs of the slow and expert learners taken into consideration in the class?

- *Encourage participation and involve learners.* Are learners encouraged to take an active part in the training? Does the trainer demonstrate a desire to involve participants in the learning process?

- *Provide opportunities for success.* Does the trainer provide positive reinforcement and help the learners succeed at answering questions and completing tasks?

- *Deal with personalities effectively.* Can the trainer interact and communicate well with a broad spectrum of learner personalities? Is the trainer adept at dealing with "difficult" learners?

- *Provide clear explanations.* Is the trainer able to explain ideas, concepts, and procedures in a clear, concise, and understandable manner?

- *Use appropriate analogies/learning aids.* Does the trainer use relevant examples, analogies, and aids to clarify the subject? Does the trainer attempt to customize the training to reflect the learner's experience?

- *Develop a rapport with learners.* Does the trainer successfully develop a rapport with the learners at the beginning of and during the training?

- *Demonstrate good listening skills.* Does the trainer show an ability to listen carefully to learner's questions without interrupting?

- *Be patient.* Does the trainer demonstrate a high level of patience with learners when teaching or helping them one-on-one?

- *Move around the room.* Does the trainer move around the room from learner to learner giving individual help and making sure the learners are clear?

- *Use a variety of instructional methods.* Does the trainer use different methods, techniques and approaches in the training? Is the style and manner of instruction varied to complement different learning styles?

- *Manage group dynamics.* Does the trainer have the ability to manage groups and group interactions in an appropriate manner?

- *Check for understanding and confusion.* Does the trainer regularly check to see if the learners are understanding or confused before moving on?

- *Avoid using their mouse or keyboard.* Does the trainer avoid helping learners by touching their mouse or keyboard?

- *Show adequate preparation.* Has the trainer demonstrated an adequate level of preparation for the class? Does the flow of the class reflect this?

- *Promote independence in the learner.* Does the trainer show a commitment to having the learner learn independently? Does the trainer encourage the learners to solve their own problems and answer their own questions?

- *Handle interruptions/distractions well.* Can the trainer handle interruptions to the flow of the class well? Is a level of calmness and confidence present when things go wrong?

When an evaluation of the trainer takes place, feedback should be offered as soon as possible. It won't be as valuable if the evaluator waits a week before sitting down with the trainer to review the results. The trainer will want feedback soon after the class.

When the trainer and the evaluator sit down to review the results, the conversation should be as objective as possible. Opinions and "shoulds" ought to be kept to a minimum. Stick to "you did this," or "you didn't do that," rather than "I think you should be doing this." If the trainer has a commitment to improve, he or she will naturally ask for suggestions or guidance—at which time it is appropriate to give it. Otherwise, stick to the observable, objective facts.

When evaluating someone, try not to spend an inordinate amount of time focusing on the weak areas. Spend as much time pointing out the strengths of the trainer. Being evaluated should also be an opportunity to see how successful and effective the trainer is.

Some training organizations have a system of trainer mentoring, where a more experienced trainer offers guidance, coaching, and support to less experienced trainers. Trainer evaluations are often more effectively done by such a mentor because the mentoring trainer has already established himself or herself as someone whose responsibility is to assist and promote the trainer's professional development. Being evaluated by someone you know and whose goal is to help you improve is very different from being evaluated by someone you have not developed a relationship with.

After being evaluated, a trainer can see some areas that might need attention and can concentrate on improving in these areas. It is good to follow up with a plan of action after an evaluation rather than just have it be a report on performance.

Keep in mind when evaluating that an observed class will always be slightly different from an unobserved class. The fact that the trainer is being evaluated inevitably alters the trainer's behavior to some extent. Also try not to make generalizations about a trainer based on one evaluation from one person. A few evaluations carried out at intervals by different evaluators would give a more balanced perspective.

Evaluating a trainer is only one element in evaluating the effectiveness of training. Just because you have a group of wonderful computer trainers who know how to teach effectively does not mean that the training is going to be effective. Measuring the effectiveness of training is not the same as measuring the effectiveness of a trainer, as discussed in chapter 4.

Continuing your own learning

A good knowledge of the software you are teaching is a prerequisite for a computer trainer. Without this, the best training techniques in the world amount to nothing. It is therefore important to continue to learn and update your own software knowledge as new products are developed and new versions appear on the market. Stay current with the latest software and increase your own knowledge. Apart from updating your own skills and credibility, it puts you back in the role of learner, which is a perfect place to be for a trainer.

Although many computer trainers tend to teach themselves new versions or new products, I highly recommend taking a class to upgrade your skills. The experience of being a learner in a classroom environment is invaluable to the trainer. Not only will you upgrade your software skills, but you will develop a deeper appreciation of computer training from the learner's perspective and get insights into your training that would never occur to you when you're on the other side.

If you predominantly teach introductory, end-user classes, consider upgrading and teaching more technical classes. You'll find that enhancing your skills with more advanced classes will not only give you a broader teaching background, but will add depth and interest to your introductory classes. Try not to get too comfortable teaching the same piece of software for too long just because you know it inside out and it's easy to teach. Constantly stretch yourself and learn. The more you experience learning, the better trainer you will become.

Observing your peers

Whenever you have the opportunity, ask one of your fellow trainers if you can sit in on one of their classes and observe, even if it is only for a few hours. Let them know you want to pick up some new ideas and techniques and remind yourself what it's like to be a learner. Unless you have set up some formal trainer evaluation, don't offer any advice, suggestions, or coaching after the class unless asked to do so.

Observing another trainer will be an opportunity to

- Sit in the learner's seat and see a class from their perspective

- Gain new training ideas, techniques and approaches

- See how other trainers deal with challenges during the class

- Observe learners more closely and see how they respond to the trainer

- Get a feel for the room ergonomics (Are the seats comfortable? Is there enough room? Is the overhead clearly visible?)

- Learn some new analogies, ways of explaining, and different examples

- Pick up a few new jokes

After you have attended someone's class, don't forget to thank them for the privilege and let them know how you benefited. Always keep it positive. Never give advice if it wasn't requested or give covert coaching like "the class was great . . . I'm sure no one minded that you didn't cover tabs, they probably won't need it."

Videotaping your training

The next best thing to observing someone else train is to observe yourself. Although most trainers fear being videotaped more than death itself, it is a wonderful way of evaluating your training. If you have ever recorded your voice on tape, you know how surprising it can be. The tone, vocal variety, level of enthusiasm, and number of "ums" and "ers" can be quite different from what you imagined.

By videotaping, you can step back and evaluate yourself a little more objectively than you usually do. You notice things you never realized you did—or never realized you didn't do. An hour of training is all you really need to record to discover some of your training traits. When you do this and play the tape back, have a pen and paper ready to jot down things that you feel didn't work so well and also things that worked very well. Don't just have it be an exercise of picking yourself to bits. Acknowledge yourself for those things you do really well.

Look for the following characteristics:

- *Voice.* Did you use a fair amount of vocal variety in your speaking, or did it seem more like a monotone? Would you like to listen to you for six hours? Did you speak clearly and without too many "ums" and "ahs?" Did it seem like you were loud enough?

- *Movement.* Did you stand in one spot all the time or move around? Did you turn your back to the class many times? Talk to the whiteboard? Did you use your hands and arms to add emphasis to what you were teaching?

- *Posture.* Did you seem poised when you were standing, or did you slouch? Were there any distracting mannerisms like jiggling coins in your pocket or scratching your nose?

- *Delivery.* Did it seem like there was a structured flow to your teaching, or did it seem disjointed in any way? Did you get sidetracked in any way? How well did you use the instructional media? Were your explanations clear and concise? Were your diagrams easy to follow?

- *Interaction.* How did you seem to relate to the learners? Did you appear patient, concerned, and understanding? Did you listen carefully to each question? How did you respond to questions? Did you ask them enough questions? Did you wait long enough before you answered your own questions? Did you ask enough open-ended questions?

Re-read your notes and comments from time to time and, most importantly, before you teach a class. Remind yourself of what you need to concentrate on and remind yourself of what you do that works really well. Do this consistently for a month, and you'll greatly improve your training.

Trainer certification

The certification of computer trainers has increased dramatically in recent years and shows no signs of slowing down. Certification of skills is becoming an important part of the computer training profession. Some of the driving forces behind the need and importance of certification are technological advancement, business pressures, and government initiatives.

As technology advances, the computer industry produces more information and more sophisticated systems. Systems such as networks are critical to the day-to-day operation of a business, and downtime can be very costly. Because of the complexity of network software and the importance of reliability, an organization must be assured of the technical skills of a network administrator. Management has no real way of knowing this person's skill level. Certification can be an objective way of assuring that people have the requisite skills for the job. The same holds true for the trainer who is teaching these skills—there must be some way of objectively assessing competence level.

Certification is also being driven by government initiatives such as Goals 2000: Educate America Act. Here, the government is becoming involved in helping define skill standards and advancing certification of skills through voluntary partnerships. There is a considerable push to develop skill standards in the United States; we are behind most other countries in the industrialized world in defining and measuring competencies.

The sophistication of software, the explosion of information, the pressure from businesses, and the push from government initiatives make certification for computer trainers almost a prerequisite in some cases. Without some type of certification, career advancement will become more difficult. If you have the opportunity to get certified, especially if someone else can help foot the bill, take it.

Who exactly benefits from certification?

Benefits of certification for *the trainer* include the following:

- Training organizations and clients can more easily recognize a trainer's software expertise. They no longer have to guess at whether a trainer really does know his or her stuff.

- The services and skills of the trainer are often promoted by the software publisher. The publisher can put potential clients in contact with certified trainers.

- The trainer can gain access to the latest software information, technical information, and, often, beta copies. It makes it easier for the trainer to keep skills current.

- The trainer can have access to special training events around the country.

- Certification can put the trainer in touch with other training professionals. He or she becomes part of a community of technical specialists and can share information and expertise.

At the same time, *the organization* benefits by certification in these ways:

- Certification provides a standard, objective method for gauging technical proficiency. It provides a consistent measure of expertise around the globe.

- Certification assists organizations in developing their trainers and recognizing their accomplishments.

- The organization can objectively demonstrate the level of expertise of its trainers to clients.

- By encouraging the development of skills within the organization, the organization increases its technical self-sufficiency. Upgrading skills internally alleviates the need for reliance on outside expertise.

- Certification can provide a reliable standard for hiring and promoting within an organization.

Finally, the benefits of certification for *end users* include these:

- Certification provides an objective means of choosing trainers or training companies.

- End-users are assured that the trainer has attained a certain level of technical knowledge.

- Training is consistent from place to place.

- The end-user has access to the latest updates and technical information on the product.

Some concerns

Some people in the training field have concerns about certification and its usefulness. The expense, the need to constantly recertify, questions about the overall return on investment, and the primary emphasis on technical skills are some of the common complaints about certification. Some training organizations feel that the fact that their trainers posses certification is not enough to instill confidence in their clients as to their training ability. It is one thing to be technically competent, and another to be able to train effectively.

Software publishers are taking note of some of these concerns and are beginning to include effective training-delivery elements as part of the overall technical certification. Because of the importance of this and the duplication of certain parts of certification programs from different software companies, "cross-vendor" certification is being developed. One element of this is the Certified Technical Trainer (CTT) program by the Educational Testing Service (ETS), which has been endorsed by the major software publishers. The CTT program certifies technical training competencies. It might become a recognized component in many of the existing certification programs from the software publishers.

Certification on the Net?

With the increasingly sophisticated browsers, delivery systems, and improved security on the Internet, some software publishers are looking to the online universe to deliver self-administered certification tests for technical expertise. This might even be possible via interactive TV in the not-too-distant future. Rather than have to schedule a test at the nearest testing center, a trainer will be able to take a test when and where it is most convenient—in the training center at work, or maybe even at home. In addition to having the test online, studying for such a certification will be simplified by providing study materials and support online.

A great book on certification issues and their importance is *The Complete Guide to Certification for Computing Professionals* by Drake Prometric (see the bibliography).

Instructor meetings

Trying to improve and grow as a trainer in isolation is difficult. It's hard to be objective when you're the subject. Interaction and association with other trainers is a much more powerful way of developing your training skills and techniques.

Try to schedule instructor meetings on a regular basis, perhaps once or twice a month. Make it clear to those attending that the purpose of the meeting is to discuss and exchange training ideas, techniques, and issues that relate to delivering the training in the classroom. Have a main topic to focus on at each meeting, such as dealing with fast and slow learners in the same class, or teaching Windows. Discuss approaches to teaching, find out how other trainers teach the classes you teach, what examples or analogies they use, and how they deal with particular problems. Trainers love to talk and share their knowledge. When everyone participates and exchanges their training ideas, you'll discover there's a gold mine of information in the room. you'll come away with some tips and techniques you never thought of before.

Computer training can sometimes feel a little isolating—many of the trainer's challenges and concerns happen in the company of learners, as opposed to their peers. Trainers are often reluctant to discuss some of the challenges they face when talking to other trainers. Being given the opportunity to bring these challenges and concerns out into the open in such a meeting can be very refreshing and therapeutic.

Very often, just the fact that other trainers are dealing with the same concerns and challenges is heartening. The opportunity to lick your wounds, share war stories, and learn from your fellow trainers can be very energizing and beneficial. Everyone leaves with new ideas for teaching, a renewed enthusiasm, and a level of camaraderie with other trainers. It can be a small investment with a surprisingly large return.

Creating a computer-training support group

An extension of an instructor meeting within one organization is a computer-training support group for trainers from different organizations. The benefits of such a group are much the same as internal instructor meetings, except that the trainer has access to a wider background of trainers and training environments.

Such a group is particularly valuable for contract or independent trainers who lack the support structure and benefits of training with an organization. The sense of isolation or "unconnectedness" that independent trainers can experience is sometimes a challenge. The independent trainer meets hundreds of people, but gets to know relatively few on an ongoing basis. This can often be stressful. The support group is a perfect way of giving such trainers a sense of support and community. Independent trainers face unique challenges; to be able to share these with trainers with similar concerns can be very energizing and satisfying. Another advantage of such a group for independent trainers is being able to exchange job leads and employment opportunities.

A typical group might meet once a month and offer perspectives, insights, tips, and learning opportunities. When new software or upgrades appear, it is useful to have members of the group give mini-training sessions to help keep everyone current. Because each member has their own software specialties, this can be a wonderful way of keeping abreast of the latest software and information.

Contact the computer trainers you know, get some phone numbers and e-mail addresses, and start networking with other trainers and organizations. Within a month, you can have the seeds of a successful, supportive, and productive group.

Fine-tuning your training

The process of training doesn't end when the class finishes. After planning, preparing, and delivering the material, the trainer needs to evaluate his or her performance and fine-tune. The trainer needs to constantly ask, "How could I improve? What worked well and what didn't work so well? How could the next class be better?"

Look back at the class and consider these issues:

- *Timing.* Was there too much or too little material for the class? Was the material presented at a comfortable pace, or was it rushed?

- *Content.* Were all the most important concepts and procedures covered? Was there too much or too little emphasis on any particular topic? Which topics seemed to be most valuable to the participants?

- *Courseware.* Did you use the courseware appropriately during the class? Did the participants find it easy to follow? Did they find it useful?

- *Exercises.* Did the learners find the exercises valuable? Did the exercises cause any confusion? Did the exercises seem relevant to the learners?

- *Explanations.* Did you feel your presentations and explanations were clear and understandable? If not, how could you make things clearer next time? What examples could you use?

- *Rapport.* Did you develop a good rapport with the participants, or did things seem a little strained? Did anything get in the way of developing a rapport? Did the learners participate and ask questions?

- *Media.* Did the overhead, LCD panel, video, etc., add to or in anyway detract from the class? Did you use enough visual aids? Did you use too many?

- *Room setup.* Was the layout of the room conducive to learning? Could you move around the room and assist learners one-on-one? Did they have enough room?

After giving thought to each of these, you can update the class, iron out any problems, and regroup for next time. Fine-tuning and evaluating your performance after a class is critical to continually improving as a trainer.

6

Courseware and documentation

"What is the use of a book," thought Alice, "without pictures?"
— **Lewis Carroll**

Types of courseware and documentation

After attending a computer training class, the user will need help and support. No amount of training can provide the answers to every question or problem that might arise back on the job. Part of this support is the courseware or documentation that has been provided. Different types of courseware and documentation are used in computer training. Each type is suited to a different need, and it is important to choose or create the right one for your purposes. Typically, the following sources are available:

- *Reference manuals* are usually comprehensive and detailed manuals that cover most of the functions of standard software applications. These are the huge tomes that frighten new users. ("I have to read that?!") They are not advised for instructor-led-training use, but they are an important resource for a learner to have back at the office.

- *Teach-yourself books* are produced by some software publishers and third parties for an individual to sit down and attempt to teach themselves. They are usually organized as a structured, step-by-step approach to learning the basics. Although not necessarily designed for instructor-led training, they are sometimes used for this purpose.

- *Classroom courseware* is designed to be used in computer training classes. Courseware covers specific topics, tasks, and features, and is usually divided into levels or modules. It is written with class objectives and time constraints in mind. It includes practice exercises or scenarios for the learner to complete. Some courseware can be used as a self-teaching manual.

- *Handouts* include anything that focuses on a specific task, topic, or feature. Unlike courseware, handouts can be used in a training session to teach or illustrate a particular area of interest. For example, you might create a handout on mail-merge or macros—something specific. Trainers quite often create these themselves to supplement the courseware or to teach a class that highlights only one or two topics.

- *Job aids* can be "cheat sheets"—simple memory aids with shortcuts, reminders, or procedures that can be used by someone back at work to assist them with remembering basic keystrokes or menus. They are designed to help the user "get the job done."

- *Online documentation* refers to help, information, or any reference that is delivered online, as opposed to in physical printed form. Examples of these include Help menus embedded in a program and Internet-accessed materials. Because of the increasing volume of learning and training necessary today, online documentation is becoming more and more prevalent.

Let's look at typical classroom courseware in more detail. Courseware designed for classroom use can vary quite considerably, but usually falls into one of these three basic types:

- Self-teach courseware is written in such a way that the user can follow along step-by-step without necessarily needing the trainer's guidance. It is usually quite specific about exactly what procedural steps to take.

- Instructor-led courseware is specifically written for the trainer to use in the classroom. It is designed to be complementary to the instructor-led training and is not designed to be used as a self-teach manual.

- "Combination" courseware is a mixture of the previous two. It has some step-by-step procedures that the user could follow independently, but the trainer needs to provide much of the direction and explanations.

There are advantages and disadvantages to each type. Self-teach courseware, for example, is usually very comprehensive and specific. It usually contains detailed step-by-step procedures for each task. The drawback with this type of courseware is that because of its detail, it is harder for the trainer to adapt it to his or her own style. Using the courseware as suggested by the publisher requires that the trainer follow the book page by page, using the same examples and exercises. The training can become highly structured and lack the flexibility needed to adapt to the moment. Most learners do not respond well to trainers who go through the courseware page by page. They feel that this is not much different from reading and following the book back at the office.

In the instructor's version of this type of courseware, you will sometimes see timelines mentioned, for example, "This section should start at approx. 2 p.m." In an ideal, best-case scenario class, this might be reasonable. However, in most real computer classes with questions, discussions, and the odd challenge, a timeline can be a little idealistic. I've seen trainers rush learners through sections in courseware to stick to the timeline and confuse the heck out of them. It's better to spend a little more time than to risk any confusion.

Instructor-led courseware is designed to be used during a computer class. On its own, it might be incomplete. It covers the main concepts, vocabulary, and procedures, but it leaves the trainer to determine how the information is taught. It leaves enough flexibility for the trainer to teach in his or her unique style, and choose examples and practice exercises as needed. Because instructor-led courseware is less detailed and less comprehensive than the "self-teach" courseware, many learners prefer it. They find it easier to locate information and find the procedural steps they need. They have courseware that contains all the pertinent information, but in a more concise format.

It is often easier for them to locate information and find out how to carry out a procedure. They don't have to wade through pages of examples and detail.

Interestingly enough, when choosing standard courseware, an organization often selects that which seems thorough and comprehensive—the self-teach type. They feel that more detail is better. Most trainers, however, tend not to follow such courseware page by page, and end up using only relevant parts of it. When the learners get back to the office, they generally prefer to refer to a concise "how-to" booklet. They find the more detailed, self-teach courseware hard to use for finding solutions quickly. So, ironically, the courseware chosen by the organization doesn't always completely satisfy the trainer or the learner.

Choosing courseware

Some trainers and training managers need to purchase courseware. What should you buy? What should you look for when choosing courseware for your computer training? The first thing to do is to ask yourself a few questions:

- What function must the courseware serve?

- Is the courseware to be used in a classroom, as a reference, or in a self-study environment?

- How experienced are the users—what level of detail is required? If they are very familiar with the computer environment they are currently using, they might not need courseware that gives directions like, ". . . and then press Enter." Instead, a brief overview of procedural steps might be all that's necessary.

- Should the courseware be more procedural or conceptual? Do you need to concentrate on users understanding the "big picture," or do you want to focus on specific procedural steps?

- Does the courseware cover all the topics you need to teach? If you are only teaching a few specific tasks or procedures, then a standard piece of courseware might not be appropriate. In this case, you might consider creating your own courseware or purchasing some customizable courseware.

- Do you need to be able to customize your courseware? Again, customizable courseware will best suit your training. You can create publications that cover only the topics you need.

- Do your users have a preference for types of courseware? Show some samples of courseware to the end-users. Which do they like? Which do they feel would support them in their jobs best?

- Does the courseware include relevant examples and exercises?

- Are there enough hands-on exercises and examples? Are these relevant to the job functions of the learners?

- Is the courseware well-designed and easy to read?

- Is it well-produced? Is information easy to locate? Does it have lots of white space, screen shots, and diagrams? Does it have an index and table of contents?

After you have a clear understanding of your courseware needs, you might have several possible courseware publishers from which to choose. Look for clarity, simplicity, consistency, and organization. Work through some of the sections yourself. Try any examples. Are instructions clear? Are procedures easy to follow? Are there enough explanatory diagrams or screen shots? Will it be easy for your learners to install the sample files? Are the examples used relevant to who will be taking the training?

After working through some of the sections and examples yourself and answering some of these questions, you'll be better able to make a decision. Remember detailed, comprehensive, large, and popular are qualities you sometimes don't need. Some of the best courseware I have ever seen for instructor-led training was about half as thick and detailed as some of the most popular courseware available. It was simple, graphical, to the point, and easy to teach from, and the users loved it.

The only way to truly test courseware is to use it for a while in your training. After you have invested in courseware and used it for some time, you might find that it doesn't work as well for your training as you first thought. Always be willing to try other courseware from other publishers.

Are your practice exercises effective?

A critical part of a computer training class is the unassisted exercise, when the learner is asked to complete a task without explicit directions from the trainer. This is usually done with an exercise from the courseware or a question sheet handed out by the trainer.

The purpose of the exercise is to see if the learner can carry out the necessary procedures without direct assistance. This gives both the trainer and the learner an idea of what has been understood and retained, and what has not. It is a perfect opportunity for the learner to practice skills and to clear up any confusion that might exist.

Carrying out an exercise successfully should indicate that the learner has understood the work and can apply the knowledge to complete a specific task. The exercise should be designed to test understanding and application, not simply remembering keystrokes, mouse clicks, or directions.

In exercises and examples, make sure the emphasis is on demonstrating understanding rather than following steps. For example, take a look at these instructions:

Click on File and then Open.
Choose ABC.DOC from the list of files and click OK.
Press <CTRL> <END> to go back to the end of the document.

These are very clear, easy-to-follow steps, but they do not encourage the learner to think, only to follow instructions. The learning gained from steps like this is through repetition and rote. Learners can go through pages of exercises with instructions like this and learn very little. They can "successfully" complete an exercise without understanding a thing. A much better approach would be

Open the file ABC.DOC.
Move to the end of the document.

The learner has to read and understand the instruction and then recall the information covered in the class. It becomes problem-solving rather than step-following. In this case, learners are encouraged to learn skills when less information is given, not more. (This is the same logic that applies to the trainer asking questions, rather telling someone how to do something, as discussed in chapter 1.)

Take a closer look at the exercises you are asking the learners to complete. What abilities are they testing or promoting? Are they leading learners through a myriad of steps, or are they encouraging them to think?

If you find that too many of the courseware exercises are the step-by-step type, then consider creating some new ones that encourage learners to think a little more. I often use my own exercise sheets in addition to the ones in the courseware. I keep them very simple, and try not to explain how to carry out each and every step. If participants don't know what to do, I encourage them to look at their notes, use the Help menu, and use any other resources available to them before I provide an answer.

This reflects the real-life scenario back at work. They will have a task to complete and will not have step-by-step instructions for everything. They will have to work it out themselves.

When choosing or creating exercises, also consider how relevant they are to the group you are teaching. If you are teaching staff in a legal office how to use macros, then choosing a macro to create a pleading might be more valuable than choosing one to create a simple memo. If it's relevant, it's more likely to be remembered (see page xxx).

An exercise that provides value does not have to be something pre-planned or printed out. Some of the best exercises are made up at the spur of the moment. When you discover that a particular feature or function is going to be useful to the group you're teaching, sketch out a few diagrams or steps for them to follow, saying something like, "Why don't we try to create one of those with two columns and smaller margins similar to the form you use at work?" Create a short exercise, giving any necessary information the group might need. Participants end up with something they might actually use at work. They can immediately appreciate the value of what they have just learned.

Don't let courseware dominate your training

Courseware is an aid in computer training. It can help provide guidance during the training and be a useful resource after the training. However, it should never be the focus of the training. The learners should always be the focus of the training. If there is a choice between covering everything in the courseware and having the participants leave a little confused, or covering 90% and having them understand and feel confident, I recommend the latter. Covering the material is not as important as making sure that what is covered is understood. This is not to say that the courseware shouldn't be an important, integral part of the training, but it shouldn't dominate it. What should drive the training is what the learners need at each moment in time.

For example, you might be halfway through teaching macros and find that very few learners are following you or understanding the examples in the courseware. You planned on teaching another topic before lunchtime. Rather than move on, it is best to ensure that the current topic is clear and understandable first. It's tempting to move on anyway to keep with the plan of the courseware, but when you do this and squeeze in that extra topic, the learners go to lunch feeling confused. The worst thing you can do in training is have them leave for lunch confused. Their confidence and capacity to learn start to plummet. Finishing the class in this manner would not serve the needs of the learner—only the trainer's sense of "I covered everything." Courseware should support the training, not define it.

Guidelines for creating your own courseware

Suppose you have decided to create courseware for your training rather than purchase it. The first thing to do is to decide what type of courseware you need, as discussed at the beginning of this chapter. Do you need detailed, step-by-step courseware that learners can use to teach themselves, less detailed, instructor-led courseware with just the core topics and procedures, or a little of each?

Ask yourself these questions:

- Who is it designed for?

- What will they use it for?

- How will they use it?

- What does it need to include?

- Will I need to add to it later?

Schedule enough time

Creating good courseware is not something you can do in your spare time. The time to create it needs to be scheduled. Trying to squeeze it into lunchtimes and evenings on top of everything else you do won't work. Creating something worthwhile takes time to plan, design, test, and rewrite.

If you are creating courseware for the first time, plan on taking about twice as much time as you initially estimate. It's like buying a hard drive: whatever capacity you think you need, multiply by two. Also, plan on time to update and fine-tune it after you have tried it out in a class. You might decide to add or remove sections or exercises after it has been "road-tested."

Keep it consistent

Make certain you use templates and styles so you keep a consistent format throughout. Every main heading should look the same, as should every subheading, every caption, and every practice exercise. Readability is very important—spend a little time deciding on an appropriate format for each style. Make it clear and easy to read. Try not to use more than a couple of fonts, even though you're eager to try out the other 250 on your system.

When you show typed entries, function keys, or menu commands, have a convention that is consistent, as shown in Fig. 6-1. Make it easy for the reader to distinguish between descriptive text and the keys or menus that need to be selected.

If you are creating courseware for a graphical user interface like Windows, try to use pictures of the buttons or menu items to illustrate more clearly what the user will see. Keep it consistent, clear, simple, and organized.

Saving the presentation

Do this

1. Choose
   File

   Save As...

2. Make sure the **example** directory is selected

3. Type **present1**
   Click on
   OK

6-1 *Showing clearly what to choose, type, or press.*

Use diagrams and screen shots

When possible, and especially when explaining a concept, try to use simple diagrams and pictures (see page 79). Written explanations are not always the best way of understanding software concepts and procedures. Learning software is a very visual experience, and the courseware should reflect this. Don't explain what the user will see, show it! Use screen-capture software to get pictures of the actual software. Let the users see exactly what they'll get on their screen when they carry out the procedure.

The more graphics and the less text, the better. If you look at many of the older computer reference books or courseware, you'll see pages and pages of words and explanations. No wonder people got intimidated by computers! Nowadays, many software manuals and references are full of pictures, screen shots, diagrams, and cartoon characters—and they sell like hotcakes. People want to see what happens, not read an explanation of what happens.

Use white space

Most people who are familiar with desktop publishing know how important white space can be. If your goal is to have someone want to read a newsletter, flyer, advertisement, or pages in courseware, it needs to have an inviting quality about it. White space, which is the area of the page that has nothing printed on it, can help achieve this. Look at the diagrams in Fig. 6-2. Which one looks interesting and inviting, and which looks like hard work?

Blank areas in the margin can also allow the learner to make notes during the class. Consider having quite a large left margin or a blank left-hand page for notes. Don't try to cram as much as you can on a page in order to save paper or cut down on the number of pages. You might save a few pennies, but lose your learners.

Provide the right amount of detail

The level of detail you provide in your procedures and step-by-step instructions should reflect the audience for the courseware. If it is to be used in a class and as a reference afterwards, less detail is required than if it is to be used predominantly for users to teach themselves. The common tendency is for the courseware developer to give very detailed instructions regardless of who the user is. A more computer-literate group, however, would not need procedural steps such as these:

1. Click File, then Page Setup.
2. Click the Margins tab.
3. Change the left margin to 1.5".

Simply

Change the left margin to 1.5".

would be good enough.

One way of determining how detailed you courseware needs to be is to test it out. You will soon see if the detail you provided is adequate when your learners begin to use your material.

State the objectives for each module

It is important, especially for courseware with a lot of detail, to state the objectives or topics covered for each module or lesson. This gives the learners a quick overview of what information is covered in the section and what skills they might expect to learn. Objectives are also useful to the trainer when teaching, so that he or she can preview what is going to be covered.

The Basic Commands

Listed below are a few of the commonly used menu commands.

Style/Number Format - will enable you to change a specified range on the spread-sheet to currency, percentage, fixed decimal places, date or other format. Using the format icons is the easiest way to choose commonly used formats.

Style/Alignment - will allow you to set a label alignment for a range of labels such as Left, Center or Right. The Alignment icons on the icon palette is the simplest way to align worksheet entries.

Edit/Clear - will erase the contents of all the cells in the range that you highlight. <Del> will delete the contents of the highlighted cell(s).

File/Close - will close the current worksheet. If you do this make sure you have saved it first.

File/Open - will open or load a specified worksheet from a disk. You can use the icon for this. More than one worksheet can be open at one time.

Style/Column Width - allows you to change the width of the current column. This becomes necessary if ********* appears in the column where a number should be. The easiest way to change a column width is to drag the column separator line between the column letters. Row height can be adjusted in a similar manner.

Edit/Insert - will insert new, blank columns or rows into a worksheet. To delete columns and rows use Worksheet Delete.

Edit/Copy Down   Edit/Copy Right - used to quickly copy formulas down or to the right of the currently selected cell.

Edit Cut and **Edit Paste** - these are used to "cut" cells or ranges of cells and paste them back at other locations.

Range Fill - used to enter numbers in ascending or descending order in a range incrementing or decrementing by any step. Saves time entering.

Pressing <Esc> will take you out of a menu.

Rather than use these commands as selected from the menus you can use the icons at the top of the screen. These are mouse shortcuts for many of the commands. The icons can also be customized to suit your particular needs. The next page shows a list of the icons on a standard menu and some of the other available sets of icons.

6-2a *Lack of white space.*

Try not to include too many objectives for each module. Don't over-burden the user with too much information or tasks at one time. Covering 10 separate topics in one module can be overwhelming—better to break it into two smaller modules.

Tell them three times

Use the "three times" rule that is used when presenting any information to anyone, anywhere, using any medium: Tell them what you are about to tell them. Then tell them. Then tell them what you told them.

The Basic Commands

Listed below are a few of the commonly used menu commands.

Style
  Number Format
will enable you to change a specified range on the spreadsheet to
currency, percentage, fixed decimal places, date or other format.
Using the format icons is the easiest way to choose commonly
used formats.

Style
  Alignment
will allow you to set a label alignment for a range of labels such as
Left, Center or Right. The Alignment icons on the icon palette is
the simplest way to align worksheet entries.

Edit
  Clear
will erase the contents of all the cells in the range that you
highlight. <Del> will delete the contents of the highlighted cell(s).

File
  Close
will close the current worksheet. If you do this make sure you
have saved it first.

File
  Open
will open or load a specified worksheet from a disk. You can use
the icon for this. More than one worksheet can be open at one
time.

Style
  Column Width
allows you to change the width of the current column. This
becomes necessary if ********* appears in the column where a

6-2b *Appropriate white space.*

Translated into courseware terms, this would be mean

1 Tell them at the beginning of each module what the module
is going to cover.

2 Cover the information in the module.

3 Review or summarize what you covered at the end of the
module.

Explain concepts

Include explanations of concepts before showing procedural steps. Give the "big picture" information first. Procedural steps are not that useful unless the underlying concepts are understood. Use diagrams if at all possible.

Show procedures clearly

When you are showing the keystrokes or menu commands that need to be chosen, make sure you clearly distinguish what is typed, what is chosen from a menu, and what is simply pressed. Have a different convention for showing each. (The legend for these should be included at the beginning of the courseware.) The user needs to see simple, clear, and unambiguous steps. Try to keep the procedural steps short and to the point. Consider having a column alongside the procedures to provide explanations of each step, as shown in Fig. 6-3.

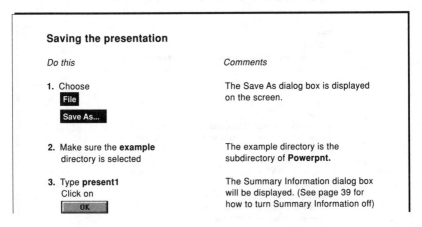

6-3 *Using two columns.*

When you are writing procedural steps, show the icons to be clicked or keys to be pressed graphically. Try not to describe an icon, button, or key; show it, as in Fig. 6-4.

Provide appropriate exercises

When you design exercises for skill practice, consider the following:

- *Are the exercises relevant?* Do they reflect "real-world" scenarios that the learners can relate to? Are they relevant to what the learners might be doing back at work?

Moving text

1. Select the text

2. Click the ✂ button

3. Click at the bottom of the paragraph

4. Click the 📋 button

6-4 *Using icons in the text.*

- *Do the participants get to practice everything?* Do the exercises allow the them to practice every new skill or feature that was covered in the module? Make sure you give them a chance to use everything they learned.

- *Do the exercises build confidence?* How easy is it for them to feel successful after completing an exercise?

- *Are the exercises cumulative?* It is often useful to have each exercise build on the previous one so that learners can see how the skills relate to one scenario. Are your exercises totally independent of each other? Would having each one build on the previous be better? If so, can someone start a new module without having finished the exercise in the previous one?

- *Are the exercises simple to follow?* Sometimes the instructions in an exercise can confuse rather than clarify. Are the instructions clear and understandable? Avoid having too much introductory text to read before the exercises.

- *Do you have exercises for faster learners?* It is a good idea to include extra "challenge" exercises for faster learners. While others are finishing off the standard exercise, the fast learner can get to explore a few new features and functions. This helps avoid the situation where the fast learners are tapping their fingers or playing solitaire, waiting for the rest to finish.

- *Have you provided answers?* Consider including answers for each practice exercise at the end of the courseware. This way, you can encourage the learners to evaluate their own work (see page 155, "Encourage self-evaluation").

Include a quick reference

Include a quick reference or "cheat-sheet" in your courseware. Some learners only need a push in the right direction to recall a technique or procedure, and a quick reference of commands, shortcuts, or function keys is valuable to them when they return to work. Searching through the courseware text to find a few procedural steps can be tedious. You might consider designing the quick reference so that it can be removed from the courseware and use it independently.

Include a glossary

Most tasks and processes have associated terms and vocabulary. Unless this new vocabulary is understood, the concepts and procedures become meaningless. Give explanations or definition of any new vocabulary words at the beginning of the section where they are used, as well as in a glossary at the end of the courseware.

When you are giving a definition for a vocabulary word, try to keep the audience in mind. Don't be technically accurate at the expense of not being clear. Use language that your audience will understand.

Include a table of contents and index

It is important that your courseware includes a table of contents in the front and some type of index in the back. The reader needs to see an overview of what the courseware covers and where to find the information.

Add headers and footers

Headers and footers can assist the reader in knowing where they are in the courseware. Have something like "Lesson 3—Tabs and Indents" that shows where you are and what the section is.

Make sure your page numbers are easy to read. Avoid putting them in the middle or near the inside edge of the pages. Have them on the outside edges of the pages in an easy-to-read font.

Use a spiral binding

It is preferable to use some type of spiral binding on your courseware. Participants prefer being able to lay it flat on the desk or fold it back rather than having to try and keep the pages open with their hands. Avoid using bindings that don't allow this, even though they might be better for your budget.

Consider adding appendices

Appendices are useful to include extra features, more review exercises, more advanced work, or special information. Any extra information that you might like to provide for the user but that would be out of place in the body of the courseware can be placed in an appendix.

Fine-tune

Courseware that you create yourself will never seem complete. With every class it's used in, you will think of extra sections or features to add, or parts to delete. What's more, when you finally decide it is finished, you'll probably upgrade your software! Test and fine-tune your courseware as soon as you can. Use it in a class, and then ask yourself some questions, such as:

- Was it suitable for the length of the class?

- Did the learners seem to find it easy to follow?

- Did the trainer find it easy to teach from?

- Were the practice exercises too short or too long?

- Were there enough exercises to suit the types of learners?

- Was it valuable to the learners after the training?

- Could you add or delete anything to make things clearer?

After testing the courseware a few times, try to revise it and then produce a "final" version. Don't spend the rest of your life trying to constantly update and polish it.

7

Designing training

◆◆◆

"If you're not sure where you're going, you're liable to end up someplace else."
— **Robert Mager**

If a company needs to train its staff on how to graph accounting data, sending them to a six-hour Excel class that covers graphing in the last hour would be a waste of training dollars. Sending a group of office personnel to an advanced WordPerfect class, if all they need to know was how to create tables, would also be a waste. Training has to reflect specific needs in order to be valuable.

When you design computer training, you need to carry out certain processes (Fig. 7-1) to ensure the final product is relevant, useful, and satisfies needs. When these elements of training design are missing, you are simply throwing mud at a wall in the hope that some of it might stick. When you do not have the time or resources to carefully design the training (as is often the case with public classes), you still need to consider each of these steps, but at an accelerated pace before and during the training itself (as discussed in "A word about JITT," later in this chapter).

Identifying needs

The first step in designing computer training is to identify needs. You will be providing training because there is a *perceived* need for it. You

Designing Computer Training

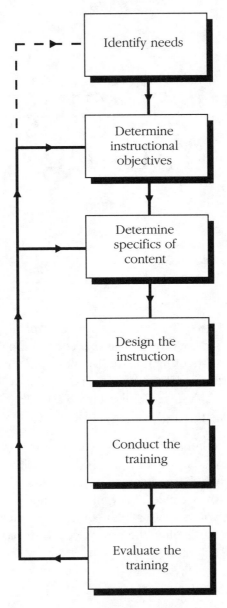

7-1 *Steps in designing training.*

must also identify and analyze the *actual* needs. These actual needs might be quite different from the perceived needs.

Typically, you identify needs by carrying out what is usually termed a "needs analysis" or "needs assessment." You find out who is involved in the training and what their specific needs are. There might be different needs:

- The organizational needs

- The learner needs

- The task needs

The organizational needs center around how the training affects the overall goals and objectives of the organization. Is the training going to forward the goals and objectives of the organization? Will the training be a short-term fix or a building block for future learning? Will the investment in training give returns by helping to increase productivity?

The learners' needs are a little different. Will the training satisfy the learners' need to feel competent and comfortable in carrying out particular tasks? Will the training help the learners become knowledgeable enough to solve their own problems? Will the training make their lives easier? Another level of learner needs are *intrinsic needs*, such as giving the learner a sense that the organization is willing to invest in their learning, providing the learner with a sense of self-confidence about using new technologies. Quite often these intrinsic needs and benefits in training are as productive and valuable as the extrinsic ones. An individual who derives a sense of self-direction, competency, and self-confidence from training is an asset to the company as well as his or her own sense of self.

Task needs are those required to carry out a specific task or tasks, that is, the skills or knowledge required to do the job. Does the training provide relevant information and practical skills for solving the real workplace problems? How much of the training focuses on the specific processes and tasks that will be needed back on the job? How will the training affect the way tasks will be carried out?

When analyzing needs, you should be conscious of all three areas. Try to develop training that addresses them all.

How can you carry out a needs assessment? There are many different ways to collect this information, including interviews, surveys, questionnaires, observations, and informal conversations.

Interviews

You can talk with the learners or the learners' supervisor about what is required from the training. Sometimes, the learners' perception of needs varies somewhat from that of the manager or supervisor. It is important to consider both perspectives. Interviews can be a useful way of getting a feel for what is and isn't needed in the training—something that is not so apparent in surveys or questionnaires.

Surveys and questionnaires

Surveys and questionnaires can save time interviewing individuals, but they need to be put together carefully if the feedback is to provide useful information. Spend time developing the right questions so that the answers can provide specific guidance to the training developer. A question like, "Are you familiar with the basics of your spreadsheet program?" is not as valuable as, "Can you use your spreadsheet program to multiply two cells together, add a column of numbers, and calculate an average?"

It is important to collect the right data, and then interpret the data to determine its effect on the training needs, and on the support needs after the training. It might turn out that the information highlights different needs than originally intended. The training might need to be adapted accordingly.

When designing questionnaires, try to develop questions that address learners' preferences, attitudes, and concerns, as well as specific job-related skills. Questions can be included that gauge the learners' preferred ways of learning, job stress levels, experience, educational background, and so forth. This information is as valuable to the developer as information about the tasks and processes that are being carried out. A whole training program could be developed that teaches exactly the right skills needed to complete workplace tasks, but overlooks the need of the learners to feel more comfortable with and less threatened by the technology.

Observation

Another method of assessing needs is to visit the workplace and observe what the people to be trained are actually doing and how they are using the software tools to achieve results. What tasks need to be carried out, and how could the software be used to best satisfy these needs? Sometimes, actually observing work processes is helpful because the training developer can see new ways of solving existing problems. Rather than develop training to solve existing problems with old approaches, you might be able to help create whole new approaches to the problems.

Informal conversations

A lot of valuable information can be unearthed by being around the workplace and listening. Some of the most important elements in creating a training class can result from listening to conversations at the photocopier or water cooler, or in the break room. Often the most important elements that the training needs to include are those which people tend to moan and complain about. Keep your ear to the ground and take note of the occasional comment, concern, or complaint as a potentially useful contribution to the design of your training.

From my files

When delivering training to individuals from a large corporation, I listened to several people complain that they had to remember yet another password for the e-mail program I was teaching. This was obviously a major concern to many of the learners, so I decided to add a 15-minute section to the class entitled "Dealing with password stress." The response was gratifying. They seemed relieved that someone had acknowledged one of their concerns. Just adding that section helped bring a little more levity to the classroom and seemed to decrease the resistance to training that some of them had. Training needs are often attitudes as well as skills.

Determining instructional objectives

Once needs are determined, they can be used to develop instructional objectives. What does the training need to provide? What skills should the learners possess after the training? Here are some examples of instructional objectives:

- To have users be able to create and print charts

- To have users print reports from a database

- To have users be able to link information from the spreadsheet to the word processor.

This helps the course designer outline the overall focus of the training and is an important first step before getting into specifics.

Why objectives are so important

Objectives are key elements of course design. If there are no objectives, there can be no basis for selecting content, methods, and media, and no foundation for evaluating the computer training. Training without objectives is like a road trip without a destination.

Objectives provide

- A basis for planning the training

- A roadmap for the learner as to what to expect

- A basis for evaluating the effectiveness of training

The objectives of the training don't have to be exactly the same as the objectives in the courseware. Sometimes your objectives may need to change or be adapted as you go. This is particularly true when it comes to public computer training classes—the objectives of all the participants will be slightly different and the trainer's objectives should adapt accordingly.

Determine specifics

The broad objectives for the training can then be dissected into the specifics that need to be taught. Exactly what concepts and procedures need to be taught? What new vocabulary needs to be learned? What specific tasks do the learners need to be able to carry out? Specific objectives might include the following:

- Understand the terms X-axis, Y-axis, linear, nonlinear, combination chart, trend-line

- Use the chart tool to create a simple column chart

- Plot a chart from two columns in a simple database

The specifics are what you refer to later when evaluating the effectiveness of the training.

Designing the instruction

Now that you know what the training needs to deliver, the next step is to determine the most appropriate way to deliver it, and then design the instruction accordingly. It's one thing knowing you need to teach learners how to accomplish a specific task, but another thing to figure out how to do this. Consider questions like these:

- What learning principles should the training reflect?

- What are the criteria you wish to evaluate?

- How should you design your method of evaluation?

- What behavioral change, if any, do you wish to achieve?

- What are the resistances to training in the learners?

- What method and media should be used to deliver the training?

- Are job-aids or "cheat-sheets" required?

- Does courseware need to be developed, or can it be purchased?

- What exercises or practice sessions would be appropriate?

- What will the prerequisites be?

- Will the method of delivery suit the audience?

- What support will learners receive after the training?

- What time constraints are there?

Answering these questions should provide the course designer with the information needed to fine-tune the structure and design of the class. The training design should be such that it maximizes the similarity between the training and the workplace.

Conducting the training

At this point, the objectives have been determined, and the training method and design have been finalized. You then conduct the training in accordance with the design.

Let me mention something about being flexible and adaptable. You might have spent considerable effort assessing needs and designing your training, and have your strategy all laid out, but you should never let your training plan overrule what might be needed in the moment. After careful planning, you might have decided on an approach to training that doesn't seem to be working as you hoped it would. Perhaps you opted to use an example exercise from the courseware and find it is producing more confusion than clarity. You need to adapt the class on the fly. You must respond to what is needed in the moment and be flexible enough to alter your course.

Evaluating the training

The final step in the process of designing computer training is evaluating the training. How will you know if the training was successful? What are your criteria for determining success? What methods should you use in measuring the effectiveness of the training? If there was a problem, was it due to documentation, courseware, method of delivery, or the instructor?

After designing a valid test or method of evaluation, you need to continually adapt and fine-tune your training so that it is responsive to the learner's needs. The information gleaned from evaluating the training can be fed back to the design process, so that the training is constantly adjusted and balanced.

Evaluating computer training as an independent exercise—that is, not using it as a feedback mechanism to fine-tune training—has limited value. It would be like asking your participants if the room temperature was okay, but not doing anything about it if it wasn't. Evaluation should always be fed back into the design process.

A word about just-in-time training (JITT)

Increasingly, computer training is needed "just in time." Waiting a month or so to have training delivered will be unacceptable. This does not mean that the six steps in the design process outlined here need to be overlooked. It simply means you have to carry them out in a very short time period.

Each step is still critical to the design process, but needs to be adapted to the timeframe available. For example, the needs analysis might end up being a few telephone conversations with the client about content and objectives. The specifics and design might end up being the customization of existing courseware and discussions with the trainer about the delivery of the training. Just-in-time training doesn't mean neglecting the elements of design, it just means we carry them out more quickly.

What's wrong with classroom training?

There are many reasons why instructor-led classroom training works well. There are also reasons why it doesn't work so well. By looking at what doesn't work so well, you are in a better position to improve your training and explore other learning options. By knowing your weaknesses, you can develop your strengths.

Generic training

Most users who attend prepackaged, end-user computer training find that only 20 to 30 percent of the information they learn is immediately useful to them. Sometimes, a trainer spends a few minutes answering a question about something not included in the outline. Often, for the learner, this can be the most valuable part of the class. Standard end-user classes are certainly valuable, but because of their general nature and the differing needs of the participants, they are not always time- and cost-effective.

Ability levels

A typical instructor-led class has people with differing skill levels. At best, this means the learner will progress at the average speed of the class. At worst, the learner will be either bored or confused. Classroom training cannot avoid differences in ability levels, and therefore, training cannot be fully customized to a learner's style and speed.

Learning-style differences

People learn fastest and most effectively when information is presented to them in their preferred learning style (see Chapter 16). Some people learn better with the written word, while others prefer pictures and diagrams. Some learn better sitting quietly with no interruptions, while others prefer background music or like to move around when they learn.

As much as a computer trainer attempts to satisfy the learning needs of everyone, there is compromise. The learner has no choice but to accept the information provided in the mode the trainer decides to use.

Peer fear

Most learners are quick to compare themselves to the other participants in a training room. They rapidly rate their perceived ability levels in the class and relate to the trainer and the other participants with this self-measurement. "I know I'm the slowest one here, but . . ." or, "This is probably a dumb question but . . ." are phrases trainers tend to hear a lot.

More often than not, the fear of making a mistake or looking dumb in front of others prevents any questions or comments. The presence of coworkers or strangers does not always encourage participation and self-expression. As a result, the learning becomes less effective.

When scheduled

Because of the nature of classroom computer training, it is not always provided when needed, but rather, when scheduled. Often, computer training is required to satisfy an immediate need. Indeed, learning is most effective when it is an immediate response to a need. When learning is delayed, the impact of the training is reduced.

The hidden benefit of classroom training

Apart from the primary benefit of computer training, that is, the acquisition of useful knowledge and skills, there is a secondary benefit: the social aspect of training. Everyone needs to be part of a group or a community. The classroom provides an opportunity for people to relate and connect with each other on a fundamental level. Face-to-face communication satisfies a basic human need and is very different from communication via telephone, e-mail, or computer.

When the learner is in a room with other learners, there is a sense of common purpose, a sense of working toward the same goal. The class is more than just a collection of individuals—it has its own character and energy. When someone asks or answers questions, it stimulates ideas and interaction with others in the room. It's also comforting to the learner to know that others are experiencing similar challenges.

In short, there are many social benefits of instructor-led training. When designing computer training and looking to other methods for delivering learning, be aware of these secondary benefits. The more you can include some of these social elements into other methods of computer training, the more successful and satisfying the training can be. Their absence might not affect the skills learned, but might affect the overall sense of community and warmth the participants gain from the class.

8

Training media and technologies

"Words, like eyeglasses, blur everything that they do not make clear."
— **Joseph Joubert**

Using data panels and displays

There are many types of training display systems. The most common for computer training are LCD panels, portable LCD projectors, video projection systems, large TV data monitors, and "networked" displays. Each has its particular qualities suited to particular needs.

LCD panels
LCD panels are liquid crystal displays that can are placed on top of an OHP (overhead projector) to project the monitor output onto a screen. LCD panels are cheaper than most of the other alternatives ($1000 to $4000). They are also portable, easy to set up, and relatively small. On the other hand, unless you have a very powerful OHP, the display intensity is poor. You need quite a dark room to see the information onscreen clearly. Even then, your audience won't be able to see the movements of the mouse cursor unless you invest in the more expensive active-matrix type of display.

Portable LCD projectors
With portable LCD projectors, the LCD system and the light source are built into one unit. These are far more expensive than the stan-

dard data panels. Although they are portable, easy to set up, relatively small, and often produce a much greater light intensity than regular LCD panels, portable LCD projectors are relatively expensive ($6000 and up).

Video projection systems
Video projection systems can display a large image of the computer screen (or video) onto a projection screen. They are often used at conferences and large presentations.

Video projection systems produce very large, high-quality images. The light-intensity level is better than LCD-type displays, and they can be used for projecting video images as well as computer displays. They are very expensive, however, ($10,000 to $30,000) and not very portable.

Data monitors
Data monitors are large-screen TVs with data-quality output. (It is possible to use a regular large-screen TV with a video converter as a data monitor, but these systems lack any clarity and result in poor displays.)

Data monitors are relatively inexpensive ($2000 to $4000). They can be used in a room without dimming the lights, the display is bright and clear, and they can be set out of the way on a wall or hanging from the ceiling. On the other hand, the screen size is not as large as you could get with other types of display. As a result, the audience needs to be quite near the monitor.

Networked displays
Another method of displaying screen data is to have the trainer's display sent to all the participants screens. In this networked setup, you have the option of observing the learners' screens or display the trainer's screen.

Networked displays can be inexpensive ($250 to $400 per computer) while maintaining high display quality, and they can also be used in a room without dimming the lights. Also, the trainer has control over each station, and there is only ever one screen to look at. There are disadvantages to networked displays, however. This system encourages the trainer to stay at the front of the room and not interact with the learners. It is also harder for the trainer to know if she or he has everyone's attention. Finally, it encourages very structured training.

Adjusting the lighting

When you are using some type of projection system, strive to have a way of dimming the lights rather than having them either on or off, so you can adjust the light to the most optimum level. Just having light or no light can be distracting to the learners. If you do have to turn the lights completely off, consider having small reading lamps by each computer station so that participants can see the courseware and the keyboard. Avoid having them strain their eyes to read courseware in a dimly lit room.

Screen positioning

When you are projecting an image, position your screen such that everyone can see the image without moving or straining their necks. Avoid using a side wall in a classroom or the whiteboard. Instead, use an actual screen. The reflective properties of a plain wall, and especially a whiteboard, do not provide the best display. The reflections they cause can be distracting.

Try to have the screen perpendicular to the light source so the image doesn't get skewed. There's nothing worse than having to look at an image of the screen that is wide at the top and skinny at the bottom. Try to angle the projector or the screen if this is a problem.

Learning with other media

This book primarily focuses on instructor-led training (ILT), but there are other methods of training that can be effective, either used on their own, or as a complement to ILT. The most common are videotapes, audio cassettes, and multimedia training or CBT (computer-based training).

Let's look at when video, audio, or computer-based training might be a viable alternative to instructor-led training:

- When your volume of learners is large
- When the training is recurring, not a one-time event
- When the training needs to be consistent
- When instructor-led training is expensive

- When the learners are geographically dispersed

- When the learners have varied work schedules

- When the learners have not responded well to traditional training

- When training rooms are unavailable

- When trainers lack the necessary skills to teach the course

If any of the above situations are present, it might be worthwhile to complement your instructor-led training with one of these other forms of training. The advantages and disadvantages of each method are shown in Table 8-1.

CBT

CBT, often called multimedia training, is a popular learning technology. It can range from very simple text- and graphics-based software on a floppy disk to quite sophisticated interactive multimedia from a CD-ROM or file server. Modern CBT has evolved into a learner-centered, interactive training medium that takes full advantage of photographs, still graphics, animation, sound, and motion video. It is being used in many areas of training, including "soft-skills" training—not just computer training. The effectiveness and cost benefits of CBT added to the fact that the training can be anywhere and anytime make it a viable alternative to instructor-led training for many organizations.

One of the advantages of CBT and interactive multimedia systems is that the learner uses the computer to actually carry out keystrokes and mouse clicks as he or she would in an actual program. Many of the CBT/multimedia learning programs have sophisticated sound and graphic elements that make learning much more fun and engaging. They generally allow the learner to choose the tasks or features he or she wishes to learn, and assist and encourage the learner throughout the training. Many CBT programs also have some method of assessing skill levels after completing a tutorial.

What good CBT looks like
The quality of CBT varies enormously. What features should good off-the-shelf or customized CBT have?

Table 8-1. Training media.

Media	Advantages	Disadvantages
Video tapes	Inexpensive consistent content, easy to distribute, convenient, can review easily, has visual appeal.	Expensive to produce custom videos, not interactive, user divides attention between two screens, linear approach to learning, not well-suited to skill practice, sometimes difficult to see computer screen details, not easy to customize.
Audio cassettes	Inexpensive, consistent content, easy to distribute, convenient, can review easily, good for providing information, user can focus on the actual software when learning.	Not interactive, not suited to non-auditory learners, linear approach to learning, not easy to customize.
CBT/Multimedia	Off-the-shelf CBT is inexpensive, consistent content, easy to distribute, interactive, multisensory, user has more control over what to learn (nonlinear), easier to customize, can provide feedback and testing.	Custom CBT can be expensive to produce.

One of the most important features is the learning model on which the CBT is based. All too often, CBT takes the learner down a very linear road and teaches in a very structured procedural manner. "Click this, now this, then this . . ." The emphasis is usually on repetition. Do the tutorial enough times, and you'll learn it. Not enough CBT includes elements of conceptual learning (see page 280), where there is also emphasis on understanding the big picture. Much of the CBT currently available doesn't allow the user to go in any direction he or she wishes. CBT will be much more effective when it is designed so that users can learn in a nonlinear fashion, which better reflects the way people master most skills.

Here are a few other things to look for when considering investing in or creating CBT:

- Is it instructionally sound? Is it based on the principles of adult learning?

- Is it easy to use and understand? Are the instructions wordy, or simple and clear?

- Is it easy for the user to navigate through the program?

- Is it varied in its use of media? Does it include an appropriate amount of animation, graphics, audio, and video?

- What happens when an error is made? How many times must the learner fail to do something before the CBT responds with a hint or answer?

- Does the CBT give guidance and encouragement, or just report correct and incorrect entries?

- Does it prompt users to learn and think, or does it just tell them how to do something?

- Does it maintain interest? Is it fun and gratifying for the learner?

- Does it include any way to assess skill levels? When the learner has completed a task or a set of procedures, is there a way that progress can be shown?

- Can the user jump to any lesson or tutorial without having to go through earlier ones?

- Does it use meaningful examples? Do they relate to your learners' experiences?

- Is the level of the CBT suitable for the users? Can the CBT be used for different levels of users?

When you have answered all these questions, you'll be in a much better position to make a decision. And don't forget to talk to the person who can tell you the most about the effectiveness and suitability of the software—the learner.

Electronic performance support systems

Electronic performance support systems (EPSSs) are increasingly being used in organizations to enable people to perform job tasks more efficiently. These systems were developed to meet the need for improved job performance because of the increasing complexity of information systems, while minimizing the cost and inadequacy of training. They are changing the way people work and learn with information technology and therefore will impact the work of the computer trainer.

What exactly is an electronic performance support system? Here's one definition:

> *An EPSS is a closely integrated system that offers immediate and context-sensitive access to information, advice, and learning that enable a person to perform a job with a minimum of support by others.*

In other words, it is very sophisticated software that is integrated with the work environment at someone's computer to help him or her perform a task, access information, and learn. For example, a worker might need to fill out a complicated insurance claim form and be unfamiliar with the procedure. Rather than seek help from coworkers or consult the manual, the worker clicks a button on the screen and is guided step-by-step through the procedures necessary to complete the task. During these procedures, help screens, tutorials, or databases that relate to this particular task can be accessed.

An EPSS typically includes a hypertext database, an expert system, and some modular CBT. It is a truly customized software system, designed to provide guidance and learning when and where it is needed and therefore increase job performance. Such a system can be used to support any type of computer-based task. Rather than sending workers to expensive, off-the-job, time-consuming training hoping that the requisite skills will be learned, an organization can install a sophisticated EPSS and cut training time and costs dramatically. The EPSS provides the task information and the learning when it is needed on the job.

How might this affect computer training? The traditional approach to improving job performance has been to send a worker out to training to learn a particular software application. After understanding the capabilities of the software and learning how to complete different general tasks, the worker would go back and attempt to apply the new skills to real job tasks. The learning preceded and was separate from the job tasks.

In EPSS, the job task and the learning are concurrent, not separated in time and space. The worker no longer needs a thorough understanding of the software application or the work procedures before completing a task—the necessary skills or procedures can be learned or accessed when needed. As a result, the need for training is reduced. The training focuses less on the application or job skills and more on how to use the EPSS. Many businesses have already implemented such systems and found significant increases in performance while drastically reducing their need for traditional training.

Trainers of all types are naturally concerned about the trend to implement such systems. One of the common criticisms of EPSS is that, although performance and productivity are increased, the worker might ultimately understand much less about the overall system and its functioning. The dependence on the machine will increase, and the value placed on experience and accumulated knowledge might decrease.

When more EPSSs (or whatever they might be called next year) start to appear in the workplace, the trainer's role might change in the organization. It might become one of learning and performance consultant, and you might well find yourself working with the system's designers.

9

More training suggestions

◆◆◆

"A man with a new idea is a crank until the idea succeeds."
— **Mark Twain**

Technical training

Most training departments and organizations separate training into application training and technical training. Application training generally deals with end-user software, such as word processors, e-mail systems, presentation graphics, spreadsheets, and so on. Technical training deals with higher-end products, such as operating systems, networking systems, CAD products, programming languages, and so forth. Technical training is often for professionals who teach, support, or use these products in their day-to-day work.

This book is geared primarily toward application training. The examples and scenarios are related to end-user software. However, because of the increasing amount of technical training being delivered in organizations, I want to highlight some differences. For the most part, everything in this book can apply to technical training, but some areas demand a slightly different approach.

Differences in technical training

- *Experienced users.* Prerequisites are crucial in this type of training. Most people in these classes are experienced computer users. The participants are familiar with computer concepts and terminology, and you usually find a high level of computer expertise in the room.

- *Less "hand-holding".* Because of their level of expertise, the learners in technical training classes do not require as much "hand-holding" and step-by-step examples as those in an application class. It is usually enough that they understand a concept and the procedure for implementing it—extensive practice sessions are usually not necessary or desired by the learners.

- *More lecturing.* Most technical training, by definition, has a significant amount of conceptual material. Understanding the concept or the logic of the software is even more important than it is in application training; as a result, more information is delivered by lecturing. Application training is usually simple concepts and lots of hands-on practice, whereas technical training is usually more complex concepts and less hands-on practice.

- *Importance of concepts.* In most technical training, many concepts build on the understanding and integration of other concepts. Often several concepts are the building blocks of a new concept. A full grasp of each new concept is crucial to understanding further concepts.

- *More memorization.* Frequently in this type of training, large volumes of material must be covered and new terms and vocabulary introduced. The amount of pure memorization is greater than in application training. The material is often very terminology-intensive with lots of acronyms.

- *High expectations.* Technical training classes can cost many thousands of dollars. When paying out such large sums of money, organizations and individuals expect to have their needs met. Participants expect a lot and often are critical if they feel their needs are not met.

- *Real-life experience.* Trainers typically do more training than hands-on work, such as installations and troubleshooting. Participants in technical training classes value the practical experience of a trainer. Very often one of the first things a technical learner wants to know is what experience the trainer has had in the "real-world". They become concerned if they feel the trainer is a theoretician rather than someone with practical experience.

- *Time constraints.* Many technical classes cover enormous amounts of information in a relatively short time. The opportunities for leisurely discussion of a topic or consideration of related issues are usually limited. The trainer typically has to keep to a tight time schedule and maintain focus and direction.

Suggestions for technical trainers

Because of these differences in teaching technical classes, the trainer should adapt his or her approach. Technical classes cannot always be taught like application classes—the audience and the material are different and require a different training style. Here are some suggestions and tips for teaching technical classes.

- Make sure all participants have the required prerequisites. Try to find out in advance of the first day of class. Make sure anyone registering for a class is clear about exactly what will be covered and exactly what the prerequisites are. Avoid any surprises on day one!

- If at all possible, find out who is going to be in your class, what their backgrounds are, and what they hope to get out of the training. Although not always possible, sending out a questionnaire or making a few telephone calls can prepare you for what to expect and what topics might be important to the participants. Talking with participants before the class is a great way to develop rapport and get a feel for what their concerns and interests might be.

- Explain to the participants your style of training and the approach you will adopt during the class. If they need to do a fair amount of reading or you will do a lot of lecturing, addressing these issues up front. Prepare them for what to expect. If the approach you are adopting is a little different from what they might be used to, then give your reasons for using that approach.

- As with applications training, the trainer should know considerably more about the software being taught than the class outline specifies. This is even more important in technical training—participants will expect you to be knowledgeable in all aspects of the software (even though this may be an unrealistic expectation). They expect you to be an expert.

- Widen your experience and knowledge of the product whenever you can. Gain as much practical, hands-on experience of the product as you can. Avoid being a "book" trainer who has all the correct answers but little on-the-job expertise. Learners understandably feel much more comfortable with trainers who actually use the software they teach.

- Completely understand each concept that you teach and be able to explain each concept in your own way. Your explanations and analogies should be clearer than the explanation in the manual. Avoid reading from the courseware and expecting learners to gain a full understanding from the printed text. Be sure you check for understanding before moving on.

- Have a diagram, an analogy, or even a story ready for all the concepts that are central to the understanding of the course material. Most learners relate much better to diagrams and analogies than they do to purely verbal explanations. Because of their background, technical trainers often end up talking through material rather than demonstrating with an example or a sketch. Technical training doesn't mean the presentation should be technical or dull.

- Be aware of using new vocabulary or terminology without first giving an explanation or a definition. Technical training is packed with terminology and acronyms, and it is easy to assume that people know what you're talking about. They are often reluctant to ask for a definition or clarification because they feel they should know it (and assume everyone else does). Just because they are experienced users doesn't mean they don't get intimidated.

- As with application training, be sure that your learners completely understand a concept before carrying out the associated procedures. Very often a trainer mixes the explanation of the procedural steps with the explanation of the concept. This method confuses the learner, who is trying to carry out a procedure without quite understanding why. Whenever possible, present the concept before the procedure.

- If you are teaching a class to prepare participants for a certification exam, consider emphasizing the importance of certain core concepts and ideas that might crop up in an examination. However, avoid saying things like, "They'll ask you this in the test..." or "One of the questions in the test will be..." It might help some people, but most organizations that create certification tests frown upon such a practice. Also, if you say something like this, and it doesn't appear on the test, you are doing yourself and your training organization a disservice.

- Manage the time of your class carefully. Most technical classes are information-intensive and getting sidetracked or moving too slowly can make it very difficult for the trainer to cover all the material. Covering all the material is a little more important in technical classes, where participants may be preparing for a certification test. The learners won't be too happy if they have to omit important material because of your lack of time management.

  Stay focused and on track, and, if necessary, assign some independent reading outside the class times. If you are asked questions that don't directly relate to the material you are covering, offer to address them at a break time, lunch time, or after class.

- Be prepared to not know the answers to some questions. Training at this level involves concepts and ideas that often spill over into many other areas of expertise. You should, of course, know what you're teaching, but you can't know everything about every related subject. Be honest when you don't know. Never try to avoid or fake it. The participants will respect you much more if you tell them you don't know but are willing find out. Be open to learning from others in the class. Because the level of computer expertise of learners in technical classes is generally high, you might often have the opportunity to learn from your learners.

- Although you need to cover material at a reasonable pace, try to allow for a certain amount of class discussion of the more challenging topics. Discussion and inquiry allow for a greater understanding of the material.

- If you are teaching an intensive class, avoid scheduling too many other appointments each evening. You might need the time for planning, reorganizing, or just relaxing. Technical classes can be extremely draining—your learners deserve a refreshed, stress-free trainer each day.

Trying something new

Breaking the pattern of your normal training routine is good for the creative juices. Trying new approaches and implementing new ideas can add interest and breathe life into your training. It takes a little more planning and effort, but the rewards in terms of improving your training and developing your skills are great. If you try a few of the suggestions in this chapter, you will discover new ways of training that you will want to adopt permanently. You might also come up with a few really creative training insights.

Introductions

Instead of your usual way of having the learners introduce themselves, try something different. If you usually go around the room asking them to introduce themselves, consider having them interview their neighbor and have their neighbor introduce them. Ask them to write their job title as well as their name on the name tent. On the inside of the name tent, ask them to write down what they would like to learn. Use a game or quiz. Use any new method you feel would work well, but don't use your default method—the one you usually do. Try this for a few weeks, adding something different for every class.

Courseware

If you tend to teach by following the courseware closely and teaching from it, try teaching a class where you don't follow it page by page. Create a teaching guide (see page 65) to give you structure, but teach the concepts and procedures in you own way. Include your usual exercises and page references, but teach your own version of the topics.

Exercises

Don't use the example exercises you usually use. Create some different ones, or ask your participants for examples that would be relevant to what they are doing at work. Try creating exercises that give less explicit directions and prompt them to figure out more for themselves (see page 148). Include some simple topics in the exercises that you haven't taught yet—suggest to the learners that they figure it out themselves.

Teaching style

Find out what your preferred learning (and therefore teaching) style is (see Chapter 16), and teach your next class with the minimum of that type of instruction. For example, if your mode is very visual, that is, you tend to draw lots of diagrams and pictures, then use more verbal or written explanations. If your tendency is verbal explanation or written instructions, try a much more visual approach. See what it feels like to get away from your own preferred style. You might find it is actually better for some of your participants when you change your style.

Break times

Try taking two five- or 10-minute breaks in the morning and afternoon, rather than one longer break. Try "learner-controlled" breaks—have them decide during the class when they would like a break. Consider having "homework" for the break time—challenge the participants to figure something out before they return from break.

Movement and posture

Give learners the option of doing something other than sitting upright in a seat for hours. Encourage them to lounge, put their feet up, stand (without blocking anyone's view), or walk around the room if the need arises. Let them do whatever they need to do to feel comfortable and relaxed when they're learning.

Anonymous suggestions

Provide everyone with a preprinted slip of paper with the following written on it:

- You're going too fast for me.

- You're going too slow for me.

- The speed is just fine.

- I'm getting very confused.

- I'm getting a little confused.

- I'm following everything.

- Suggestions for improvement:

Before you break for lunch, have the participants check the ones that apply, and possibly add a short suggestion for improving the class. Have them drop these off in a box as they leave. Read them before you start the afternoon session.

Names

Try to memorize the names of everyone in your next class (see page 29). Use their names twice as much as you usually do, for example, "Let's suppose Sheila needs to create a query to . . ." or, "So we're going to create Pete's Web homepage. . . ." When you do sample exercises, blend their names in with the examples. If you are doing a payroll example in a spreadsheet, for instance, use the names of everyone in the class as the employees.

Teach backwards

Decide what you consider to be the most difficult topic you have to teach in a class. Introduce any new vocabulary or basic concepts the learners absolutely have to know, and teach this topic first. Teach the easier topics later to the class.

Quick evaluation

At the end of each class, jot down on a piece of paper what seemed to work really well, and what did not work so well. Write down a few suggestions for teaching the class next time. Give yourself a grade. Place this inside your instructor's manual or teaching notes so that you see the note the next time you teach the same class. Compare your grades each time you teach the class.

Review "Jeopardy"
Rather than do your usual review of the work, set it up in "Jeopardy" format. "It creates a hypertext link . . .," "It helps you create Gantt charts. . . ." Award "incredible" prizes like Lifesavers, M&Ms, Twinkies, or other nutritious foodstuffs.

Change the seating
If your training session is longer than one day, consider rearranging the seating. Ask everyone to move to a new position somewhere else in the room. The learners might be a little reluctant to do this after getting "settled," but it can be reenergizing, providing new interest and different class interactions.

Instant rapport
Make an effort to speak with every participant before the class formally begins. Find out what they do, what they know, and what they hope to gain from the class. Let them get to know you before you formally start the class. When you do start, the atmosphere will be much more relaxed and informal. You will already have a considerable rapport.

Get out of the way
Spend 50% less training time at the front of the room, and 50% more time walking around. Spend 50% less time demonstrating, and 50% more time having them do exercises. Cut what you say by 50%, and increase what they say by 50%.

Topic voting
List all the topics and features to be covered on the board or flipchart at the beginning of the training. Ask the group to vote on which topics they feel are most important, prioritize them, and teach them in that order. Also, find out if there is a topic everyone would like to learn that is not covered in the class outline. Tell them you'll teach this extra one as a special treat if "they're good."

Figure it out
People love a challenge. After teaching a procedure that you are sure everyone has understood, try teaching a related procedure by challenging them. "Okay, let's see if you can figure out how to do. . . ."

State the objective and watch them teach themselves. Prompt and guide the slower learners if necessary.

Award ceremony
Have some preprinted award certificates made up. At the end of the class, have awards for things like "Most Persistent," "Most Humorous," "Best Notetaker," "Nicest Tie," "Most Punctual," "Worst Windows Color Scheme," etc. Make them light and humorous, and make a particular effort at recognizing the qualities of the slower, less able learners.

Taking a break

At the start of a class, the trainer sets the scene and lets the participants know when the breaks will be. If it is a one-day class, then perhaps there will be a break in the morning, a lunch break, and another break in the afternoon. The lunch break generally has to be a set time, such as noon to 1:00, so that people can plan their day. You probably don't have too much flexibility there. What you usually do have flexibility with is the morning and afternoon breaks.

Too often in computer training, trainers will determine the time for a break by looking at their watch. The trainer thinks, "It's about 10:30, we should take a break." Try picking your break times using different criteria. If possible, the breaks should complement what is happening in the class.

At the end of a section

A computer class is typically broken down into sections that address different ideas, concepts, and procedures. A good time to take a break is after the completion of such a section or procedure, When the trainer feels the concept or procedure has been understood and is clear to learners. Participants take the break feeling a sense of completion and satisfaction that they have comprehended the subject.

If the trainer determines it is time to take a break because it happens to be 10:30, it might cause unnecessary confusion or anxiety because there is a break in continuity. Let's suppose the class is three-quarters of the way through learning how to edit macros. The trainer looks at the time and says, "Well, it's 10:30 . . . let's take a break."

By taking a break at this part in the class, the trainer has put the concept or procedure on hold. There is no sense of completion or full understanding. Those learners who might have been a little confused in places take their confusion along with them at break time. On the other hand, the learners who were following along quite nicely have a sense of incompleteness. They were brought along so far, but never got to the destination. It's like being told a joke without getting to the punchline.

It's far better to choose to break a little later when the train of thought, concept, or explanation has reached its conclusion and has been understood by everyone. Whenever possible, avoid taking that break until the end of a logical section and until everyone in the room "gets it."

Setting up for after the break

Whenever possible, when you take a break, set up an exercise, challenge, or practice session for the participants to work on when they return. Even though you probably specified a time to return from the break, there will be participants who return earlier and will want to continue to learn. Having set up an exercise for them before the break allows them to start working whenever they feel inclined to during the break. It is good for some slow learners because it gives them an opportunity to "catch up" or spend a little more time practicing. You do not need to wait for everyone to return to their seats before resuming the class—you can wander around helping those present with the exercise until all the participants get back. This way, nobody is kept waiting and everyone can continue learning when they choose to do so.

Assisting slower learners

A break is an ideal opportunity to deal with any concerns or problems that participants might have, especially those who seem slow or confused in the class. You might be covering a topic or concept that isn't quite clear to one of the learners. Rather than spend an inordinate amount of time during the class to clarify the information, use the break to sit down with the individual and help get him or her up to speed. By helping the learner this way, you are not taking up valuable time in the class. In addition, you are taking the pressure off the individual by helping them one-on-one.

Sometimes when I am teaching a class and someone is confused and rapidly becoming frustrated, I decide to take a break and clear up the confusion. By doing this, I prevent the learner's self-esteem from sliding downhill and get them back on track quickly.

Dealing with difficult learners

Another good time for a break is when you are confronted with a difficult learner. The class is going along quite smoothly, but you have a character in the class who begins to test your patience and is disrupting the class. It could be anything from making calls on a mobile phone to making inappropriate comments. The first step, of course, is to try to deal with the situation within the class. When this is not possible, the best thing to do is to take a break and address the issue with that individual. It is much more effective to take a break and immediately address a problem than to try and work your way around it during the class.

Avoiding brain overload

There will be occasions when you are teaching some quite technical or conceptually difficult topics, and you'll look around the room and observe a sea of vacant faces. Information overload has set in. You realize you have been giving them too much information, too fast, and you are beginning to lose them. This can be a good time for a break.

Even the shortest break will reenergize the brain, improve the level of attention and allow the new information to be digested. Choose your break times by observing what the participants are doing and what their needs are. Read your learners so that you can introduce breaks at appropriate times. Avoid taking breaks just because it's 10:30 or because someone just paged you.

Getting them back from breaks

One of the most important parts of a computer training class is the unassisted exercise, the time when learners get to practice what they have learned. Sometimes the trainer sets an exercise and lets the participants know that after they have finished, they will be taking a break. In a group where there is a wide range of ability levels, this can become embarrassing for a slower learner. Other people finish the exercise, get up and go for a cup of coffee, and the slower learner is still sitting there struggling.

A much better way is to introduce the exercises before the break, and tell participants that they can start on them after the break. The slow learners can then take a short break with everyone else, and if they want to, return earlier to get a head start on the work. This is much less intimidating for them. The more experienced, more confident user, meanwhile, can choose to start the exercise a little later without missing anything.

Another reason for doing this is so that everyone knows exactly what to do when they return from break. Someone who is a little late coming back from break will jut miss some time on the exercise rather than miss out on something new you might be teaching.

Other suggestions

A method that works very well for getting your group back on time is to enlist the help of one of the participants. Appoint one of the group to be responsible for making sure everyone is back on time. You'll find that people actually enjoy being given such a responsibility; it brings a measure of fun to the task and it removes the burden from you. Choose a different person at each break.

Another method that works well is to tell participants just before you break that the first three members back from break will receive a "punctuality prize." Tell them it will be either an expenses-paid trip to Hawaii or something almost as exciting. Present the first three with the "exciting" prize—a cheat sheet, quick reference, shareware disk, candy bar, key ring, pen, etc. A prize that helps someone learn, is useful, or rots the teeth usually works well. Watch out, though, for those who might want to sue you for misleading advertising!

Ice-breakers

Sometimes it's tense, formal, and quiet at the beginning of a training session. An ice-breaker or warm-up exercise reduces tension, gets people involved, opens up communication, and introduces some fun before you get down to business. Strive to create some original ones of your own rather than using just the old standards. Try to make them interesting, humorous, and interactive, but avoid putting anyone on the spot or making anyone feel uncomfortable.

Ice-breakers can be a wonderful way of starting your training and will help develop an immediate rapport. The following sections provide a few examples.

Interview your neighbor

Pair up the class and have each person interview his or her neighbor to find out three interesting things this person has done—one of which is a lie. Each person has to guess which of the three things about the other person is not true. When they are done, ask them to share any surprises with the rest of the class. It's usually quite hilarious, and you will be amazed what a weird and wonderful group you are about to teach!

Name tents

As well as having them put their name on the name tents, ask participants to open up the card and on the inside finish the following sentences:

- Right now I would rather be . . .

- I hope this class won't be . . .

- I'd really like to learn . . .

After they have done this or later on during the class, ask if any of the learners would like to share what they have written. It's entertaining and the responses you get will help you teach the class.

Cartoon

Try putting up a humorous computer-related cartoon on the overhead before the class starts. Try to find one that reflects the way participants might be feeling about the class.

Finding matches

Have everyone write down the names of the other class members who:

- Have the same taste in food as they do

- Have the same color eyes

- Have had the same problem with their software

After participants walk around the room to do this and report on their findings, the atmosphere in the room is totally different. There is a rapport, a sense of fun, and an anticipation. This is also a very valuable ice-breaker for getting to know people's names.

What's different?

Have people get into pairs and then ask them to stand with their back to their neighbor and change four things about their appearance. One of these four changes has to be very silly. Ask them to turn back around and try to figure out everything that's different. When they're done, they get to sit down. There will not be a person in the room without a broad smile on their face. You will immediately get to see who the bold extroverts are, and who are the more conservative participants.

Brown-bag training

Brown-bag training is a computer-training session that is scheduled for short time periods, usually at a lunch. This type of training helps keep users up to speed on new features, functions, and upgrades without the expense or inconvenience of a full-blown training class. Typically, the participants sit and eat lunch and learn something new from a fellow worker or company trainer.

Everyone who wishes to learn more about new software or some new tips and tricks about existing systems can attend and add to their knowledge. Brown-bag training is brief, informal, and usually focuses on only one or two topics. It is a great way of providing a little extra computer training in an organization. It is in-house, short (and therefore easy to maintain attention), does not entail major training expenditure, doesn't necessitate any lost working time, and yet can provide some very valuable software tips and techniques.

Specializing your skills

There was a time when a computer trainer could teach and have an in-depth knowledge of most of the standard end-user software. Those days are gone. In order to stay current with all the software out there and know it well, you would have to go without sleep and spend your whole life in front of a monitor. The rate at which software is being produced and the rate at which companies need to train and retrain is increasing dramatically. It's impossible to keep up with everything—you can't know it all.

So rather than become overwhelmed and spread yourself thin, specialize. Pick a few software packages (that are not going out of style!)

and focus on those. Become an expert in a few programs rather than trying to learn everything under the sun. The trend is towards offering more technical and network training these days, so you might consider moving into those areas.

Suggestions for training managers

The relationship between a training manager and the classroom computer trainer is precious. This is especially true for training companies that use contract trainers. The quality of this relationship can be the difference between delivering excellent training and mediocre training. Here are some suggestions for training managers to make the most of this relationship.

- Get to know your trainers well. Meet with them whenever you can.

- Have an "open-door" policy so that your trainers feel comfortable expressing any of their training concerns to you.

- Visit trainers in the trenches. Stop by at the beginning, end, or during a class. Observe them in action.

- Thank your trainers for their contributions on a regular basis.

- Read all the instructor evaluations as well as the student evaluations, and follow up with the trainer promptly when necessary.

- Consider teaching a class once in a while. Get to see things from the trainer's perspective.

- Make sure training policies and procedures are clear to every trainer. Don't let a problem arise before making these clear.

- Get the trainers' input before you decide on new courseware, forms, procedures, or equipment. The trainers will be the ones actually using them, so they need to have a say.

- Get all the trainers together on a regular basis for an informal mixer.

- Do not get too involved in "managing" training and forget your product—quality training.

- Offer trainers incentives to learn new software and develop themselves professionally. Encourage and support trainer certification.

- Attend training and learning conferences. Find out what other organizations are doing.

- Offer "train-the-trainer" classes for your instructors.

Trainer evaluations

An evaluation that is sometimes overlooked is the trainer's evaluation of the class. When a training manager is reading through the class evaluations, it is also important to read what the instructor thought about the class. Without this, the person attempting to evaluate the class has incomplete information. Comments on a few evaluations mentioning that the trainer went too fast could be seen in a different perspective when the trainer evaluation notes that several participants did not have the prerequisites for the class. Comments about how the class went, any challenges, suggestions, or complaints, and any feedback regarding the software and hardware are all extremely valuable to anyone concerned with delivering quality training.

The instructor evaluation might include questions like these:

- Overall, how do you feel the class went?

- What worked well in the class?

- What didn't work so well?

- Please comment if you had any problems with:
  ~ Classroom setup or courseware
  ~ Hardware or software

- Do you have any suggestions for improving the class?

Each section should have plenty of room for comments.

Even with the simplest evaluation, the message to the classroom trainer is that his or her opinions are valued. After a challenging class, the instructor has an outlet for expressing any needs and concerns. This ultimately serves the training manager as well as the instructor.

Without voicing these concerns in some way, a frustrated trainer is likely to feel unsupported and unappreciated.

Make absolutely sure to follow up on any problems noted in the evaluations. There is nothing more irksome to a trainer than to spend time providing feedback only to find they go unread. An immediate follow-up, on the other hand, shows the respondent that his or her comments were read and appreciated, and will be addressed. It is an excellent way of maintaining a good working relationship with your trainers and your trainees.

Giving your opinion

People often view the computer trainer as an authority on software and hardware. They are inclined to ask for your advice and opinions on certain programs or computer systems. This is a time for you to be as objective as you possibly can. Most trainers have particular favorites when it comes to a particular type of software or a hardware manufacturer. They feel that some are far superior than others.

When someone in a class asks which is the best word processor or spreadsheet, you need to answer carefully and appropriately, not like a trainer I knew who once said something like, "Oh, WordPerfect is a piece of junk." One of the participants then asked why the training organization was a WordPerfect Authorized Training Center.

It's not a good idea to share all your opinions about software you don't like with your class. You can't effectively compare one program to another unless you are intimate with them both. A trainer who uses one word processor more than any other is not qualified to objectively compare word processors. Suggesting a particular product is poorer quality or "really buggy" is obviously inappropriate. Be honest, but don't be scathing.

Suppose someone asks you a question like, "What's better: WordPerfect or Word?" If you have always preferred Word, a tactful answer might be, "Well, I don't know as much about WordPerfect as I do Word, so I'm not really in a position to give a good comparison. I personally like to use Word. I find it a great program, but both of them have many of the same features—it's really just a question of personal preference."

Being tactful and objective applies to hardware also. Suppose someone asks you what you think of XYZ computers and you tell them they are best used as doorstops. Several people in the room might have XYZ computers, and they won't be too happy. "Are these any good?" says a participant, pointing to one of the training center computers. Measure carefully what you say in response.

Ending classes early

There is often a tendency for trainers to want to end classes earlier than scheduled. Participants are usually excited about the prospect of "getting out early," and it is easy for the trainer to make this happen. Trainers end classes early for several reasons:

1 All of the class topics have been covered.

2 Participants say they have to leave early.

3 Everyone wants to get a head start on the freeway traffic.

4 The trainer wants to leave early.

These are rarely good reasons for finishing the class earlier. For one thing, each class is usually paid for by a company, department, or individual based on a particular number of hours specified as part of the contract. They paid for an eight-hour class, but they get your services for only seven hours—and the individual paying the bill might not even know it. This is not the best way of promoting yourself as a professional trainer. Let's address the reasons trainers give for finishing early.

All the class topics have been covered
If all the topics or tasks have been covered, the extra hour or half-hour can be a perfect opportunity to review the work or perhaps give some extra information that is not in your outline. I often use this time for a review quiz or game—get all the participants involved in asking and answering questions about the work that was covered. Not only is this useful to clarify the work, but it also has them leave the room on a high note—most people love to have their knowledge tested in a team environment.

Participants say they have to leave early

Sometimes a participant will let you know sometime in the class (often toward the end!) that he or she needs to leave early. This might be for a bona fide reason, but sometimes it is just so that person can go home earlier. You obviously cannot prevent anyone from leaving, but strongly encourage participants to stay for the whole class. When individuals start to leave your class early at the end of the day, it can take the life and energy from the room. It's distracting for the trainer, and the participants remaining often feel less enthusiasm for learning in a half-empty room. Ask before you start the class whether anyone needs to leave early. When you do this, you will generally find there is less of a tendency for people coming up to you at afternoon break whispering, "Actually, I have to leave a bit earlier, you see my cat . . ."

Everyone wants to get a head start on the freeway traffic

It might be more convenient for everyone, including the trainer, to leave an hour earlier to avoid the traffic or the rush. The participants will all be sitting there with their hands together appealing to you to "let them out" earlier, just like you used to do in school. Once again, in most cases, avoid this. In certain circumstances, it might be valid, but when the organization or individual footing the training bill is unaware of it, this practice is not altogether professional.

The trainer wants to leave early

Okay, let's be honest. There's often a temptation to try to get all the work done in the class early so that you can be on your merry way. You might subtly manipulate the class so that it's 3:30 and you've covered everything. How convenient! "Well, I've covered everything. We can either review the work or . . . go home early. What do you want to do?" We all know which one the participants choose. It works out perfectly: you get to leave early and you get to blame them for the decision should there be any repercussions!

Tempting as this might be, avoid organizing the class schedule to fit your agenda. When you're thinking of what is convenient for you, you are being a less effective trainer. Never ask the participants whether they want to leave early—they will always say yes. As I have mentioned before, if you want to become an exceptional trainer, your focus and commitment should be always on the learners and their learning. Your agenda should always be secondary.

If you are ever in doubt as to whether you should end your class ear-lier (or anything else for that matter) try this. Imagine you are a learner in your own class and you paid full price for the training out of your own pocket. You want to learn as much as you can about the software, to get the most from the class. Would you feel you were get-ting your money's worth if your class ended early? If the answer is no, avoid doing it.

10

The future

"We should all be concerned about the future because we will have to spend the rest of our lives there."
— **C. F. Kettering**

No one can accurately predict the future of a technology or a profession, but we can look at some social, business, and technological trends and see in what direction they are pointing. Areas that will affect computer training and learning in the years to come include

- Technology

- Economics

- The nature of "work"

Technology

Technology is unstoppable. Advances in hardware and software make new learning technologies possible. The sophistication of systems makes new modes of learning available to users. CBT, multimedia, video teleconferencing, Internet learning, and other avenues of computer learning continue to grow and mature, and become more accessible.

The idea of having a portable computer the size of a notebook was unthinkable 10 years ago. They are now an accepted part of our lives. In 10 years' time, we will have learning technologies that are equally unimaginable today. As electronic technology has developed, it has increasingly put access to information in the hands of the end-user.

Technology encourages the trend of self-directed learning by providing the end-user with opportunities to learn in nontraditional ways.

In addition to providing new ways of delivering learning, technological advances create a continual need for training and retraining. The need for computer trainers (or more accurately, learning facilitators) will continue to expand and grow in the future.

Economics

Competition is becoming fiercer. Organizations are reinventing, re-engineering, and restructuring in an attempt to improve efficiency and cut costs. Sending workers to computer training is very expensive. Organizations are looking at cheaper and more efficient ways of training their employees. For many companies, instructor-led classroom training is not the best solution to their training needs. They are looking to other technologies to provide cheaper, faster, and more effective methods. These needs are becoming a driving force behind new approaches and new technologies for learning. When any type of resource is scarce, humanity usually experiences a period of creativity and innovation. This might well be the case in computer training and support.

The nature of work

Increasingly, in this information age, work is becoming "virtual." Work is less often physical activity and more often collecting, managing, and analyzing information. The work being done is also not static. People are not just doing the old work with more and more sophisticated software tools, they are creating new types of work with new tools. The character of work is changing, as well as the tools to carry out the work. Added to this is the challenge of the ever-increasing speed of change in the work people do.

The result of this is that learning, rather than being an activity separated from work, is now becoming an integral part of it. In some cases, it is the work. The division between work and learning is becoming less defined. More and more, people are in a constant process of learning and relearning, and the successful businesses are those that can learn continuously and fast. This process of learning and change is also effecting life outside of work; it is not separate from it.

In short, learning and work are becoming one and the same. For the trainer, this means that computer learning is ceasing to be a separate activity from working and is becoming an integral part of it. Trainers and training companies of the future will need to satisfy the need for fast, continuous, and user-directed learning.

Under the influence of improving technologies, increasing competition, and changes in the nature of work, computer training is changing. In the future, instructor-led classroom training will be complemented, and in some cases replaced, by sophisticated learning technologies such as

- CBT and interactive multimedia

- Electronic performance-support systems

- Web-based training

- Interactive video teleconferencing

Most of these technologies are still in their early stages with regard to training, but they will soon become effective and affordable methods of learning.

Other changes you might see in the future include these:

- More research on the effects of training, performance, and return on training investment

- More appropriate use of technology-delivered instruction

- More and more learning taking place outside the classroom

- Business success being measured by the ability to learn faster

- More learning and more working taking place at home

- A greater variety of learning media and ways to learn

- More user-directed and user-controlled learning

- Shorter, more customized, and more modular learning

- Organizations integrating their training, support, and performance functions

- More cross-vendor support for training solutions

- Cheaper alternatives to classroom training

- EPSS and expert systems replacing training, support, and help desks

- More online resources available to learners

Distance learning

Training and education are playing an increasingly important role in enabling organizations to stay vital and competitive. Training that workers receive today becomes obsolete within two to five years. Businesses are finding that they need to provide more training for their workforce with less financial resources.

Distance learning is a possible solution to these needs and constraints. Distance learning is any method of delivering training or support interactively to one or more locations separated by proximity or time. It includes, but is not limited to, the following:

- E-mail

- Bulletin board systems (BBSs)

- Internet access (such as Web-based training and Microsoft Online Institute)

- Remote CBT and multimedia

- Audio and video teleconferencing

Such methods are being considered as a viable alternative to traditional training for several reasons:

- Training increasingly needs to be "just-in-time."

- Competition is fiercer, and a successful organization is one that can learn continuously and fast.

- Technology can provide viable alternatives to traditional learning.

- There is a need to serve lifelong learning requirements for organizations and individuals.

- Distance learning can be more cost-effective than traditional training methods.

- There is a need for training to be consistent throughout an organization.

- Distance learning can be less disruptive than traditional training.

- Distance learning can be more flexible and more easily adapted.

- Distance learning can provide access to instructional resources that might otherwise be unavailable.

One organization researched the cost and effectiveness of providing instructor-led training and compared it to a distance-learning approach using interactive video training. In the distance-learning approach, the trainer was at a remote location providing instruction through two-way video links, where learners could use the computers and interact with the trainer in real-time. For training a group of 40 learners, they found a savings on the order of 10 to one. In other words, distance learning cost them ten times less than the typical instructor-led approach. Tests on retention and understanding compared favorably with the instructor-led training, and most learners found it to be an effective alternative.

Because of results like these and the need for cost-effective solutions to workforce training, distance learning will become more widespread in the years to come. Whether it is via the Internet, an organization's network, or satellite video links, training will be delivered remotely to the learner's workplace when it is needed. For large corporations, this will increasingly complement traditional, instructor-led training.

There are, of course, drawbacks. One of them is the "low-touch" nature inherent in learning at a distance. A subtle, secondary-level benefit of instructor-led training is the social content of the course. Many learners gain a significant amount of comfort, socialization, encouragement, and sense of belonging from interacting with other people in the room. This socializing aspect of traditional classroom training is often overlooked. Quite often, the interaction with the instructor and other participants gives the learner an experience with a quality that is absent in most distance learning. This should be a serious consideration when designing new approaches to learning. Distance learning and other types of technology-aided learning will be unsuccessful in the future unless they have enough "high-touch" features built into them.

Web-based learning

Delivery of information via the Internet is in its infancy. Right now, the Internet can deliver textual information and still graphic images efficiently, but sound, video, and real-time interactivity have a long way to go. One of the limiting factors is the bandwidth available through the standard telephone lines. Learning is already being delivered on the Worldwide Web to a limited extent, but as ISDN (Integrated Services Digital Network) lines become more widely used, along with cable and optic fiber systems, the suitability of the Web for true interactive learning will improve dramatically.

Learning on the Web has many advantages:

- It can provide learning anytime and anywhere. Internet access is growing exponentially both at work and at home. When it becomes as common as cable TV, people will be able to choose when and where to learn. Learning could take place at home, at work, in the airport, or sitting in a cafe.

- It can access a global library of resources. Because the whole world will be using the same delivery method for information, any learning program can be linked to a vast array of worldwide information resources.

- It can be used to track performance. It will be easier for a learning organization to track progress and performance. The standardization of the delivery channel will allow tracking and performance testing to be much more easily realized.

- Training can easily be customized and updated. Unlike CD-ROM-based training, training delivered via the Web can be very quickly and easily customized and updated. Training updates on new versions of software can be immediately available. Training programs can be edited and customized for an organization in seconds.

- It's a popular and exciting medium to use. When an informational medium is popular and fun to use, its potential for providing learning (and entertainment) increases significantly. Learning becomes easier and more engaging when it is multisensory and interactive.

Before long, a person will be able to browse computer learning companies on the Web, choose an appropriate course, register and pay online with "cyber-cash," and be ready to start the interactive learning experience. The learning program will include graphics, sound, high-quality video, and lots of interactivity, and adapt itself to the person's preferred learning style.

There might be pre- and post-tests embedded in the learning so that learners can get an objective measurement of their progress and skills. In large organizations, people at widespread locations will be able to receive the same training at the same time at their desks, while asking the trainer questions via the interactive video on their computers.

These types of applications are already being developed, along with enabling technologies such as video servers, video compression, real-time voice converters, 3D modeling, and intelligent Web browsers. When the technology for online interactivity matures, not only will the Web be a source for learning, it might end up being the source for the software itself. Software applications might begin to migrate from hard-drive space to a location in cyberspace. For more information, see "Online learning" in chapter 15.

11

Managing stress in computer training

◆◆◆

"Stress is like the body's warning light. It lets you know
something needs to be changed or serviced."
— **Paul Clothier**

Stress is what happens when perceived threats chronically activate
the body's "fight or flight" response. Another, not so precise definition
of stress is "the confusion created when one's mind overrides the
body's desire to choke the living daylights out of some jerk who desperately deserves it."

Stress is useful up to a point. A little of it can give you an edge on
performance and keep you on your toes. When it becomes persistent,
however, it has debilitating effects. When you are stressed, you cannot communicate as effectively; you can get irritable, tense, and defensive. Stress affects your physical as well as your mental well-being.
If you have been a computer trainer for at least a few years, you have
experienced some of the stress it brings and perhaps some of the
symptoms of "burnout."

The causes and symptoms of stress

There are many factors that contribute to stress in computer training. They include teaching too much, being unprepared, not managing time well, confronting challenging learners, lack of support, lack of resources, inability to implement new ideas—the list is long. Some of these are organizational issues and must be addressed with peers, supervisors, or management. They are not directly under the control of the trainer. However, there are some causes of stress that are under the control of the trainer and that can be eliminated or at least reduced.

Before getting into any of the specifics, I must make one thing very clear, and it is vitally important to understand and accept this before looking at any "solutions" to stress reduction. Stress is a personal reaction to a specific set of circumstances. A situation that causes stress in one person might have a totally different effect on another. One trainer might have an adverse reaction to loud and assertive people and get very stressed, while another might have no problem whatsoever relating to such a person. Blowing an overhead bulb might be a very minor irritation for one trainer, and yet cause another to explode. A stressful situation is really a reflection of the attitudes and perceptions of the trainer, not the situation itself. Likewise, a problem is only a problem because you have defined it as such. Actually, it's just something that happened; your reaction to it determines whether it is a problem or not. When you really begin to appreciate this, you'll find it much easier to deal with stress. It's important to realize that the causes are internal, not external.

Sometimes people don't realize they are stressed. It just seems like they're having lots of bad hair days, are grouchy and tired all the time. If some or all of the items on this list describe how you feel, you are probably experiencing stress:

- Lack of enthusiasm and interest

- Loss of sense of humor

- Lack of patience with others

- Focusing on failures rather than successes

- Tiredness and irritability

- Lower back pain or tension in the shoulders and neck

- Inability to relax

Managing the training

There are two areas to look at to reduce stress levels: your training and yourself. You can manage your training environment so that there is less opportunity for situations to cause stress. You can also manage what you do and how you relate to the environment.

Know your training environment

You don't want to be discovering problems or finding your way around your training environment during a class. You won't instill much confidence in your learners if you are unfamiliar with the equipment, the room, or the building. This might not be a problem if you are training in the same location all the time, but if your training takes you to different sites, familiarity with the room, equipment, and supplies is critical.

If you are going to train in a new environment, become familiar with it before the class. Either get acquainted with it a week or a few days before the training, or if this is not possible, arrive at least an hour early at the new training site. Never attempt to train at a new location by only allowing yourself 15 minutes to get set up. This would be like requesting extra portions of stress in your life. Get there early so you can get comfortable with the equipment, the supplies, and the layout.

Turn on all the computers. Are they all working? Are they networked? Do you need to know any logins or passwords? Run the software you are going to be using. Is everything working? Are all the systems consistent? Are all the software defaults set? Have the exercise files been installed? What directories do you have access to? Do you have access to a printer? Is the correct printer driver installed?

Check out the teaching aids. Do you have a whiteboard or a flipchart? Enough marker pens? Enough flipchart paper? Set up the overhead or display. Ensure that it is working and focused. Where are the spare bulbs if one blows? Familiarize yourself with its controls. Where are the light switches? Can the lights be dimmed?

Can you easily move around the room? Can you move from the trainer's station to the overhead screen easily? Is anything blocking you from moving around the room to give assistance to each learner?

Find out where the bathrooms are located. Where can the learners get coffee? If the learners will also be new to the training site, where can they get lunch? Where are the nearest telephones that participants can use?

When the learners arrive in your classroom and you have a comfort level with that environment, you will get off to a good start. When participants are confronted with a trainer who seems unfamiliar and unsure of the equipment and environment, it will not be a very inspiring start to their training day. They are expecting you to teach them advanced macro programming, and you can't even focus the overhead!

Be prepared

It is not unusual for computer trainers to agree to teach an unfamiliar software package with only a week in which to learn it. In some cases, it's the next day. You might reason, "I'll study it tonight—I should be okay." Avoid doing this unless you have enough time to fully prepare the class. Teaching a new piece of software is not just a case of learning it. It is vitally important that you prepare for your new classes. The first time you see the courseware manual and work through the practice exercises shouldn't be when you're in front of a room full of learners.

A good computer training class needs preparation. The courseware needs to be studied and worked through before the class. Any exercises that the learners are expected to attempt, the trainer should complete beforehand. Are there any parts of the courseware or the exercises that require special guidance? What are the key points? Do the exercises seem clear or might some confuse the learner? Which sections will you include or omit? Do you have extra exercises for the faster learners?

Preparation is critical. Lack of preparation increases stress. Being unsure, fumbling, discovering errors, or not knowing can make for a very stressful day. When you walk into the training room, you need to know the software, the courseware, and the exercises, and have a clear outline of how the class will be structured. If it means staying up until midnight to make sure that your preparation is complete, then so be it. You will be glad of it the next day.

Manage your time better

Time runs our lives. We fill every second with activity. We rush to work, and we rush home. We schedule meetings at lunchtime when we should be eating. We are on the telephone checking voice-mail at break times when we should be relaxing with a cup of coffee. There doesn't seem enough time to get everything done. When your life and training day is like this, it is no wonder you feel a little stressed. In order to relieve some of this, you need to manage time a little differently and set different priorities.

You wouldn't think of scheduling yourself to teach a class at the same time you are teaching another class. You wouldn't schedule a meeting that conflicts with another meeting. However, when it comes to "free" time, it's always up for grabs. You might schedule meetings, phone calls, and conversations just before a class, at break times, or at lunch, trying to squeeze in what you can, where you can.

You might think you're getting more done this way, but you will probably end up being less effective, less energized, stressed, and impatient. To be effective as a trainer, or anything else for that matter, strive for balance. Everyone needs some times, however short, in which to relax and recuperate. Give these times a higher priority on your "to-do" list. Schedule times during your day where you are not running around doing things.

Consider getting to a class earlier than usual and having 15 minutes to relax with a cup of tea or coffee. Don't do anything except sit and sip. For most of people, it's not as easy as it sounds. When you have a morning break, don't rush to the nearest telephone to return calls or check your voice-mail. Take a break with your participants. Talk with them for 10 minutes. Manage your lunch break so you can actually eat and digest your food uninterrupted.

Something else you can do in managing your time is to write appointments and "to-dos" down. Make sure everything you need to attend or do—classes, meetings, appointments, etc.—are written down. Writing things down frees your mind from concerns about what you need to be doing. I do this with problems as well—I get them out of my head and onto paper so that I can confront them a little more objectively and get some clarity. It works! Instead of walking around worrying about what needs to be done, you just follow your schedule.

Don't overbook yourself when you schedule appointments. Don't schedule your appointments so close together that you are rushing around. Leave enough time between them so that you have time to regroup. Learn to say no, or reschedule an appointment if you can't make it without rushing. Allow yourself more time. At first it will seem as if you are going to get less done in your day, but the clarity, calm, and creativity that result will allow you to be more productive and much less stressed.

Keep on track

A certain amount of flexibility is important in computer training, but just as important is the ability to keep on track and stay focused. When people ask questions, a trainer will often digress from the class outline to give an answer. This is appropriate if it helps clarify an issue or an idea for someone, but it is also important to get back on track as soon as possible.

Getting sidetracked by questions or by your own enthusiasm often prevents the necessary material being covered in the given time. When this happens, it becomes a source of concern and anxiety for you. Be flexible, but stay focused on your outline. When you answer questions or digress into some related areas, get right back on track. Don't spend inordinate amounts of time answering questions that move the class in a different direction. Address questions, but get right back to the concepts or procedures you are teaching. If people seem to be taking up too much time asking unrelated questions, tell them that you will help them at a break or after the class. Try saying things like, "Let me cover that with you at the end if we have time," or, "I don't want to get into detail about that right now, but let me show you the steps at break." Don't feel the need to answer every question at the time it is asked. If it is not relevant to the work at hand, or it is off-track, don't get into it during the class.

When you're training—just train!

When you lose yourself in an activity and are completely focused on what you are doing, you are at your most effective. You become more creative, relaxed, and focused, and temporarily forget any anxieties or concerns. When you are not focused, when there is a background conversation going on in your head about what you should do today, what you didn't do yesterday, what calls you need to make, and so on, effectiveness is reduced. One of the factors that contribute to stress is not being able to give your full attention to any one thing, allowing other concerns, fears, and anxieties cloud your thoughts.

This often happens while training. Part of your mind is thinking about returning telephone calls, addressing that problem with a coworker, getting your car fixed, calling the dentist, or planning dinner. When you are conscious of other concerns in your training, you are not fully engaged with the learners, and your training is less effective.

When you shut the door to your training room, shut the rest of your life out. Leave all those concerns outside the room. You won't be able to do anything with them while you're training anyway, so set them aside. When you are in the training room, just train. Completely focus on what you are doing, and lose yourself in your training. Your concerns, anxieties, and problems will still be there after the class. You can deal with them then.

Managing you

In addition to managing your training environment, there are several ways to manage yourself to reduce stress.

Be yourself

One of the causes of stress in life is the effort people exert trying to portray themselves in a favorable light. It might seem like you spend half your life trying to look good and the other half trying not to look bad. In computer training, especially, it's natural to do all you can to look like you know what you're talking about and avoid making any embarrassing mistakes. You hope that the learners think you are good at what you do. You hope they like you.

The ironic thing is that when you concentrate on portraying yourself in a favorable light, you are not yourself, and not relaxed. Rather than being effective and building rapport, you are doing just the opposite. Being yourself can alleviate a lot of stress in training. When you expend energy maintaining a certain "trainer" persona that isn't the real you, it takes effort and ends up adding to your stress level. Being yourself (your best self) and letting people see the real you when you're teaching is one of the best investments you can make in your training and in yourself.

Relate to others

When you are stressed, there is a tendency to withdraw and avoid interactions with others. You take lunch alone. The bathroom seems like a good place to hang out. Your training is over and you rush to grab your things and leave. You don't feel like being part of the group or community—you'd rather do your own thing.

Rather than help you reduce your stress level, this can often end up adding to it. You isolate yourself and don't communicate what you are thinking or feeling. It takes more effort to communicate than not when you are feeling stressed, but the effort is always worth it. Have a cup of tea or coffee with your friends or colleagues, join them at lunch, spend some time with them. Share some of the challenges you are facing or frustrations you are experiencing. It doesn't have to be whining; just talk about some of your concerns. Just expressing your feelings lightens the load and can be stress-reducing. Try to let others in—don't shut them out.

Maintain a balance

Computer trainers spend a large proportion of their week either in front of a class or in front of a computer. When learning new software or planning classes, most trainers end up working on their computers at home. They go to work, train, go home, and start working again. This can be okay for a while, but when it gets to become a habit, the trainer's life can become a little unbalanced. Instead of working and then relaxing, exercising, and socializing, the trainer constantly works. People, family, relaxation, diet, exercise, and having some fun become secondary to sitting in front of the computer. The excitement, challenge, and joy of life start to fade.

When you arrange for a little more balance in life, you become more productive, more creative, and experience a lot less stress. You might have a deadline to work with, but some time spent away from the screen relaxing, exercising, or doing what you want to do is an investment in your productivity and effectiveness. Two hours working with enthusiasm, creativity, and a relaxed frame of mind is more productive than four hours working when you are feeling tired, stressed, and overworked. Temper your workload with relaxation or a change of focus. Try not to let your work overpower everything else in your life.

Diet and exercise

When people are stressed, they tend not to take so much care of themselves. Diet and exercise programs suffer, making the effects of stress even more damaging. A balanced diet is as important as a balanced lifestyle. Make time to eat well. Never train on an empty stomach. Avoid missing lunch to get some more work done or grabbing those not-so-nutritious fast foods on the run. When the body is dealing with stress it needs a nutritious, well-balanced diet.

When you exercise, you produce endorphins in the body that act to counteract the effects of stress and give a sense of well-being. As well as being good for the body, exercise is good for the mind. After an intense day of training, you probably feel tired and exhausted, and the thought of going to the gym, jogging, swimming, or walking doesn't always sound too attractive. This tiredness is usually more mental than it is physical—teaching a class all day can be emotionally draining. Exercise is a great remedy for this. It reduces the effects of stress in your body, provides a greater sense of wellness, and is reenergizing.

Take a walk

Taking a walk can be a great way to help alleviate a little stress. It provides a change of scenery, a change of focus, and is an opportunity to take a few deep breaths. When things start to become a little overwhelming and the tension is building, consider setting aside 10 minutes to go for a walk, preferably outside. Simply spend 10 minutes walking around taking a few deep breaths. Get out of the training room or office and experience a different environment for a while. Don't think about work or problems—just walk, breathe deeply, and try to relax.

Self-talk

Another useful approach to stress at work is to engage in a little encouraging and nurturing self-talk. A great way to do this is to imagine you are talking with one of your very good friends or a loved one. Imagine explaining to them how you are feeling, what your frustrations are, and what is causing stress in your life. Imagine what they would say to you. The encouragement, advice, support, and understanding they would provide would be very different from the conversations you have with yourself.

Most of your familiar self-talk is about what you didn't do, what you should have done, why you aren't as good as you could be, and so on. Put those aside and try to be to yourself what your supportive friends and family would be to you. They wouldn't say, "Yeah, you really did teach a lousy class. Imagine making such mistakes! Perhaps you should get out of computer training." They would be understanding, sympathetic, encouraging, positive, and love you regardless. Try being more of a supportive, nurturing best friend to yourself. When you feel the negative feelings and the stress creeping in, give yourself a little encouraging self-talk.

Plan some quiet time

Set aside 20 minutes a day to sit and relax, unwind, or meditate. Schedule some quiet time into your busy schedule. Find some place where you will not be disturbed, sit still, and try to clear your mind. Don't try to do anything except sit, breathe, and let go. Closing your eyes helps. A good technique to practice is to think about relaxing your whole body, letting go of the tension in every muscle. Start at your feet and concentrate on having every muscle in your feet relax and let go. Then move to your legs, abdomen, and so on until you end up at your scalp—all the time concentrating on relaxing the muscles. Try to do this every day or whenever you feel a little strained.

And don't give me the excuse that you haven't got the time in your busy schedule to do this. Saying you can't find time to do this is like saying that you don't have enough time to stop for gas because you are driving so much. This quiet time provides the fuel for your busy schedule.

Some extra stress-busting tips

Here are a few more tips to keep stress at bay:

- *Schedule your relaxation.* Be as consistent and reliable about scheduling your own relaxation and recreation as you are about scheduling your work activities. You'll get more done in the long run and have more creative energy. Don't let R-and-R be at the bottom of your priority list.

- *Be a kid.* Children rarely experience the type of stress that adults do. They do lots of fun things, are spontaneous, laugh a lot, express their emotions freely, are enthusiastic, dream, and totally focus on what they are doing in the moment. Incorporate a few more child-like qualities into your life and your training.

- *Focus on your achievements.* Most of us constantly focus on what we haven't done, haven't got, should have done, and could have got, instead of what we have achieved. After a day of training, run through the accomplishments and successes of your day. Celebrate the things you did well.

- *Laugh.* Children, on average, laugh about 500 times a day. The average adult laughs about 10 times a day. Laughter floods your body with endorphins, the body's natural pain reliever and learning drug. Bring laughter into your work and your training.

- *Personalize your work area.* Redesign your desk or work area. Add pictures of your family and friends, put up artwork, decorate your computer, and bring in a comfortable chair. Surround yourself with pleasing and uplifting images.

- *Recognize others.* It is gratifying to give recognition as well as to get it. Let people you work with know how much you appreciate what they do. Let your learners know how much they contribute to you.

Trainer "burnout"

Certain computer training stresses can mature into burnout after several years in the profession. Burned-out computer trainers don't enjoy training, have lost the magic of teaching, and find it all a chore. A trainer who continues to train in a state of burnout does the computer training profession a disservice—like a doctor practicing bad medicine.

Before looking at some of the remedies for trainer burnout, you first need to look at the symptoms. For many trainers, these symptoms begin to appear after a few years of full-time training. The early enthusiasm, excitement, challenge, and sense of fulfillment have worn thin and have been replaced by routine, cynicism, tiredness, and stress. In the early days, you looked forward to actually teaching the class. Now, you look forward to actually *finishing* the class. In the beginning, the class left you with a real sense of achievement; now it just leaves you with a sense of relief.

Here are some other symptoms of imminent burnout:

- You don't look forward to teaching a class. "I have to teach tomorrow," you say with a sigh.

- You begin to lose a sense of humor. People who laugh and have fun in the class just serve to irritate you.

- You begin to lose patience with slower learners. It takes all your willpower not to grab them by the throats.

- You are easily upset when things don't run smoothly. The overhead bulb blows, and you think of quitting the profession.

- You seem to be getting more and more strange and annoying people in your classes.

- All you ever talk about to other trainers are training horror stories or problem students.

- You avoid your learners during breaks, lunch, and after class.

- You are much more tired after you teach classes than you used to be.

- You avoid implementing any new training ideas or approaches that might change your comfortable pattern of teaching a class.

- You start to judge your learners harshly.

- You can tell just by looking at certain people in the room that they are going to make your life a misery.

- You seem to be given all the "bad" classes.

- You take advantage of any opportunity to finish your classes earlier.

- You talk down to slower learners.

- It's a good class if they just press the right keys, follow your instructions, and get the right answers.

- You wonder how you ever got into computer training.

If you find yourself represented in many of the above, then you are a prime candidate for burnout. It doesn't have to stay that way. There are ways of dealing with and overcoming trainer burnout. All it takes is a little time, effort, and commitment. Here are some suggestions:

- *Teach less.* Sometimes one of the causes of burnout is teaching too much. Try to arrange to limit the number of hours you actually train in the classroom. Avoid teaching a class every day of the week.

- *Create some new approaches to teaching the same classes.* Use different examples and different training methods. Change the order of what you teach. Involve the learners more. Review the work by using games or quizzes. Resolve never to teach the same class the same way.

- *Vary your training schedule.* If you primarily do classroom training, try to arrange to do more one-on-one training or consulting. A change is often as good as a rest. If you train a lot, try to teach less and take on other jobs.

- *Talk to your peers about your training.* Ask them how they teach particular concepts or procedures. What analogies do they use? What are their challenges in training? Set up trainer meetings and get some other trainer's perspectives. Become a member of a computer training support group as discussed in chapter 5.

- *Sit in a class and be a learner for a day.* See what it feels like to be on the other side. This is one of the most valuable activities you can do as a trainer. It will give you a wonderful insight into your training.

- *Get one of your peers or managers to be your training mentor or coach.* Look for ways of improving delivery, presentation techniques, and communication. Even less-experienced trainers can provide you with valuable feedback.

- *Stay current on software.* Learn about what's going on in the software industry. When are the new versions coming out? Learn some new tips and tricks of your favorite software program. Consider teaching more advanced levels of the classes you teach.

- *Teach different applications.* Don't just stick to teaching one software program. Consider learning a new one. Expand your repertoire. Ask one of your peers to help teach you.

- *Follow up with some of your learners after the class.* Find out if they are using much of what they learned. What was the most valuable topic they learned in your class?

- *Set some career goals.* What do you want to be doing in two years' time? What could you be doing now to help achieve that? Have an idea of the direction you want to move in with your organization.

- *Get to know your learners.* Get to know more about your learners during the class. What are their jobs? What software do they use? What do they love about their computers? What do they hate about them? How has the computer changed the way they do their jobs? What are their biggest concerns when taking a class?

- *Attend computer training conferences and seminars.* Learn more about your profession. Network with other computer trainers to find out how they deal with some of the challenges of training. Learn more about the resources available for computer trainers.

12

Dealing with difficult learners

"Why be disagreeable, when with a little effort you can be impossible?"
— **Douglas Woodruff**

Let me first define the term "difficult learner." By difficult learner, I mean one or more individuals who interrupt the flow of an instructor-led class and demands special attention; people whose skills or attitudes become a real challenge for the trainer. This could be anything from a very slow learner to someone who is loud and aggressive—the types of learners who test your patience and your interpersonal skills. Perhaps more accurately, they should be described as "challenging" learners—the difficulty is with the trainer, not them.

Before getting into specifics, though, I need to mention one important fact about "difficult" learners that will make dealing with them a whole lot easier. It's very simple to say, but not the easiest to acknowledge. It is this:

Difficult learners are only difficult because of the way you react to them.

Read that again. What these learners really are is just different. Only when they frustrate you do they become difficult. When they don't, they are just another learner. Have you ever noticed how some instructors always seem to have difficult students, while others rarely come across them? What is difficult and frustrating for one trainer is

225

often no problem for another. It is all a question of personalities, temperament, and communication. If you want to master dealing with difficult learners, you must be willing to adapt, change, and be flexible. This is the hardest part for most people.

Another thing to remember is

> *You can't change the learner's behavior; you can only change your attitude to it.*

Your goal with a difficult learner should not necessarily be to try to change his or her behavior, but to change your reaction to it. You probably know people who you thought were awful when you first met them. You couldn't relate to them. Later, when you got to know them and began to understand them a little better, it became much easier to be around them. They didn't change; you just changed your view of them. It is the same with many of the difficult learners in computer training.

You can group challenging learners into two types: those whose skills challenge you and those whose attitudes challenge you. Challenging learners under the skills heading would be those whose skill-level effects the class—people who are slow on the keyboard, slow to learn, fast learners, and classes with widely ranging abilities (an all-time favorite). These people are generally the easier of the two groups to deal with because the challenges predominantly involve skills, not personalities.

The group that is a little harder to cope with and a little more emotionally draining are those whose attitudes and personalities you find difficult. Here, you get to confront head-on your own attitudes, personality, and temperament—not always a comfortable experience. However, by re-reading the suggestions and techniques in chapters 1 and 3 and by trying out some of the ideas outlined here, you will be amazed how different your relationship to these "difficult" learners can be.

Skills

Challenging classes usually have learners who are in some way slower than most of the group, faster than most of the group, or both.

The slow learner

If participants are too slow or do not have the correct prerequisites, they need to be encouraged to reschedule. They should not be in the class, and it is unfair to the other participants. Here are some other tips for dealing with slow learners:

- Have sufficient practice exercises that range from simple to challenging. Give slower learners less challenging exercises that cover the very basic skills.

- Consider pairing them up with more adept users, if appropriate. (Ask for permission first.) A more experienced user is often quite happy to give assistance now and then.

- Devote more time to slow learners when walking around helping others. The faster learners need less of your time.

- If they feel self-conscious about needing extra help, reassure them at break time that they are not a problem.

- Get them up to speed during a break, or enlist one of their coworkers to help. Be sensitive about having coworkers help, however—sometimes this can be a chore for them.

- Have them practice or prepare for the next session if it is a two- or three-day class.

- Suggest they get back from lunch 15 minutes earlier and help them get up to speed.

- When everyone else has finished the practice exercise, and you are still waiting for the slower learner, ask questions of the group or review the work until the slower learner has caught up.

- Never let the slow learner dictate the speed of the class. Teach to the majority.

Slow on the keyboard

Don't make the mistake of thinking that someone who is slow on a keyboard is a slow learner. He or she might be a very quick learner, but lack typing skills. Try these tips:

- Have exercises available that don't involve large amounts of typing.

- Reassure the slow typist that typing speed is not as critical as understanding the work.

- If participants are having enormous difficulty with the keyboard, suggest (privately) that they reschedule and/or practice.

- Don't press any keys for them or allow anyone else to do the same.

Slow on the mouse

As with a slow typist, don't make the mistake of thinking that someone who struggles with the mouse is a slow learner. Here are some helps for slow typists:

- Try to gauge mouse skills before class. If necessary, have participants hone their skills on a Windows tutorial or with a game like Solitaire.

- If they are having enormous difficulties with the mouse, suggest they reschedule and/or practice.

- Slow down the mouse tracking and double-click speed.

- Have someone who's having trouble with the mouse sit near you so you can easily assist them.

- Avoid seating them next to another person who has difficulty with the mouse.

When you are helping slower learners, don't give the impression that they are in any way a problem or an interruption of the class. No covert sighing is allowed! They are doing the very best they can do and deserve the utmost respect and patience. When you start to see improvements, let them know. Give them lots of genuine encouragement.

The fast learner

There are many ways to accommodate fast learners:

- Have more challenging practice exercises for faster learners.

- When they finish a practice exercise, provide a challenge, saying, "See if you can . . ." These learners generally won't need much guidance—just a goal.

- Show them extra tips and tricks and have them experiment with different features.

- It is often worth saying something like, "Sue, you're a bit more advanced than most people in the class—you'll have to bear with me." Fast learners will usually take this as a compliment and be much more open to being patient with you and others in the room.

- When someone asks a question frequently, direct it to the fast learner. Challenge them with other people's questions.

- Avoid having fast learners sit idle, waiting for the rest of the participants to finish an exercise. Keep them active and involved.

As with slow learners, don't give the impression that a fast learner is anything other than a valued participant in the class. Rather than a challenge, they can be a distinct asset to the trainer. Have them bring their skills into the class. Thank them after the class for their patience and assistance.

The wide range of abilities

Quite often, you'll have slower and faster learners in the same class. This doesn't have to be as difficult as it sounds. Just apply the suggestions listed above for slow and fast learners and do a bit of juggling. Also, read the section entitled "Juggling ability levels" in chapter 1.

The key to teaching a wide range of abilities is to gear the training to the average ability range, but make allowances for the extremes. Also try to arrange the class so that you can do numerous unassisted exercises. This will give you a chance to offer lots of one-on-one help. It is far easier to deal with ability ranges when you are walking around giving individual help than when you are teaching the whole group at the front of the room.

Attitudes

When you are confronted with attitudes that interrupt the learning process, it's natural to become frustrated. It's easy to forgive someone for the fact that his or her skill level is a challenge for you, but when it comes to personality and attitude, an instinctive first reaction is to judge the participant harshly or become defensive.

The key to dealing with attitudes is to avoid judging people and to instead deal with their behavior. When something is getting in the way of the learning, address the result of the behavior, not the personality. For example, consider these two responses to a "compulsive answerer":

- "I'd love to give someone else a chance to answer that one, Pete."

- "Pete, can you please not interrupt me when I'm asking someone else a question?"

The first has no implicit personal judgment. It is simply a statement. The latter comes across as a reprimand and a personal judgment about Pete. In order to deal effectively with anyone's difficult attitude, remember that the person generally has no idea he or she is a problem. Relate to that person as you would anyone else, with respect and consideration, while at the same time addressing the behavior that is affecting the learning.

Talkative people

If just one or two members of the class are particularly talkative, try these tactics:

- Ask them a question. If Sue is not listening, ask, "Does that make sense to you, Sue?"

- Suggest they pay attention: "Sue, I don't want you to miss any of this."

- Continue teaching and talking, but walk over to them or stand behind them. (This always works!) Stop in mid-sentence, look at the person, and wait. When he or she looks up, ask, "Do you need some help?" The person will get the message.

- Never stop and scowl at anyone.

- If it continues to be a problem, talk to the class member at break time. Remember to talk about the behavior, not the person.

A talkative group is usually only a problem when the group is all from the same department or company. When they are all strangers, it rarely happens. If you feel this might be a problem because you know ahead of time that all the participants are from the same department, address the issue before the class gets underway. Ask for their assistance—they are usually quite happy to give it. Also, before the class, set some ground rules. Let everyone know that one of your rules is that when anyone asks or answers a question, everyone else listens. If not, you'll disconnect their mouse. Try these other tips as well:

- If someone is asking or answering a question, and the rest are talking, stop and say something like "Hold it. I'd like you to listen to what Sue's saying." Keep it positive. Avoid saying anything like "Would you please listen!"

- Stop talking and wait. The participants will soon look up and wonder what's going on. When you have their attention, ask "Is everybody with me?"

- If all else fails, hand out an exercise. They realize they have to do something and start to settle down to work.

The compulsive answerer

You have probably come across the individual who is either very motivated, or who wants to display his or her knowledge of the subject and answers every question you ask. You can deal with this in several ways:

- Ask another person in the room specifically: "Bill, what do you think?" This way, the "answerer" is less likely to respond.

- Interrupt them, politely: "Just a second, Bob, let me see if anyone else can answer that."

- When the "answerer" responds to a question, turn to someone else and say, "Sally, what do you think?" Don't confirm the correct answer until a few people have offered their opinion.

- If this person still doesn't get the message, talk to him or her at a break. For example, you might say, "Bob, I appreciate your answering all the questions, but I'd like to give the others a chance to answer some too." He or she will generally understand and comply.

The "I don't want to be here" learner

Some people make it known that they are not having fun, and that they were "forced" to come to training. Here are some ways to handle people who appear to have little interest in learning:

- Ask them what they hope to get out of the class. Just listen to their story or complaints without comment or judgment.

- Later in the class, when you have the opportunity to talk with these people one-on-one, try to find at least one thing you're covering that might be of benefit or interest to them.

- Avoid trying to convince them that they should want to be there, or trying to persuade them how useful the class will be for them. This is probably what they expect you to do.

- Regularly ask them questions during the class; make sure you involve them.

- If you can, ask them to help other learners with something. This works well for thawing them out and gaining their participation.

The lost and confused person

Sometimes you'll have a learner who is either confused or getting completely lost and is beginning to feel upset and stressed. This attitude is often accompanied by mumblings of "Oh, I'm so dumb, I'll never learn this stuff." This person is often ready to smash the mouse, or leave. Try these tips to help these learners relax:

- Give a lot of assistance to this person without bringing too much attention to him or her.

- Keep close by (without making it too obvious) and guide the learner through the procedure. Don't touch his or her keyboard or mouse, though.

- Quietly, one-on-one or at a break, let him or her express what the frustration is. Listen carefully and attentively.

- Don't give this learner any indication whatsoever that he or she is causing a "problem" in the class or is slowing anyone down. Make clear that it is perfectly okay for him or her to be struggling.

- Suggest a solution. Provide help during a break or lunch time. If appropriate, have a neighbor assist this person. Make sure the source of confusion is cleared up as soon as possible.

The key to dealing with frustrated learners is to make them feel as comfortable as possible, let them know that whatever they are feeling is perfectly fine, and help them get back on track. Once the embarrassment or pressure is lifted, learning becomes a whole lot easier for them.

The angry or aggressive person

Upset learners have a problem with something or someone—the class, you, the boss, the day of the week—and relate to you in an angry or aggressive fashion. Their behavior is usually distinguished by sharp, argumentative comments like, "well, I think it's stupid!" or, "Aren't you supposed to know these things?" Here are some ways to handle these learners:

- Listen carefully to whatever they have to say, no matter how they express it.

- Try not to take anything they say personally. It probably has nothing to do with you.

- Never embarrass them. Sometimes when you feel like you're being attacked, you become defensive and throw back inappropriate comments. Avoid this, however tempting.

- Never reflect their attitude. It takes two to tango—their attitude will subside if you just receive what they have to give.

- Make a genuine effort to understand what they are saying. Listen to what they say, not how they say it.

- Respond with something like, "I can understand what you're saying," or, "You know I could be wrong. . . ." Don't use comments like, "I disagree with you," or, "You're wrong about that."

If this person continues to be a disruptive influence, you need to take a break and address the issue with him or her. Say something like, "I need your help. It's difficult for me to teach the class when you . . ." Don't be defensive or offensive. Talk about the behavior, not the learner's personality.

The quiet individual

Some learners sit at the back, never ask questions, and never offer to answer any questions. It's often hard to know if these people are understanding the work because there's no feedback. Here are some ways to draw these learners out:

- Make things comfortable for them. Make it easy for them to answer. Don't put them on the spot.

- Start by asking them a few simple questions and then build up to answers that require more discussion.

- When you ask a question to the class, make eye contact with a quiet person so he or she is encouraged to answer.

- Use these people's names if you can do so without embarrassing them or putting them on the spot. "How do you edit the macro? Bill, what do you think?"

- Try some paired learning so that they get into conversation with their neighbors. This can often draw them out.

The quiet group

Occasionally, you'll get a whole group where no one asks questions and no one answers any of your questions. You're unsure if they're "getting it" or not. This usually happens when no one knows each other.

- Use some type of ice-breaker. Get them involved in an activity.

- Try some paired learning exercises. Get them talking with their neighbor.

- Ask questions and wait for an answer. If no one answers, repeat the question. Continue to wait for an answer. There might be an uncomfortably long pause, but eventually someone will answer. When they know that you will continue to wait for a response, they'll answer more readily.

- They might be quiet because they are unsure of you. Try to create an open, easy, informal atmosphere where they get to know you and feel comfortable with you.

- Avoid saying something like, "You're all very quiet, what's up?" This will not encourage them to participate or share their thoughts with you.

- Don't change your energy level. There is a tendency sometimes to teach more quietly and less energetically to a quiet group. Don't do it. Teach with the same vigor you always do.

If nothing seems to work, talk casually with them at break to find out if there's a problem. It's sometimes a reason outside of the training. In one class I taught, I discovered that half the participants had lost their jobs the day before.

The "busy bee"

Have you ever had someone who rushes in 10 minutes late, brings in a cellular phone, and rushes out 10 minutes later to talk on the phone? You can't get them back on time from break or lunch because they're checking voice-mail. They sometimes tell you at 2 p.m. that they have to leave at 3 p.m. Here are some ways to deal with this type:

- Set ground rules. If you come across such a participant, you need to let him or her know the ground rules up front: no telephones on in the class, beepers must be on vibrate, and please use break and lunch times to attend to business.

- Suggest that this person reschedule if he or she can't honor the rules. Salespeople and agents, in particular, sometimes insist that they have to use the telephone/beeper and respond to calls. If this is the case, and it disrupts your class, ask them to reschedule or suggest that they take a more appropriate form of training, such as one-on-one, CBT, or video.

- Just before break or lunch time, specify the exact time you will restart. "We'll start again at 10:45. Will everyone be able to get back here by 10:45?" This works much better than saying, "We'll take a 15-minute break."

The know-it-all

Some people want to constantly let you and the rest of the room know how much they know. They often try to stump the trainer or make the trainer wrong. For example, when you say, "RAM is typically 16 megabytes," they might say, "Don't you mean 16,384 bytes because a kilobyte is actually 1,024 bytes?" Their main goal is to display their knowledge and be right.

The first and most important thing to do in this case is to listen to what they have to say. Never cut them off. Let them say what they want to say initially, then compliment them on their knowledge, "You're absolutely right, Connie. You obviously know a fair amount about the program." If they are mistaken in their comments or answers, respond with something like, "Well, I'm not familiar with that. Perhaps you could show me at break time." Try not to tell them they're wrong or argue a point with them. It is not worth it.

Rather than discourage their participation and hence prompt their know-it-all comments, encourage it by directing questions to them, such as, "Connie, I bet you know the answer to that." If another person asks you a question, respond with, "Let's see if Connie knows that one." By doing this, you are satisfying their need to express their knowledge, and you'll find that they will begin to quiet down. You need to make sure they feel that their comments and knowledge are valued.

If it is appropriate, ask them if they wouldn't mind helping other learners when they get stuck. If everyone is working on an exercise, and the know-it-all has finished, ask, "Connie, would you mind giving Joe a hand while I'm helping Sue?" They are usually only too eager to help another member of the class.

As with any "difficult" learner, if none of the suggestions seems to have any effect, you must address the issue with them at a break in a nonconfrontational manner. Try an approach such as, "Connie, I know you're familiar with a lot of this work, but it's difficult for me to teach when . . ."

Upgrade upset

The learner or learners who have been using a particular piece of software for many years and who are "forced" to learn a new package might very well feel upset. Their organization is upgrading or changing the software, but they think it's a bad idea and resent having to learn the new package. They are expecting you to tell them how wonderful the new software is.

Be familiar with their old software and its functions and features, so that you can relate to it as you teach the new software. It's much harder to show and compare useful new features if you're not familiar with the old ones. Relate the keystrokes or procedures in the new software to the old. "You remember <Shift><F3> in WordPerfect? Well, you can press <Ctrl><F6> to do the same thing here." Relating the old to the new will help the participants feel more comfortable. The question they will always want answered is, "I used to do this. How do I do it now?"

If a whole group has this attitude, start the class off with something like, "How many of you would be quite happy using your old program instead of learning this new one?" This is usually a relief for them. You have made it clear that you understand their position. Ask them what they liked about their old software and what they don't like about the new software. Don't try and convince them at this point how wonderful the new software is. They are expecting you to do this. Again, the point is to help them unload some of their thoughts and feelings.

Ask them to interrupt you during the class if they come across a feature they find was easy in the old program, but difficult in the new one. When they do this, show them an efficient new way of accomplishing the task. If it is more difficult, be honest with them: "Yes, you're right. It's a little easier in the old program."

Let them know that it usually takes time to adapt to new software—encourage them to be patient. Give them a personal experience of yours where you were once attached to a favorite program and didn't want to change.

Above all, avoid saying anything disparaging about their old program, even if you know of some of its poorer qualities. It will immediately alienate the learners. They want empathy, they don't want your opinion.

Summary

As you might have noticed, there are a few threads that run through each of the "difficult" learner suggestions in this chapter. I want to summarize them here because they are the key to dealing with any difficulty with learners. If you can implement these, you should rarely have problems:

- Actively listen to any complaint or concern. Don't interrupt or make judgments. Just listen.

- Try not to view anyone as a problem. They are simply expressing their thoughts and feelings, which might differ from yours.

- Try to understand what the learners' needs are and satisfy them without negatively affecting the class.

- Don't take anything personally. Never reflect their attitude.

- If you address a concern with someone, focus on the behavior, not on his or her personality.

- Develop more patience.

13

Teaching Windows programs

◆◆◆

"A picture shows me at a glance what it takes dozens of pages of a book to expound."
— **Ivan Sergeyevich Turgenev**

Teaching less

Teaching Windows programs is somewhat different from teaching text-based programs. Windows and other GUI operating systems are specifically designed to be graphical, consistent, and intuitive. Because of this, your approach to teaching the software needs to be different. Programs for DOS, UNIX, and other text-based operating systems are, on the whole, less intuitive to use. The less intuitive a program is, the more guidance the trainer needs to provide. With Windows programs, the guidance from the trainer can be reduced. This doesn't always happen, however. Many trainers teach Windows programs in exactly the same way they teach text-based programs. As a result, less information is taught, and users are encouraged to concentrate on procedural learning when they should be becoming independent. Instead of taking advantage of the intuitive nature of the program, the trainer simply tells the learner which mouse-clicks and keystrokes to use.

To guide the learner in a Windows-based class, teach by asking questions as discussed in chapter 1 and try to encourage learning by discovery. "What do you think that button does?" "See if you can figure out what this option gives you." Learning by discovery and experimentation is much more appropriate in a Windows environment because it helps the learner understand the logical, intuitive nature of the software and promotes independent thinking. To independently discover what a particular button on a toolbar does is a much more powerful way to learn than being told what it does. Windows programs give people a much greater opportunity to learn this way.

Prerequisites!

What is one of the most common complaints from trainers when teaching Windows programs? The participants don't have the prerequisite skills needed to be able to learn the software. It is crucial for anyone taking a class in some Windows software to understand and be reasonably adept at the basics. People should not be registered in classes if they do not have the necessary prerequisites. Allowing learners into a class without prerequisites, perhaps to fill a class or in the hope that they will "catch on," causes frustration for the trainer and is unfair to the other participants.

What prerequisites
are needed for a Windows class?

Ideally, before taking a class for a Windows program, a learner should understand and be familiar with the following:

- The keyboard

- Different mouse cursors

- Clicking and double-clicking

- Dragging and dropping

- How to use scrollbars

- Maximizing and minimizing

- How to select items from menus

- How to select options from dialog boxes

- The concept of the clipboard and cut, copy, and paste

- The concept of an active window

- Closing, moving, resizing, tiling, and cascading windows

- Opening, closing, and saving files

- The concept of multitasking

- The concept of folders, directories, and subdirectories.

If participants understand and are comfortable with these basic ideas and skills, then teaching the class will be much more productive for them and less challenging for the trainer. What too often happens, as you well know, is that not all users have these prerequisites and a large part of the class time is spent in helping people with these basic skills. This is typical for teaching most Windows applications, but it should be avoided at all costs. You will never get a situation where every single person in the class has exactly the same skill level, but if you or your training department can make prerequisites a higher priority, the effectiveness of your training will improve dramatically. Think of how much more you could teach if you never had to worry about teaching mouse clicks, selecting text, or how to save a file! Your classes would be very different.

How can you make sure that users have prerequisites?

Make sure learners are aware of the prerequisites for each class that is available. Encourage them to read the prerequisites carefully and take them seriously. Don't allow users to sign up for a class if they do not have or cannot demonstrate the prerequisite skills. Avoid having people sign themselves up for a class without someone confirming that they have the necessary skills.

Make the training sales staff or whoever books classes aware of the importance of prerequisites and have them ensure anyone booking a class has them. If possible, consider having the training manager or the trainer call participants or supervisors to verify that everyone has the appropriate skills for taking the class.

Give the participants a pre-test before scheduling them for a class. Don't let it become a simple questionnaire—people often inflate their skill levels to get into a class. Instead, try to have some simple online, interactive software that can objectively rate skill levels.

Mention the need for prerequisites at the end of classes in which learners might be taking the next level. Encourage them to consult training managers or trainers as to the suitability of their skills. Have a system for helping users who lack the basic Windows skills. Provide access to videos, CBT, courseware, and other learning aids.

If all else fails, try to gauge before you teach the class, or early on in the class, what the users' skill levels are. Do a quick little conversational survey to discover what skill levels you're dealing with. Don't wait till you are halfway into the training to discover that no one has the basics.

A different approach

Have you noticed that it is easier for the user to get off track or get into trouble in a Windows program? It is so easy to move around, play, and discover new features that users are apt to experiment and click different parts of the screen. All of a sudden, they're looking at a different screen and have five versions of Solitaire running in the background.

This can often be a challenge for the trainer. When software is non-intuitive and more difficult to learn, the trainer has control. The learners listen for every instruction and every step. When the software is easy to use, intuitive, and fun, the trainer loses some of that control. The users begin experimenting, clicking and playing, and occasionally getting stuck. "I don't know what happened, but my screen doesn't look like yours" is a phrase you've probably heard. The challenge when teaching Windows programs is to not stifle that urge to discover, explore, and learn independently, while at the same time trying to ensure that you provide a degree of direction.

Synchronous training, where you say things like, "Okay, now everyone press F1 on the count of three . . ." is less effective in teaching Windows programs. You need to let go of the need for strict control of the class and allow for a lot more learner independence. Have participants follow your general guidance, but be flexible enough to have them get there in their own way. For example, rather than saying something like, "Click File, Open, and double-click the document called Memo," say, "Go ahead and open the Memo document." This way, the learners can open the document in any one of three or four different ways, whichever is easiest for them. They get away from strictly following the trainer's mouse clicks and keystrokes, and find their own best way of doing things. After all, Windows was designed to have several methods of doing the same thing so that users can suit their own preferences. Of course, there are procedures where this is more difficult to implement, but whenever there is an opportunity for you not to lead them step by step through a menu, you should take it.

To ensure a reasonable amount of control and to make sure the learners don't drift too far off track, address this issue at the beginning of the class. It can be very frustrating to keep interrupting a class to help get someone back on track who has been "exploring" all the buttons and icons. I start off the class by explaining how easy it is to get off track and into other screens and menus. I ask participants to try and follow along with me, tempting though it is to get sidetracked and explore other things. Try to maintain that subtle balance between keeping them all on track and allowing a certain amount of independent learning.

Typical problems

There are certain recurring problems users have when learning Windows programs. Here are the most common:

- Being unable to control the mouse movement

- Not using the very tip of the mouse cursor

- Being unable to double-click

- Knowing when to double-click

- Moving the mouse when clicking

- Confusing the different types of mouse cursors

- Having windows disappear

- Not selecting text or graphics before choosing a function

- Trying to select a whole section of text from the middle

- Running multiple versions of the same program

- Accidentally erasing selected text by pressing Enter

- Not being able to use the scrollbars

When you are teaching a Windows class and someone encounters one of these problems, make sure that you not only help the learner correct the problem, but you have him or her understand the reason it happened. When, all of a sudden, the Help window disappears, it is not enough for you to correct it or explain how to get it back. You need to quickly explain what happened and the concept behind it. If you merely tell learners how to get back on track, they miss a valuable opportunity to learn.

Users often struggle with some of these common problems for months, not really understanding what is going on. If you can take the opportunity in the class to briefly explain and clarify concepts for them, you have provided a valuable contribution to their learning. As well as helping the individual with his or her problem, there might be two or three other people in the room who will benefit from such an explanation.

Because these typical problems and areas of confusion get in the way of teaching a Windows program, try spending a few minutes at the beginning of a class reviewing these basics and making sure they are clear to everyone. These skills should, of course, be prerequisites, but spending five or 10 minutes reviewing the ones that will crop up in your class can make a big difference to how people follow along when the class gets going.

Being a mouse novice

It is very easy in a class to see people struggling with the mouse, assume that they are slow learners, and then proceed to relate to them as slow learners. Not being totally adept at using the mouse does not mean anything about an individual's capacity to understand software concepts. Try not to confuse the two. I once made this mistake when teaching a spreadsheet class. I saw that one fellow was constantly struggling with the mouse and getting behind. I made certain that I slowed down a bit and explained every formula or function to him very carefully. At break time he tactfully said to me, "I'm a structural engineer. It's just the mouse I'm having trouble with. I know basic math." I was most embarrassed. Don't let being slow on the mouse mean anything more than just that.

If someone's problems using the mouse prevents him or her from following along, consider providing keyboard shortcuts instead. Sometimes in a class, I will encourage a mouse novice to use the Enter and Escape keys instead of clicking OK or Cancel, and maybe one or two simple Control-key shortcuts. There is a limit to how much time you can devote to helping someone master that confounded rodent.

Analogies and icons

When using analogies and other learning aids, take advantage of the images on the buttons and icons. They are there for a reason: to assist and guide the learner. When explaining cut, copy, and paste, for instance, use the images of the scissors, the sheets of paper, and the clipboard to provide an analogy. The analogies are already there on the buttons, so you might as well use them. Make your explanations as visual as you can. Windows is a graphical environment, so give graphical explanations.

Also make sure that everyone is clear about what the pictures on the buttons or icons represent. Quite often someone is confused, not because of a concept, but because they don't understand what the picture on the icon is. "That's a disk? I thought it was a TV!" "It's supposed to be a paint roller? Oh, I get it!"

Teaching four ways of doing the same thing

One of the features of Windows programs is having three or four ways of doing the same thing. Trainers often wonder whether they should teach all the different ways. On the one hand, you don't want to confuse everybody with too much information, but on the other hand you would like to give them options. What's the best approach?

It depends on who the learners are. If you have a group of novice Windows users and it is important for them to be able to master the mouse, then showing them the commonly used icons or buttons would be appropriate. Also, if a group is new to Windows, remembering what the pictures on the icons mean is easier for them than going into menus or using shortcut keys.

If you have a more experienced group, it might be appropriate to show them a few other ways of doing the same thing. Usually, this means mentioning the buttons, the menus, and the keyboard shortcuts. This gives them the option to choose the method they prefer. If you don't cover all the different options, make sure they are included in the courseware somewhere for the participants to refer to.

In certain cases, showing many of the keyboard shortcuts will be more appropriate. If you have a class of people who just changed over from a text-based word processor to a Windows word processor, everyone would probably like to know how to use the program with the keyboard as well as the mouse. In fact, in most cases when teaching word processing, the keyboard shortcuts for bold, italic, underline, left-align, center, and right-align are more valuable than using the icons because the user doesn't have to keep leaving the keyboard to grab the mouse.

If you are unsure of whether you should offer some of the other options, ask the learners during the class. Say something like, "Would anyone like to know a keyboard shortcut for doing that?" or, "Would anyone like to know how to do that in a menu instead of with the ruler?" Let the participants determine what will be most useful to them. Avoid always giving them your favorite method of using the program—it might not suit the audience you have.

Using large screens

Using a large screen when teaching Windows programs requires certain techniques that help the user to follow you in a clear and understandable way.

Seeing the cursor

Make sure the mouse cursor can be seen clearly. On some of the less-expensive dual-scan LCD displays, the mouse cursor movement is very hard to discern. Consider turning on mouse-trails to make it clearer. If the display on the screen is relatively small, consider increasing the size of the mouse cursor. Also, consider increasing the size of the font a few points, so that everyone in the room can read the text clearly. (I've found this particularly useful when teaching spreadsheet programs, where the font is generally quite small.)

When you are showing a procedure and you want your audience to notice the position of the mouse cursor, try moving it from side to side very slightly. It brings attention to the mouse immediately. Otherwise, participants will be scanning the screen to try to find it.

Watching or following?

When you are using the display, make it very clear to the participants what you want from them. You need to let them know if you are demonstrating a procedure or if you are leading them through the procedure. There should be no confusion as to whether they need to watch or follow along with you. Give instructions like, "Now just sit back and relax for a second while I show you something," or, "Okay, grab the mouse and let's do this together." If you don't make this clear, some learners will be following, some will be watching, and confusion will ensue.

Slow down

When you are showing a procedure, you need to do everything much slower than you normally do. You need to give the learners time to see what you clicked or dragged, and be able to understand why. For example, if you are showing File/Page Setup, move the mouse cursor slowly across the screen to File, saying, "We click File. . . ." You click. Drag the mouse down the File menu until you highlight Page Setup. (Highlight it rather than immediately click it, so that the class members can see the menu item you have chosen) You pause, ". . . and then Page Setup."

Give a running commentary on what you are doing, and make sure the commentary is in sync with exactly what you are doing. If you click the right mouse button, make it very clear to the class that this is what you are doing. When you go into a menu or a dialog box, pause for a few moments so that they can see where you are. If they are following your steps, be sure to give them enough time to see and hear your instructions, look at their own screens, do the same thing, and then look up again to check whether they are at the same place you are.

Point to the screen

Sometimes when you are clicking on a small button or icon, or explaining some part of a dialog box, it is clearer to walk over to the movie screen and point to the particular item. It is much easier for learners to see where you are pointing, rather than having them try to locate the section of the screen you are describing. This is why it is good to have the screen and the trainer's computer station close enough so that, if necessary, you can jump up and point to the screen.

Many LCD data panels have a system whereby the trainer can pull down menus and clock by using a special pointing device. This allows you to demonstrate the procedure while standing by the screen pointing to different menus.

Avoid setting up the screen display from a computer at the back of the room. Although this does let you see everyone's screens, it prevents you from stopping and quickly pointing out something on the large screen. You'll end up running from one side of the room to the other.

Walk around

Although it is tempting to stay at the front of the room and run the show from there, I recommend that you walk around now and again to see how your participants are doing and to offer them some personal assistance. Often a learner will not let on that he or she is confused or not following, and just sits there without saying a word. A walk around the room at regular intervals helps you quickly scan each person's screen and check that they are all on track. It also helps you quickly discover who is following and who needs some extra assistance.

Moving around the room also lets you see the large screen from their perspective to check that it is clear, without reflections or blurs, and easy to read. Quite often, what looks readable from the trainer's perspective can be barely discernible from the back of the room.

Don't hide

Having low light intensity in a room is often welcomed by trainers, who often feel a little more comfortable when the lights are low. Trainers who experience a little nervousness or self-consciousness from time to time often overdo the use of the large-screen display. They keep the lights low and the screen display on throughout the whole class. Avoid doing this. Lower the light level only when necessary. It might make you feel more comfortable training, but spending a day in a low-light environment is not good for your participants' eyes, or their level of engagement.

14

Accelerated learning

◆◆◆

"Learning which involves the whole person of the learner, feelings as well as intellect, is the most lasting and pervasive."
— **Carl Rogers**

Our standard model of computer training—in fact, our standard model of education in general—has flaws. It works to some extent, but does not complement people's natural inclinations and abilities. Sometimes the higher up in the educational system you get, the further away you drift from the type of learning that best serves people.

A better way of learning?

The typical computer classroom model, with instruction being provided almost totally verbally in an atmosphere reminiscent of high school, does not allow learners to take full advantage of their inherent learning abilities. Other approaches to learning that better reflect human nature are available, and although somewhat unconventional, have proved very successful. These concepts together are loosely called *accelerated learning*.

Accelerated learning techniques were originally developed by Dr. Georgi Lozanov, a Bulgarian psychiatrist from the University of Sophia. Sometimes known as *accelerative learning*, they are ways of presenting information and arranging the learning environment such that learning becomes easier, is understood more readily, is retained longer, and is more enjoyable. Imagine a computer class where the learners are relaxed; find the information stimulating, easy to follow, and remember; learn more; and have fun. It might sound a little utopian for some seasoned trainers, but I assure you, it is possible.

Split brains

Before getting into the specifics of accelerated learning techniques, it is important to understand a little about the ways the brain processes information.

Most people are familiar with the notion that we have a divided brain. The two hemispheres are connected through tissue called the *corpus callosum*. In many ways, the two halves of the brain seem to act independently and have different specialized functions. For the sake of simplicity, I am going to talk here of the "left brain" and the "right brain," but in fact, many of the brain's functions overlap and are not entirely located in either half. I use the terms *left brain* and *right brain* to mean, respectively, a person's linear/logic faculty and spatial/creative faculty.

The left brain predominantly processes linear, sequential, and structured information, such as number skills, logical processes, and facts. The right brain deals with more unstructured processes, such as creativity, imagination, change, and pattern recognition. The right hemisphere can be thought of as the more creative or intuitive side.

When children are very young, they learn most things in a very right-brained fashion. Learning is predominantly kinesthetic, visual, and very unstructured. It's more like exploring, discovering, and playing. It doesn't seem to take much conscious effort and is usually fun. Interestingly, the skills you learn this way are never forgotten. Recall is immediate throughout your life.

As you get older and start to "study" at school, learning becomes more and more a left-brained activity. It is more and more auditory, wordy, and structured. It doesn't seem like fun or entertainment anymore. It's serious, conscious adult stuff. Learning conjures up studying, reading, concentrating, and struggling to comprehend. Also, the skills and information you learn later in life are usually short-term and easily forgotten. (Can you remember the definitions of sine, cosine, and tangent?)

You learn mostly with your left brain early on in life, and as you get older, shift it way over to the right. What you really need is a balance. By providing a balance in the way you learn, you can assimilate and recall information more effectively and without so much conscious effort.

Global and sequential learning

The ways of learning that are characterized by the two sides of the brain are often referred to as *global* and *sequential.* The typical computer training style is sequential, in which you provide linear, step-by-step instruction, focusing on individual parts of the whole. You show and explain individual elements and then put them together, hoping that the "whole" will be comprehensible.

The way you learned your native language as a child, and the way the human mind works, is more global. This is where you are confronted, not by a single concept or element, but with the whole thing. The brain naturally assimilates information in this holistic fashion. A child does not sit down to learn grammar and syntax. The child learns by being exposed to language in an unstructured and nonlinear way.

Sequential learning can provide some useful computer skills, but the retention rate and ability to integrate the concepts and procedures into a broader computer knowledge is limited. A global learning style in computer training is one that can increase retention rate, increase understanding, and help a learner integrate concepts.

Accelerated learning techniques

Let's look at some ways to include accelerated learning techniques in your computer training and encourage more global, right-brain approaches. These can be broken down into the following categories:

- The atmosphere

- The presentation

- Music

- Colors and images

- Relaxation

- Games

- Discovery

- Verbalizing

- Mnemonics and rhymes

The atmosphere

Perhaps one of the most important elements in accelerated learning is the immediate environment of the learner and the learning atmosphere. The less the room reflects the instructor-student hierarchy, and the more it encourages the student-student relationship, the better. People will be more open to learning if the room is physically and emotionally comfortable (see page 33). Think of how much more interaction happens in a break room where the furniture is more "socially" arranged. Also, the more colorful, warm, and inviting the room, the more open to learning the participants will be. Try decorating the walls with posters, pictures, or colorful memory aids. Have some flowers at the front of the room; dim the lights a little. A training room doesn't have to look stark, cold, and academic.

Try to start the class off on a positive, engaging note, rather than being downbeat. Don't say, "We're going to cover some quite complex concepts today." Instead, say something like, "Who would like to know how to speed up your work by 50%?" Expectation is half the battle.

The presentation

Try to get away from the purely sequential style of training. Give class members a view or idea of the finished product or task before you give them the steps to achieve it. Show them exactly what they are working towards. The steps will make much more sense if they know what the end result is. Have you ever tried putting a jigsaw puzzle together without the picture on the box?

Consider teaching the "harder" material first and filling in the specifics later. A person doesn't have to know exactly what a clutch pedal does to be able to drive a car; people can learn a skill and fill in relevant details later. Avoid spending too much time giving a thorough explanation of all the parts that make up the whole. Present the whole and then let learners see how the individual parts serve to create it.

Music

Certain types of music played in the background actually enhance the learning process and help people assimilate information more quickly. Baroque music, that composed during the middle and late 1700s, is ideal for learning. Composers like Mozart, Bach, Handel, and Vivaldi wrote music that is highly structured, yet very creative. Listening to such music actually promotes alpha waves in the brain—the brainwaves that produce the relaxed, alert state that seems to enhance creativity and the ability to learn.

Try using a portable CD or tape player and blending some baroque music in with your training. It doesn't have to be loud; a low volume is just as effective. Play it as participants arrive, before actually starting the class, at break times, and especially when they are working on exercises. You can explain the purpose of the music to them, or just say nothing and observe their reactions. Try it. It is fun, relaxing, and it works!

Relaxation

People learn most effectively when they are physically and mentally at ease. In this state, brains produce alpha waves instead of the beta waves normally running around in a fully alert, fully conscious state. Beta waves prevent people from learning as easily and effectively as they can with alpha waves. So how do you get learners into the alpha state? By helping them release anxiety and stress, and "wind down." Playing Mozart helps, and so does deeper rhythmic breathing. Breathing also helps oxygenate the blood and sharpen creativity and awareness.

Before you start the class, have everyone choose a comfortable position and close their eyes. Now have them take a deep breath, hold it for a second or two, and then exhale. Have them repeat this about 10 times. While they are doing this, you can have them visualize one of their favorite, peaceful places, such as sitting quietly by a lake on a beautiful summer's day—whatever helps them relax and let go. After you've done this, have them open their eyes and begin the class.

Now, you need confidence to do this. You need to be bold enough to pull it off without feeling "weird." If you feel uncomfortable doing it, then don't. If you explain what you're doing and why you're doing it, you'll find people quite open and interested in participating. One thing is for sure—they will not forget your class!

Games

You played more games as a child when you were learning than you do as an adult. Adults don't usually think of fun and games when they think about learning new skills. They assume it should be a serious and solemn activity.

The fact is that when people learn by playing games or fun competitive activities, the learning is accelerated. Most typing-tutor software has a typing game included because it is such an effective way to learn.

Whenever you can, introduce a game, quiz, or some fun activity into your computer training to review the work. It will be even more effective if you can get people working in groups or pairs. The social interaction adds to the fun. Even those who appear unmotivated and unresponsive seem to spring to life when they are involved in a fun group activity. Try reviewing the work with a Jeopardy-type game. "The answer is Alt-Tab. The question is . . .?"

Discovery

What is learned by discovery is better remembered and recalled than learning by being "instructed" (see page 1, "Encouraging indepenence"). Discovery entails carrying out an action, observing the result, making inferences based on the result, and then using the inference to guide the next action. This is the way young children learn, and it is an extremely effective way of learning.

Try organizing your training so that it has a rich discovery element in it. Give your learners the necessary concepts and vocabulary, and have them figure out how to carry out a procedure. This is becoming increasingly easier to do with intuitive GUI programs. Not only does discovery learning help with memorization and recall, it encourages independence and self-learning.

Examples of this type of learning that I use regularly are teaching margins and text alignment in a word processor. I rarely tell class participants how to do either. I just say, "Look at the menus at the top and figure out how to set the left and right margin to 1½ inches," or, "We need the title centered. See if you can find three different ways of doing that." Try it in your class. You will be surprised at how well this works.

Verbalizing

Verbalizing words, concepts, or procedures helps people remember them by accomplishing two important things. First, by hearing words and ideas spoken, learners engage another of their senses, which aids retention even when they are the ones doing the speaking. If you review work by reading it or explaining it aloud, as opposed to in your head, the words and ideas will be cemented more firmly in your memory.

Second, in order to verbalize a concept or idea, the brain has to structure it in the form of language. Just by speaking and explaining a concept aloud, you have to understand it and apply your linguistic structure to it. The act of doing this helps clarify the concept in the learner's own mind. If a concept is not fully understood, then the act of verbalizing it will bring this to light.

When reviewing vocabulary concepts or procedures in a class, have your participants speak the words or steps to be performed. Don't stand there reviewing it for them. Have them say it.

Mnemonics and rhymes

The lyrics to songs, poems, and rhymes are easy for people to remember. You can probably sing the words to lots of songs. You didn't make an effort to learn them. The music and the rhythm made it almost effortless.

When someone asks us how many days in the month of March, most people recite to themselves, "30 days hath September, . . ." or count their knuckles. These are two examples of mnemonics or memory aids. Mnemonics work extremely well in helping people remember because they include an associated rhythm, sound, or picture. The rhythm, sound, or picture stimulates the right brain and assists learning of more left-brain material.

Try to develop some type of mnemonic or memory aid for those not-so-intuitive parts of your computer training. For example, when I talk about hypertext links in a Windows Help menu, I tell participants to remember "green will take you to another screen." When I'm teaching about the clipboard, I sometimes tell people "you never waste it when you paste it." To teach a class how to change the paper location from the top tray of a printer to the bottom tray, I get them to remember T-O-P (Tools-Options-Printer). Use anything that is easy to remember or rhymes—the sillier the better.

Another method one trainer uses is to have the class split into groups and write a "rap" song about what they have learned. The rhyming of words and the rhythm both help to assist memorization. Apart from helping the participants learn, it's hilarious.

Keep in mind that the first time you start to implement some of these accelerated learning techniques, people are going to think you're a little strange, especially if you jump right in and try to implement the whole lot at once. Take it step by step and see what works well. Try a little music to begin with, and then when you're comfortable with that, add on another technique, and so on. If a particular technique doesn't seem effective or if you feel uncomfortable doing it, then scrap it. Remember, a prerequisite for any of these techniques is that you feel comfortable using them. If you don't, your learners will pick up on it and it will color their reaction to your techniques. Be bold, have fun, and be prepared to observe some impressive results and some fascinated learners!

15

The Internet for computer trainers

*"Knowledge is not simply the accumulation of
information. We can drown in information and still
thirst for knowledge."*
— **Paul Clothier**

A few years ago not many people were familiar with the Internet and
the World Wide Web. All of a sudden, nearly everyone seems to be
connected, surfs the Web, and has a home page. The change in the
awareness of and the use of the Internet is incredible. The increase in
Internet traffic has been exponential. The techniques and technologies surrounding the Internet are changing extremely rapidly. Because of this, some of the information here on Web sites and other
resources might be out of date by the time you read it—you might
have to use a search tool to find new addresses. The important thing
to know about the Internet is not the details of accessing it, although
this of course is important; it's understanding the impact and importance of it to computer trainers. The Net and online services are here
to stay. You need to learn about them, embrace them, and use them
wisely in your training.

Online learning

Online services and the Internet will continue to have significant effect on the way people learn and communicate. You can read a news-

paper, order pizza, learn about Web browsers, find out what's on TV, join a discussion group, take a test, buy a computer, look at pictures of Mars, shop for lingerie, and communicate with the world online. Computer trainers need to learn more about this method of communicating because it will become an integral part of their work. It is a powerful vehicle for delivering computer training; organizations are already using it to provide training to their employees at their desks, when they need it.

Online training is satisfying many needs that traditional instructor-led training cannot. Much of the online learning at the moment is informal, "free" learning—people browsing the World Wide Web, using newsgroups, reading mailing lists, and sending e-mail. Increasingly, though, more formal learning resources are emerging in the Microsoft Online Institute, CompuServe, America Online, Prodigy, and the other online services. These are fee-based services that charge as people learn.

You need to become familiar with what's happening on the information highway, learn how to use its resources, and be aware of the implications and impact it will have on training and learning in the future. As a computer trainer, you can use online services for

- Communicating and networking with other trainers

- Learning

- Delivering training

Communicating and networking
The beauty of the Internet and online services is that they can bring physically diverse communities, such as computer trainers, together in one virtual location. Newsgroups, forums, and discussion lists can provide the computer trainer with ideas, information, and support from a worldwide community of training peers. The trainer can benefit from the accumulated wisdom of thousands of other computer trainers online. Got a training challenge you need help with? Send or post a message after a day's training, and you'll get supportive replies from halfway around the globe the next day.

Learning
More than ever, being a computer trainer necessitates learning. The successful trainer is forever learning and upgrading skills. The Internet and online services such as CompuServe, America Online, and

the Microsoft Network are goldmines of information on every software product you're likely to come across. When a new version or upgrade appears, you have the information at your fingertips.

As well as information about software, these online services offer vast amounts of information and resources about learning, training, human resources, or whatever you want to know about.

Delivering training

More computer training will be delivered to end users at their desktops via online services and the Internet. The desktop will not necessarily just be in the office, but in the home as well. As delivery methods improve and communication bandwidths increase, online computer training will become more sophisticated and a more viable method of training for many organizations.

It's a good idea to learn more about these technologies and delivery methods and see how they can assist (and in some cases replace) existing classroom training. Online learning has numerous advantages over sending people to an instructor-led class. Who better to be involved in its effective development than computer trainers?

Some of the desirable aspects of delivering training on the Internet are

- *It's global.* The learning can be delivered just as easily in San Francisco as it can be in New York, London, or Timbuktu. Distance is irrelevant.

- *It's consistent.* Unlike instructor-led training, online learning can provide exactly the same content and delivery to a physically diverse learner community. Everyone learning the latest version of Word 9.0 can receive identical information.

- *It's learner-controlled, not instructor-led.* The user can control what is learned, when it is learned, and how it is learned. The information and delivery can be adapted to suit the learner, rather than the provider of the information.

- *It's open all hours.* The Internet doesn't sleep. The learner can choose to study at home before going to work, during the day, or at 2:00 in the morning. Learning can be scheduled to fit the individual's need, not the training provider's.

Online software

A trend that might affect the way computer training is delivered is on-line software, or "software on demand." One of the problems of software today is its ever-increasing complexity and the costs associated with updating it and training on it. When a new upgrade appears on the market, it costs large organizations hundreds of thousands of dollars to pay for the upgrade, install it, and conduct training. Upgrading to Windows 95, for example, was estimated to cost corporations around $800 per user.

With increased access speeds on the Internet, a computer user might eventually be able to "rent" a program online. The software provider will own the software, but rent it out to organizations that wish to use it. You might purchase a year's subscription to a word-processing program and have it downloaded quickly to your system or network already configured. At the end of the year, you would have the option to renew your subscription. When the software needs upgrading or has new features added, you simply connect to your software provider online, and the new upgrade or fix is automatically downloaded and configured.

Instead of an organization investing in purchasing software, installing it, and then having to buy and install upgrades, it would simply "rent" the software for a limited period. The organization would only need to pay for the software that is actually being used during a specific time period. This could solve many of the upgrade, installation, and financial challenges associated with new software. It would be similar to using Kinkos to make copies rather than investing thousands in photocopying equipment.

When people start to buy software subscriptions on the Internet, software providers will inevitably provide access to online multimedia training or provide downloadable multimedia training for the applications it rents. It will be in the interest of software providers to provide training along with the subscription to the software. End users might end up installing, upgrading, paying for, and learning new software without leaving their seats. If it is inexpensive and effective, you can bet it will be popular.

Training people
to use the Internet

Internet training has traditionally involved teaching people what the Internet is, what Gopher, LISTSERV, and Usenet mean, and how much Veronica WAIS. In the early days of computer training, this would be equivalent to teaching people binary and BASIC programming. When the technology, software, and accessibility become more refined, using the Internet will be as simple as changing channels on the TV. When this happens, training people how to use the Internet will change its character and quality.

Trainers will no longer be involved in teaching how the Internet works, but how to use it—not how to access the World Wide Web, but where to find information on it and what to do with it once you've found it. Net training will be more about finding, sorting, filtering, creating, updating, and managing information than it will be about deciphering Unix commands. Instead of computer trainers, you might see information trainers. Rather than teaching software skills, you'll teach effective highway navigation and search skills, where to stop for directions, where to find goods and services, and how to avoid information roadkill.

Just as computer training evolved from teaching about the tool to showing how to use the tool to get work done, Internet training will change from learning about the information highway to learning how to find and use information on it. If you are considering specializing in Internet training, look a little further than teaching techniques of how to access the Net resources; the skills needed while people are connected will become more important than the skills needed to get connected.

A beginner's guide to the Internet

For seriously Net-challenged trainers, the following is a very brief explanation of some of the techniques, terms, and resources you might come across in the cyber universe. (Mature Internauts can skip this section.)

Getting connected

First of all, get set up with an Internet service provider. There are thousands of them out there. A service provider is a company that can connect you to the Internet. It is similar to having the telephone company connect you to the telephone grid. You pay them a monthly fee (and sometimes an hourly rate), and they give you access to the services of the Internet. Your service provider will either provide or suggest Internet software, such as Netscape or Mosaic, that can be used to connect to the Net in a user-friendly way. CompuServe, America Online, Prodigy, the Microsoft Network, and other online services also provide Internet connections.

LISTSERV mailing lists

A LISTSERV is a piece of software that automates the maintenance of a mailing list. You can be added to a mailing list and have information from the list sent directly to you. Be prepared to be inundated with lots of mail, however.

Suppose you're interested in being on the mailing list for NETTRAIN, which focuses on training about and over networks. The LISTSERV address for this is

listserv@ubrm.cc.buffalo.edu

This is simply the computer name on which the mailing list exists. You send a mail message to the above, and in the message, you type something like:

SUBSCRIBE NETTRAIN Paul Clothier

Of course, instead of Paul Clothier, you put in your real name. The subject line of the mail message is ignored. The LISTSERV sends back an acknowledgment and gives you all the information you will need to receive and post messages to the mailing list.

To unsubscribe to NETTRAIN, send a message to the same address, but put

UNSUBSCRIBE NETTRAIN or SIGNOFF NETTRAIN

in the message. Simple eh?

Usenet newsgroups

A newsgroup is essentially a discussion group, or a huge bulletin board system. People post and read messages, and can reply either publicly or privately. There are thousands of newsgroups organized in a type of directory hierarchy. The main hierarchies are designated as follows:

alt   strange, offbeat, and sometimes weird, with relaxed rules

comp   computer-related topics

news   topics about Usenet and news networks

rec   recreational topics

sci   topics related to the sciences

soc   social issues

talk   conversational topics, often controversial

misc   topics that can't fit anywhere else

A group could look like this:

comp.sys.ibm.pc.hardware.networking

getting more and more specific as you move to the right.

To read Usenet newsgroups, you need software that can access them. Netscape and Mosaic provide this capability, and you simply type **news:** followed by the group you wish to access in the location box at the top of the screen. For example, typing:

news:alt.education.distance

will list all the groups under alt.education. You then simply click on where you want to go next.

The World Wide Web (WWW)

The World Wide Web is most people's favorite part of the Internet. It is a hypertext-based system designed for browsing Internet resources, similar to a Windows Help menu, with graphics and links to other resources on the Net (and sometimes also sound and video if you have the software to read them). You might be viewing a page on education, and within a few hypertext mouse clicks, you could be looking at Van Gogh paintings. The Web is very interesting, very addictive, very useful, and like the rest of the Net, very disorganized.

To access a Web page, you need its URL (Uniform Resource Locator). The URL is simply an address on a computer somewhere that holds the Web page or pages. For example, consider this URL:

http://iconode.ca/trdev.html

The *http* stands for hypertext transmission protocol and indicates that it is a document on the Web. The *iconode.ca* is the computer address, */trdev* is the directory path at that address, and *html* specifies that it is a hypertext markup language document, or hypertext document. You simply type the URL into your Web browser (Netscape and Mosaic are two of the most common), press Enter, and you'll be looking at a Web page on a computer thousands of miles away.

When you surf the Web pages and come across a cool site, you can save a bookmark to record that URL and get back to it later.

FTP (File Transfer Protocol)

FTP is a client-server protocol that allows you to transfer files to and from another computer. You can locate files in directories on the other computer and download them to yours. If you have permission, you can also upload as well.

Anonymous FTP allows you to copy data to your computer without requiring that you have a special login id or account on every machine you might want to access. You do not have to remember accounts or passwords.

FTP allows you to transfer text files, graphic images, audio and video clips, and program files. The file locations are described much the same as URLs:

ftp://ftp.ed.gov/pub/studgde.zip

The computer name is *ftp.ed.gov*, the */pub* is the directory, and *studgde.zip* is the file to be downloaded or "FTP'd," as they say. Both the Netscape and Mosaic Web browsers support FTP file transfers.

Gopher

Gopher is a document retrieval system that many Internet hosts (individual Internet computers) offer. The user is provided with a hierarchy of menus and submenus that eventually lead to text files, sound files, or graphic files. The menus are in plain English and easy to read.

A selected menu item would be represented by something like:

gopher://gopher.ets.org:70/11/readme.txt

where *gopher.ets.org* is the gopher server name and *70/11/readme.txt* would be the location of the selected file. Netscape and Mosaic also support Gopher access.

Veronica

Veronica stands for Very Easy Rodent-Oriented Net-wide Index to Computerized Archives. It (she?) lets you do a keyword search of Gopher menus or document content. It is simply a tool for finding the location of specific Gopher resources. You can find pointers to Veronica on the top or second levels of most Gopher menus.

So get connected, get online, and start playing around with all these tools, and like you always tell your learners—if you get stuck, RTFM.

Search engines

The simple way to find information on the Net is to use a search tool. There are many available, but the most common are

- Yahoo at http://www.yahoo.com, a searchable catalog of Internet sites that covers thousands of entries on every subject you can imagine.

- Lycos at http://www.lycos.com, which allows you to search a database of the entire Web with keywords. It contains a list of about 5 million Web documents.

- Web Crawler at http://www.webcrawler.com, another very effective keyword search catalog that is fast and easy to use.

- Excite at http://www.excite.com, which allows you to search for concepts as well as keywords.

When you come across one of the URL addresses that I have included in the training resources list that is out of date (as some will certainly be by the time you read this), use one of the search engines to search for the title, or use a keyword.

Good beginner guides

Want it all laid out step by step? Want to know more details than my mini-guide here? Want to decipher some Internet lingo you've come across? Here are some great online introductions to the Internet and how to use them:

- *Tour the Internet* at
  http://www.globalcenter.net/gcweb/tour.html

- *Life on the Internet* at
  http://www.screen.com/understand/explore.html

- *Glossary of Internet Terms* at
  http://www.matisse.net/files/glossary.html

- *The Internet Public Library* at http://ipl.sils.umich.edu/

Internet resources

The following is a current list of available Internet and online resources of interest to computer trainers. It is not (and cannot be) extensive, and some of the links will change with time. If they do, you might be advised of the new locations, or you can use a search engine such as Yahoo to find the new URL.

General training-related Worldwide Web sites

- Computer Trainers Network at
  http://www.crctraining.com/training from the San Francisco Bay area

- Educom at http://educom.edu/, "transforming education through information technology"

- ERIC, the Educational Resources Information Center, at
  http://www.aspensys.com/eric/index.html

- Free On-line Dictionary of Computing at
  http://wombat.doc.ic.ac.uk/foldoc/contents.html

- IBM Education and Training at
  http://www.training.ibm.com/usedu/edushome.htm

- Information on Technology Training Initiative at
  http://www.hull.ac.uk/hull/itti/homepage.html

- IT Training Magazine (from the UK) at
  http://www.demon.co.uk/ittrain/index.html

- Learning and Instruction at
  http://gwis2.circ.gwu.edu/~kearsley/ (sponsored by George
  Washington University)

- Learning HTML at
  http://www.utexas.edu/learn/pub/html.html (sponsored by
  the University of Texas)

- Learning Java at http://java.sun.com/starter.html

- The Learning Organization discussion list at
  http://world.std.com/~lo

- Learning research at the University of Pittsburgh
  http://www.lrdc.pitt.edu:80/www.html

- PC Trainer's Gateway at
  http://www.isitraining.com/gateway.html, a directory of
  computer training information from InfoSource

- Technology—Communication and Human Resources by Brian
  Croft at http://www.inforamp.net/~bcroft/

- Technology Training for Adult Educators at
  http://www.gactr.uga.edu/brad/techtraining.html (sponsored
  by the University of Georgia Center for Continuing Education)

- Training and Development FAQs at
  http://www.tcm.com/trdev/faq, an excellent training resource
  from Wave Technologies

- The Training Edge, resources for computer training, at
  http://slip-2.slip.net/~pcloth/index.html

- Trainers on the Net (a reprint of an article from *Training
  Magazine*) at http://iconode.ca/trdev/trainmag.html

- Using Technology in Education at
  http://www.algonquinc.on.ca/edtech/ (sponsored by
  Algonquin College)

World Wide Web sites for courseware information

- Logical Operations at http://www.logicalops.com/index.html

- Catapult at http://www.plot.com/plot/index.html

- ComputerPrep at http://cybermart.com/cprep/

Software publishers on the Web

- Lotus Development at http://www.lotus.com/
- WordPerfect at http://www.wordperfect.com/
- Novell at http://corp.novell.com/
- Microsoft Corporation at http://www.microsoft.com/
- Microsoft Network at http://www.msn.com/
- Microsoft Online Institute (MOLI) at http://www.microsoft.com/moli/
- Software Publishers Association (SPA) at http://www.spa.org/

Magazines on the Web

- *PC Magazine Online* at http://www.zdnet.com/~pcmag/
- *PC Week Online* at http://zcias4.ziff.com/~pcweek/
- *PC Computing Online* at http://zcias4.ziff.com/~pccomp/
- *Computer Shopper* at http://zcias4.ziff.com/~cshopper/
- *Interactive Week* at http://zcias4.ziff.com/~intweek/
- *Windows Sources* at http://zcias4.ziff.com/~wsources/
- *MacUser* at http://zcias4.ziff.com/~macuser/
- *MacWEEK* http://zcias4.ziff.com/~macweek/
- *Service News*, a subscription newspaper for computer service and support, at http://www.servicenews.com

LISTSERVs

- COMPUTER-TRAINING (moderated) at listserv@bilbo.isu.edu, the computer training digest from the Masie Institute & Simplot Decision Support Center at ISU
- COMP-LITERACY (moderated) at comp-literacy@uwm.edu, a computer literacy and education digest

- CTI-L at listserv@irlearn.ucd.ie, for issues in teaching and using computers

- DEOS-L at listserv@psuvm.psu.edu, an international discussion forum for distance learning

- EDNET at listproc@nic.umass.edu, about the educational potential of the Internet

- EDSTYLE at listserv@sjuvm.stjohns.edu, for learning styles theory and research

- EDTECH (moderated) at listserv@msu.edu, an educational technology list

- EUITLIST at listserv@bitnic.educom.edu, about educational uses of information technology

- EDUTEL at listserv@vm.its.rpi.edu, for education and information technologies

- INCLASS (moderated) at listproc@schoolnet.carleton.ca, about using the Internet in the classroom

- ITTE at listserv@deakin.oz.au, a forum for information technology and teacher education

- LEARNING-ORG (moderated and archived) at majordomo@world.std.com, learning-organization information and discussion

- MMEDIA-L at listserv@vm.cnuce.cnr.it, about multimedia in education and training

- OHIOMM at listserv@miamiu.acs.muohio.edu, a multimedia development forum

- ROADMAP at listserv@ua1vm.va.edu, an online class on Internet information and resources

- NETTRAIN (moderated) at listserv@ubvm.cc.buffalo.edu, training about networks and over networks

- TEACHEFT at listserv@wcupa.edu, for teaching effectiveness

- TRDEV-L at listserv@psuvm.psu.edu, a training and development discussions list

- VIRTED at listserv@sjuvm.stjohns.edu, for virtual reality and education

Newsgroups

- alt.education.distance, education over networks list

- bit.listserv.edtech, the educational technology list (mirrors EDTECH listserv)

- bit.listserv.nettrain, training about networks and over networks (mirrors NETTRAIN listserv)

- comp.multimedia, a general discussion and resource on multimedia

- misc.education.adult, adult education discussion

- misc.business.facilitators, for facilitation skills, techniques, and tips list (FAQs)

Gopher sites

- Educational Testing Services (ETS) at gopher://gopher.ets.org, for more information, e-mail gopher@ets.org

- Technology & Information Educational Services (TIES) at gopher://gopher.ties.k12.mn.us

16

How we learn

"The process of learning is the extraction of patterns from confusion—not from clarity and simplicity."
— **Leslie A. Hart**

To help people learn how to use computers and information technology, you need to understand the process of learning. By understanding the mechanisms of learning, you can begin to develop effective approaches to training.

Memory

Although countless studies and experiments have been carried out to gain an insight into the processes by which we learn new skills, the exact mechanisms of the memory are still somewhat of a mystery. It was once thought that information was stored in specific areas of the brain, that is, localized in particular parts of the brain just as information is stored in particular locations on a hard disk drive in a computer. Although this is often a convenient analogy to use, a far more complex system seems to exist.

The storage of information in the human brain is more like that of the information storage in a hologram. Particular areas on a hologram plate do not contain particular areas of the image. A specific part of the viewed hologram image is present throughout every part of the hologram plate. In other words, the information is not localized. Similarly, memory is not localized in a particular area of the brain, but spread out across millions of interconnecting neurons. The information is stored in a complex "web" of connections and associations spread throughout the brain. Every new piece of information coming into the brain sets up or alters the existing connections to accommodate new experiences. New information can be thought of as rearranging or re-associating existing patterns rather than creating new memory areas. This is an extremely important concept to keep in mind when considering how adults learn because of the importance of association with information previously remembered.

Short- and long-term memory

For the purposes of simplicity, assume that there are two basic memory processes: short-term memory and long-term memory. This is an oversimplification of how the memory processes work in the human brain, but it serves well here for a training model.

Short-term memory (STM) is used when you look up a telephone number and can remember it long enough to dial the number. Later on, if you are asked to recall the number you dialed, you probably will not be able to do so. Short-term memory is limited in its capacity. If you try to hold a lot of information in STM, you end up having to let go of some of it. Its capacity is small. Try remembering five new telephone numbers and you begin to appreciate its character.

Long-term memory (LTM) stores information for a long time, often someone's whole life. Long-term memory enables us to live and survive by constantly relating present sensory input and experiences to past experiences and using this information to help guide a person's actions each day. The information in LTM is rarely forgotten. The recall is often poor, but the information recorded there is permanent. The capacity of long-term memory is unlimited—contrary to what some of your learners may suggest!

How do STM and LTM work together to allow memorization? Consider the simple block diagram in Fig. 16-1. When something affects your senses—when you hear, see, and experience something—the information enters the STM, where you will consider it. Depending on various factors, including attention, motivation, your emotional state, the relevance of the information, and your past experiences, the information will either go into the LTM or be purged from the STM.

Ways to encourage the passage of the information to the LTM are considered later in this chapter. For now, it is important to under-

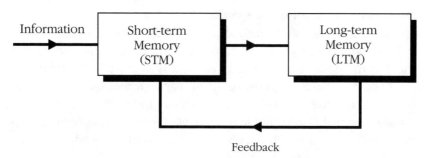

16-1 The process of memorization.

stand that the information in the LTM affects the information in the STM. This feedback determines not only if the information passes on to the LTM, but how and under what associations the information will be stored. An understanding of this relationship between what is already known and new information is critical when you train adults. This feedback loop enables the learner to determine the value of the information and also relate it to his or her own experience.

Adult learners will ask themselves, "How is this information useful to me?" They will try to relate a piece of information to their experience, and if they see it serves a useful purpose, will go ahead and pass it along to the LTM. The less-experienced learner is unsure of what is going to be useful and has fewer guidelines to determine the usefulness of the information. Because of this, the learner finds it much harder to relate the new information to past experience, and the passage to the LTM is hindered. It is your job, as a trainer, to help learners judge the value of the information you present by trying to relate its relevance to their own experiences.

Transferring from STM to LTM

Do whatever you can to assist the transfer of information from the STM to the LTM. Once the information is stored in the long-term memory, the learner can use it in the future to solve problems or generate new ideas.

So what promotes this transfer? What do you need to do in your training to ensure that the skills you are trying to develop get transferred efficiently?

Discover and develop motivation

Motivation means "stimulating the interest of." Learners come to the training with their own motivations for taking the course, which get them in the door of the training center. It is then up to the trainer to discover, as quickly as possible, each learner's motivation for being there and use this knowledge to help relate the course material. The trainer then needs to continue to motivate the individual or the group in learning the material by developing interest and showing the value and relevance of the information.

People will be more attentive and involved in the learning process if their energy level is up and they are stimulated by images, sounds, or feelings, as discussed in chapter 14. Trainers who understand this and make an effort to motivate their participants will find that transfer and retention of the material will be greatly increased.

Help the learners discover relevance

Perhaps the most important key to adult learning is how the information presented is relevant and useful to the learner. An individual might be motivated to learn but be unable to see how the material relates to his or her work. Adult learners need to know how the information relates to their experience and how they can use it. If the information presented is not seen to be immediately useful or valuable, then it is not passed on to the LTM and is forgotten. If you can help the learner appreciate how the material being taught is relevant and useful, it will be remembered.

This is why the idea of "just-in-time" training is so powerful. People learn skills when they need them, knowing exactly why the material is relevant to them. Their learning and retention is greater because the learning reflects a specific, immediate need.

Think constantly about how the material you are presenting might relate to your learners' experiences, and demonstrate its usefulness. This is another reason why it is so useful to be familiar with the background of the participants before the training, as discussed in chapter 2.

Develop attention

In order for information to enter the learners' STM, you must have their attention. It is your job as a trainer to make sure you have the full attention of the learners when new material, procedures, or concepts are discussed. This is where the skill of the trainer as presenter comes into play. The inflections of your voice, your body language, and the training environment all play a vital part in gaining the learners' attention.

"Associate" new material

Although people regularly experience new situations, encounter new ideas, and learn new skills, a large proportion of these experiences are related to concepts and ideas they already know. As a child, on the other hand, many life experiences are totally new and there are no previous experiences of a similar kind to relate to. The mechanism of learning in a child is therefore somewhat different from that of an adult. An adult needs to relate new information to existing ideas and experiences. In this way, an adult is able to blend the new information into existing memory patterns. Relating to new information in this way allows it to be fixed more securely in the LTM. I like to call this "linking." This is where the feedback loop from the LTM to the STM comes into play. If information entering the STM can be linked in some way to previous ideas, concepts, or experiences, the passage to the LTM is encouraged because the new information can "share" a memory pattern from a previous experience. Think of the new information as integrating itself with the older memory pattern. The new pattern is held in place by the "weight" of the older, familiar memory pattern.

Thus, by associating or linking the new material with something previously experienced, you encourage understanding and the ability to remember. The use of analogies in training is a prime example of this type of linking. When you explain a directory structure in terms of filing cabinets, you have done linking—associating this new concept to something that the learner is familiar with.

R. Bernard Lovell put it concisely in his book *Adult Learning*:

> *New information must fit into a structured pattern if it is to be successfully remembered. Perhaps the most important contribution the teacher can make to the adult's learning of cognitive information is to select, organize, present and translate the new material in such a way that the learner can appreciate its relationship with ideas he already has clearly established in his memory.*

One of the goals of a computer trainer is to do all you can to assist this process of linking ideas and establishing structured patterns.

Present a structure or a pattern of information

When a child learns new material at school, it is often learned by rote. This method can improve retention and recall and has its place in learning, but relying on such a technique for the adult learner is generally inappropriate. There are occasions in which learning a keystroke or technique by repetition can be useful, but typically, you need to provide the adult learner with an overall structure or meaningful pattern of the information.

We remember pieces of music, people's faces, pictures, and ideas not as a succession of individual information "bits," but as a structured whole. This is the basis of Gestalt theory that Max Wertheimer formulated in 1912. Gestalt theory suggests that the perception of the form and structure of something does not depend on the perception of individual elements making up the form. The mind perceives, and searches for, a single, organized whole to relate all the elements together as one. The mind perceives, in essence, a pattern or structure.

As mentioned earlier, the function of memory in the brain is holistic; its operation cannot be broken down into specific functioning blocks that work in certain ways when connected together. The brain remembers patterns of information much more readily than sequential lists of facts. You can remember and recall a good story that you heard because each part of the story is inextricably linked to the whole—the meaning of the whole story prompts you to recall the details. Similarly, you remember someone's face not because you made a mental note of the shape of the nose, the exact color of hair, and the width of the mouth, but because you have an integrated picture of the whole face in your mind.

Help learners evaluate and reinforce their own performances

In any learning situation, nothing is more fundamental to performance improvement than feedback. When a new skill is being learned, it is critical for the learner to receive constant feedback to see whether the actions being carrying out are moving towards or away from the desired goal. This can be done in one of two ways: *extrinsic feedback* or *intrinsic feedback*. Extrinsic feedback is what the learner receives externally, usually from the trainer. Intrinsic feedback is what the learner provides him- or herself. Intrinsic feedback is essential in computer training. A learner who relies, or is encouraged to rely, on the trainer for feedback will not be in a position to extract the most from the training.

The skills needed for learning software

There are various factors and abilities that affect how easily and successfully people learn software. The extent to which these are present determines the rate at which learning takes place. These factors are as follows:

- *Experience with software logic and concepts.* Are learners familiar with using other software? Are they familiar with some of the basic software concepts, such as saving files, copying, pasting, and formatting?

- *Basic keyboarding and mouse skills.* Do they possess an appropriate level of keyboarding skills and/or pointing-device skills?

- *Basic literacy skills.* Do they have basic reading, writing, and math skills?

- *The ability to form concepts.* How well can they visualize ideas and construct concepts, and then apply these to other situations?

- *The ability to isolate essentials.* How well can they isolate the important information from the not-so-important information? How well can they extract the essentials in an explanation or a process?

- *The ability to "link."* How well can they use the knowledge they have learned and integrate it with their existing knowledge?

- *Persistence.* How long are they willing to work at a task to solve a problem or learn a new skill? How easily do they give up when confused or not succeeding?

- *Self-concept.* Do they see themselves as able, competent, and capable of learning? Are they confident about their abilities? Are they expecting to succeed or expecting to fail?

- *Problem-solving ability.* What is their capacity for analyzing and solving problems in life? Do they have a structured approach to problem-solving, or do they have a more scattered, random approach?

- *The level of independence.* Are they used to relying on other people for answers and guidance, or figuring things out themselves? Are they self-directed in life? To what extent do they value a sense of independence?

- *The ability to memorize.* How well can they remember and recall concepts, words, pictures, ideas and procedures?

- *The level of comfort with the learning environment.* How physically and emotionally comfortable are they in the training environment?

The degree to which each of these is present determines the speed and effectiveness of the learning. When a particular skill or ability is lacking, try to complement this weakness by adapting your approach and presentation of the training.

Adapting to the learner

For the most effective training to take place, you must adapt the delivery of training to suit the individual learner. All effective and successful computer training depends on the ability of the trainer to adapt for individual differences.

Obviously, the larger the group of people being trained, the harder it becomes to adapt to individual differences. Nevertheless, it is critical that every possible effort is made to do this. This is especially important when asking and answering questions, setting practice exercises, and working one-on-one.

So how can you realistically adapt your training to the learners' skills and abilities? Let's consider adaptations to each factor in turn, as summarized in Table 16-1.

Table 16-1. Adapting to learners.

Learner lacks these abilities	Trainer response
Knowledge of software and software logic/concepts	Adjust speed of class Teach basic ideas Provide practice Give clear examples and explanations
Basic keyboarding/mouse skills	Be patient Cut down on amount of typing Teach some basic skills when appropriate
Basic literacy skills	Be understanding Be patient Teach some basic skills when approppriate
Ability to form concepts	Use more diagrams Use more analogies Use visual examples Give clear explanations Provide procedures
Ability to isolate essentials	Provide overviews and diagrams Highlight important points Use questioning Encourage inquiry/ reflection
Ability to "link"	Show relationship with other knowledge/concepts Show relevance Show practical application
Self-concept and persistence	Provide encouragement Allow sufficient practice time Build rapport

Table 16-1. Continued.

Learner lacks these abilities	Trainer response
	Nurture
	Help them succeed
Problem-solving ability	Illustrate logic of software
	Teach structured approach to learning
	Ask open-ended questions
Level of independence	Ask open-ended, reflective questions
	Encourage self-direction
	Use more practice exercises
Ability to memorize	Use visual aids
	Draw diagrams
	Use analogies
	Use mnemonics
	Allow more practice
	Use help/reference material
	Review material
Comfort with learning environment	Develop rapport
	Create pleasant, nonthreatening, atmosphere and informal

Little experience of software logic and concepts

When a learner is unfamiliar with the basic ideas and concepts of the computing environment they are working with, you can teach some of the underlying ideas incidentally during a training session (if appropriate). For example, when teaching an intermediate-level word-processing class, you assume that the participants are familiar with the basic concept of cut and paste. When this is not the case and one or two people are unsure of the concept, you can very quickly cover this idea before continuing.

Lacking basic keyboarding and mouse skills

If a few class members are struggling with basic keyboard and mouse skills (and you have decided not to have them reschedule), help by arranging for them to do less typing with practice exercises, having them sit next to more experienced colleagues, or finding time to help them learn some of the basic skills using a tutorial.

Lacking basic literacy skills

There is not much you can do when confronted with a learner who lacks basic reading, writing, and math skills apart from being understanding and patient and making an effort to clarify when there is confusion. Some people have enormous challenges in reading written instructions or carrying out basic math processes. When this is evident, help verbalize instructions or, if appropriate, quickly teach the basic math concept that is getting in the way of learning the software.

Inability to isolate essentials

Some people, when confronted with large amounts of information, have difficulty deciding which elements are the most important and relevant. They feel overwhelmed because they are unable to discern the critical from the less critical tasks or features. They feel they have to remember and recall everything that is presented to them.

You can help them by highlighting important elements or features, providing visual explanations, and asking questions that address basic ideas.

Difficulty in forming concepts

Concept formation is a critical skill in being able to think, process information, and apply knowledge. Abilities to form ideas and concepts vary enormously in people. There is not much you can do to improve this, apart from taking care to explain and clarify underlying concepts as well as showing procedures. Using visual aids—drawing charts, diagrams, and sketches—can help considerably.

Difficulty linking information

Once a concept or procedure is understood, it becomes more useful if a learner can integrate it with his or her existing knowledge base. The more someone can do this, the more able he or she is to learn and recall new skills. You can help here by showing relationships with other computer concepts and procedures, showing how the skills learned are relevant to solving different tasks, and showing practical applications of the new skills.

Lacking persistence

People are not always immediately successful when they try to learn something. With some people, this encourages them to persist until they obtain mastery. With others, it brings a sense of failure and upset and discourages them from further attempts.

Learners who lack persistence need more positive feedback, encouragement, and attention. You can also arrange the training such that they succeed frequently at whatever they are doing.

Poor problem-solving ability

Depending on previous educational experiences, environment. and upbringing, everyone has a slightly different way of dealing with life. Some people have a structured, rational way of looking at the problem, weighing the available options and deciding on a course of action. Others panic, become irrational, get driven purely by emotions, or use trial and error to solve problems. Learning how to use computer software is easier for those individuals who have a more structured approach to problems—they are more able to understand the way software works, consider a problem, and figure out an appropriate course of action.

You are certainly not going to be able to change someone's modus operandi in the space of a training session, but you can help encourage a more structured approach.

Lack of independence and self-direction

Some people like to rely on others to provide solutions, guidance, and acknowledgment. When they have a problem, they consult someone who might be able to provide a solution. When a person is dependent, learning is more difficult.

Encourage such a learner to think independently by encouraging a self-directed approach to learning and using appropriate questioning techniques (see page 1, "Encouraging independence").

Lacking self-confidence

Most learners have a preconceived idea of their abilities and limits before they ever walk into the training room. Some are confident in their ability to learn new skills, and see learning as a challenging and satisfying experience. Others doubt their abilities, feel threatened by the unknown, and fear failure. The concept they have about themselves as learners and the abilities they feel they have directly influence their performance in the training room. Their expectations of themselves are often realized.

The only thing you can do is provide some appropriate positive feedback when needed, and ensure that the atmosphere is as nonthreatening and nurturing as possible. When you have someone who doubts his or her abilities or lacks confidence, make sure that you help this person "succeed" many times throughout the class and make a point of recognizing these successes. It can make a valuable difference.

Discomfort with the learning environment

An individual might have all the abilities and prerequisites for learning, but be hindered in the learning process by the atmosphere of the learning environment. If the individual feels little rapport with the trainer and the group, feeling that his or her contributions are not valued or respected, then learning effectiveness suffers. The atmosphere of the learning environment must be open, accepting, respecting, nurturing, and comfortable.

Strive to create such an environment by developing rapport, listening carefully to what others have to say, interacting with the group, and offering encouragement.

There is no way that you are going to be able to know exactly what skills and abilities all the learners in the room have. That is something you gradually get a feel for as you teach the class. You might not know exactly what you need to do to assist a particular learner until you have a feel for his or her style and approach. Also, you cannot adapt to everyone's needs at the same time when you are teaching the class as a whole. What you can do, however, is make an effort to notice the learners' abilities and challenges and adapt your communication and training to complement them whenever you can.

The importance of forming concepts

When learning how to use computer software, or any learning for that matter, there are two fundamental processes by which people learn: *perceptual* and *conceptual*. Perceptual is when your senses perceive something: you hear something, touch something, or see something. For example, when you say "Click File, then Save," the learner touches the mouse button, hears it click, and sees a menu appear. These perceptions of hearing, touching, and seeing are how a learner gets most of his or her input in a training session.

Carrying out keystrokes, mouse-clicks, and procedural steps and remembering them is one mode of cognition, the perceptual mode. This is not unique to human beings. Animals can be taught to carry out procedural steps. (Are you reminded of your last class from hell?)

What is unique to human beings is the conceptual process of learning. This is when you observe or perceive objects, words, pictures, or thoughts, and integrate them into a meaningful pattern or whole. This integration or concept can then be used to understand and integrate other concepts and ideas. And so it goes, on through life, as you build more and more understanding from your conceptual building blocks. The degree to which an individual can successfully integrate a large number of concepts is a measure of that person's capacity to learn.

In computer training, those people who are very adept at using, understanding, and learning new software are those who have a good conceptual understanding of the computer and the characteristics of software. Because of this level of conceptual understanding, they are able to learn techniques, methods, keystrokes, and processes very quickly. If they have a task to accomplish, they apply their conceptual knowledge of the software and computer processes and "figure it out."

The conceptual mode of understanding is by far the most important in computer training. Unfortunately, most computer trainers, computer books, courseware videos, and CBT programs concentrate on the procedural, perceptual method. Pick up most computer courseware and take a look; most of them contain few conceptual explanations. It is predominantly procedures—click this, then this, press this, then that. The emphasis is always on the procedures.

Try to alter this balance in your training. Concentrate more on the conceptual and less on the procedural. Learning concepts allows people to understand and apply knowledge tomorrow; procedures merely help them get a job done today.

Preferred learning styles

There are primarily three ways in which human beings get information to their brains: seeing, hearing, and touching. The method a person prefers or the one that predominates determines his or her learning style. The learning styles, shown in Fig. 16-2, are commonly referred to as *visual, auditory,* and *kinesthetic.*

There are a number of reasons why some of these learning modes become predominant, but the important thing to remember is that different people have different preferred modes. An individual's default mode is generally the way he or she prefers to learn. If someone is used to learning by listening, then he or she most likely prefers this mode. If someone has always learned predominantly by physically doing, then this will probably be that person's preferred style.

Visual

The visual style of learning can be broken down into *visual-spatial* and *visual-linguistic.*

Visual-spatial

Visual-spatial learners process and understand information by seeing pictures, patterns, or diagrams, or constructing these in the mind's eye. A simple diagram or picture might be all they need to understand a concept or idea. They often need to visualize a process or procedure in their minds to have it be meaningful to them. They don't want

Sensory channels   *Learning styles*

Sight   Visual-spatial
Hearing ➡ Visual-linguistic
Touch   Auditory
             Kinesthetic

16-2 Learning styles.

to read an explanation of what to do, they want to see it being done. They draw shapes and diagrams when making notes.

Visual-linguistic

Visual-linguistic learners prefer to read the written word to help them understand ideas and concepts. The end result, as with the visual-spatial style, is an image in the mind's eye. Visual-linguistic learners, however, prefer the written word as a vehicle to get there. They prefer to read explanations and write notes in order to understand and remember. Words feel more concrete to them than diagrams or pictures.

Auditory

Auditory learners prefer the spoken word to pictures or the written word. They learn best by listening to someone speak. They prefer to follow verbal instructions than read or refer to a diagram. They hear words in their heads when they read, and often talk to themselves when trying to think something through. They can memorize information easily by reciting it out loud. Class discussions help them learn and understand the material.

Kinesthetic

Kinesthetic learners learn best by doing, by hands-on experience. They are characterized by, "Don't tell me or show me how to do it, let me try doing it." They are often very active, prefer to move around when learning, and need to take frequent breaks. They find it hard to sit in a chair and just listen or watch. They often solve problems by trying something to see what happens. They enjoy experimenting.

Adapting to learning styles

Keep in mind that these different learning styles are simply the predominant learning style of an individual. It doesn't mean they use only that learning style. Most people learn by a combination of different styles. In fact, in some cases, the learner will switch learning styles depending on the circumstances.

So you know that people have different preferred modes of learning and specific ways of processing information. How can this help you when you're training? How can you use this information? One way would be to figure out the learning styles of individuals and assign them to specific classes based on their preferred way of learning. When this has been done, it has created some very impressive results, but for most of us it is impractical. In the typical scenario, you have a group of individuals with different abilities and different styles. Your challenge as the trainer is to understand the various styles in which individuals learn and make certain that your training includes elements from each of these styles.

Of course, you also have a preferred learning style, but it is important not to let your style predominate. A particular trainer might learn and understand things in an auditory mode—he or she might like to learn and teach by talking and discussion. This will probably not suit all the participants, however. Use all the different styles when training so that every preference is taken into consideration.

Remember also that when you explain a concept, idea, or procedure to a learner and he or she doesn't understand, it might not be because he or she is a "slow learner." It might just be because you are using your preferred style of explanation, and it doesn't coincide with this person's style. When someone doesn't follow something, the trainer is sometimes apt to repeat an explanation using the same style, only slower. This usually doesn't clarify things. What the learner needs is an explanation using a different style, not a different speed.

Have you ever been asked a question in a class and not understood it while other people in the room know exactly what the questioner meant? This is another example of the sender and receiver using different styles of communication.

I have mentioned elsewhere in this book about the need for a classroom trainer to teach to everyone, but make allowances for individuals. Teach to a group, but adapt to each learner. This is particularly important when considering learning styles. When a learner asks a question or asks for clarification during a class, listen and watch carefully to the way the learner asks the question. You'll probably get an idea of this person's style of learning. For example, if a learner asks a question by gesticulating and drawing in the air, the chances are that a visual explanation would be clearest. If the learner asks a question by carefully choosing the correct vocabulary and wording, then perhaps a verbal answer would work best. When giving answers, try to reflect the style of how the question was asked.

There is no way that, in the relatively short time of a typical class, you are going to be able to thoroughly analyze each participant's style and preferences and adapt the class accordingly. The best you can do is be aware of the learning differences, be varied in your teaching style, and try to adapt the style of your answers to the style of the questions.

Appendix

Resources for computer trainers

Conferences worth attending

The Computer Training and
  Support Conference
SoftBank Institute
1-800-34-TRAIN

Interactive
SoftBank Institute
1-800-34-TRAIN

Training Magazine's Training
  Conference and Expo
Lakewood Conferences
1-800-707-7792

Organizations

American Society for Training &
  Development (ASTD)
1640 King St., Box 1443
Alexandria, VA 22313
1-800-NAT-ASTD (628-2783)
Membership and Information
703-683-8100 Customer Service
703-683-8183 Information Center
Internet: astdic@capcon.net

Association for Supervision &
  Curriculum Development
(ASCD)
1250 N. Pitt St.
Alexandria, VA 22314-1453
703-549-9110

Educational Testing Service
  (Certified Technical Trainer)
P.O. Box 6541
Princeton, NJ 08541-6541
1-800-967-1100
Internet: cttp@ets.org

Information Technology Training
  Association (ITTA)
3925 W. Breaker Lane
Austin, TX 78759
512-502-9300
Internet:
70720.2532@compuserve.com

International Association for
  Continuing Education &
  Training (IACET)
1101 Connecticut Ave. NW
Suite 700
Washington, DC 20036
202-857-1122

International Society for
  Technology in Education (ISTE)
1787 Agate St.
Eugene, OR 97403-1923
503-346-4414
Internet:
iste@oregon.uoregon.edu

The HUMOR Project, Inc.
110 Spring St.
Saratoga Springs, NY 12866
518-587-8770

The Masie Center
P.O. Box 397
Saratoga Springs, NY 12866
1-800-98-MASIE or 518-857-3522

National Society for Performance
& Instruction (NSPI)
1300 L St. NW, Suite 1250
Washington, DC 20005
202-408-7969
Internet:
75143.410@compuserve.com

Society for Human Resources
Management (SHRM)
606 N. Washington St.
Alexandria, VA 22314-1997
1-800-283-SHRM or 703-548-3440
Internet: 390-2491@mcimail.com

Software Publishers Association
1730 M St., NW, Suite 700
Washington, DC 20036-4510
202-452-1600
Internet: kwasch@spa.org
(president)

Toastmasters International, Inc.
P.O. Box 9052
Mission Viejo, CA 92690
714-858-8255
Internet: drex@toastmasters.org

Periodicals

Computer Training News
(newspaper)
P.O. Box 995
Yarmouth, ME 04096
207-846-0600 subscriptions
207-846-0657 fax
Internet:
aharris@servicenews.com
Articles available from
ftp://biddeford.com/pub/service
news/news stories

Creative Training Techniques
(newsletter)
Lakewood Publications, Inc.
50 S. Ninth St.
Minneapolis, MN 55402
1-800-328-4329 or 612-333-0471
Internet: sheimes@aol.com

Info-Line
American Society for Training &
Development
(see Organizations)

IT Training (magazine)
Training Information Network
Ltd.
Jubilee House, The Oaks, Ruislip
Middlesex HA4 7LF
United Kingdom
01895-622112
Internet: csteed@dial.pipex.com

MicroComputer Trainer
(newsletter)
696 9th St.
P.O. Box 2487
Secaucus, NJ 07096-2487
201-330-8923
Internet: loretta@panix.com

Performance & Instruction
National Society for Performance
& Instruction
(see Organizations)

Training Magazine
Lakewood Publications, Inc.
Internet: trainmag@aol.com

Presentations

Lakewood Publications, Inc.
(see Periodicals)

Technical & Skills Training
American Society for Training &
Development
(see Organizations)

Training & Development Journal
American Society for Training &
  Development
(see Organizations)

Books, tapes, and other training resources

Recommended Resources
  (catalog of training books and
  tapes)
Lakewood Publications, Inc.
1-800-707-7769

SkillTech Professional Seminars
SoftBank Institute
10 Presidents Landing
Medford, MA 02155
1-800-34-TRAIN

Creative Training Techniques
  International, Inc.
  (train-the-trainer seminars)
7620 West 78th St.
Minneapolis, MN 55439-2518
1-800-383-9210

The Training Edge
  (train-the-computer trainer
  seminars)
117 Lakeshore Court
Richmond, CA 94804
510-235-6401
Internet:
71203.1001@compuserve.com

Bibliography

◆◆◆

Bolles, Edmund. 1988. *Remembering and Forgetting*. New York: Walker & Co.

Brown, Mark. 1977. *Memory Matters*. New York: Crane, Russak & Co.

Bruner, Jerome. 1960. *The Process of Education*. Harvard University Press.

Buzan, Tony. 1978. *The Evolving Brain*. Holt, Rinehart & Winston.

Craig, Robert L. 1967. *Training and Development Handbook*. McGraw-Hill.

Drake Prometric. 1995. *The Complete Guide to Certification for Computing Professionals*. McGraw-Hill.

Edwards, Betty. *Drawing on the Right Side of the Brain*. J.P. Tarcher, Inc.

Gazzaniga, Michael S. 1992. *Nature's Mind*. Basic Books.

Gordon, Jack (with Ron Zemke and Phillip Jones). *Designing and Delivering Cost-Effective Training—And Measuring the Result*. Lakewood Publications.

Hart, Leslie A. 1983. *Human Brain and Human Learning*. Arizona: Books for Educators

Hoff, Ron. 1994. *"I Can See You Naked"*. Kansas City: Andrews and McMeel.

Jones, Elizabeth. 1986. *Teaching Adults—An Active Learning Approach*. NAEYC.

Kidd, J. R. 1972. *How Adults Learn*. New York: Cambridge.

Kirkpatrick, D. L. 1975. *Evaluating Training Programs*. Washington, D.C.: ASTD

Knowles, Malcolm. 1984. *The Adult Learner: A Neglected Species* (Third Edition). Houston: Gulf Publishing Co.

Loftus, Elizabeth. 1980. *Memory*. Addison Wesley.

Lovell, R. Bernard. 1980. *Adult Learning*. New York: John Wiley & Sons.

Masie, Elliott and Wholman, Rebekah. 1989. *The Computer Training Handbook*. Raquette Lake: Tools for Training, Inc.

Merwin, Sandra. *Evaluation: 10 Significant Ways for Measuring and Improving Training Impact*. Lakewood Publications.

Norman, Donald. 1969. *Memory and Attention*. New York: John Wiley & Sons.

Ramtha. 1986. *Ramtha*. Eastsound, Washington: Sovereignty, Inc.

Rand, Ayn. 1990. *Introduction to Objectivist Epistemology* (Second Edition). New York: Meridian.

Renner, Peter. 1993. *The Art of Teaching Adults*. Vancouver: Training Associates.

Rogers, Carl. 1961. *On Becoming a Person*. Boston: Houghton-Mifflin.

Rogers, Carl. 1969. *Freedom to Learn*. Columbus, Ohio: Merril.

Rose, Colin. 1987. *Accelerated Learning*. Accelerated Learning Systems, Inc.

Tapscott, Don, and Caston, Art. 1993. *Paradigm Shift*. McGraw-Hill.

Whitmore, John. 1992. *Coaching for Performance*. London: Nicholas Brealey Publishing Ltd.

Zuboff, Shoshana. 1988. *In the Age of the Smart Machine*. Basic Books.

Index

About the author

Paul Clothier is an internationally known computer trainer, speaker, and columnist. He has been teaching individuals and businesses to use information technology for more than 12 years. Originally from London, England, he started training in Tahoe City, California, and went on to help establish a computer training center in Reno, Nevada, that continues to reflect the training philosophy in this book. Paul's San Francisco-based consultancy, The Training Edge, helps organizations redesign their computer training to increase effectiveness and reduce costs.

When he is not training, speaking, or writing, Paul can be found skiing in Tahoe, hiking in the Marin hills, or trying desperately to follow the instructor in his weekly hip-hop dance class.